For Margaret Cohen
and in loving memory of Michael Cohen

'I hope that people know me well enough and realise the type of person I am . . . I would never do anything to harm the country or anything improper. I never have. I think that most people who have dealt with me think that I am a pretty straight sort of guy.'

Tony Blair, interviewed about Bernie Ecclestone's donations to New Labour, *On the Record*, BBC1, 16 November 1997

Contents

Introduction

At the turn of the twenty-first century Britain was enjoying one of the luckier moments in her history. Although British forces were often in action, their campaigns bore little resemblance to traditional wars. No foreign power menaced British territory. The threat that the Soviet Union would annihilate every soul in the land had gone. Even the dirty little war in Northern Ireland, which had claimed 3,000 lives in 30 years, settled down into an uneasy truce. With the peace came plenty. Inflation was low, and crime rates went through the floor. If unemployment wasn't down to the levels of the golden age after 1945, it had fallen back to below two million and kept falling, a blessing those of us who endured the Thatcher years thought we would never see. The incomes of the working and middle classes rose while the incomes of the rich rocketed. The stock market soared to almost 7,000 in December 1999, a peak unimaginable a few years before. House prices and consumer debt followed its ascent. 'Things can only get better,' the government had promised, and millions put their money where the Prime Minister's mouth was and borrowed against his optimism.

The boom was powered by the millenarian belief that technology would bring a capitalist paradise. The Net and the wider improvements in telecommunications were meant to herald a veritable revolution which would tip old ways of living, old hierarchies and the old rules of economics into the dustbin of history. To anyone who knew the history of capitalism the Utopian faith was a screaming warning of a coming disaster. But the British Prime Minister talked as if he believed that history was at an end. All that held Britain back, he told the 1999 Labour Party Conference, were 'the forces of conservatism, the cynics, the élites, the establishment'. The British had nothing to fear but puerile mockers who refused to leap into the future with evangelical enthusiasm, and the hidebound élites who wanted to hang on to their outmoded privileges and keep the sovereign people down.

His condemnations seemed like prize-winning hypocrisy. Blair and his entourage looked, smelt and sounded like an élite. They had abandoned the Labour Party's traditional hope of creating a more equal society and cheered on the rich. For the aristocracy of wealth, which mattered more than the aristocracy of birth, Blair was everything it could have desired. Its wiser members knew that the Tories couldn't stay in power forever. By changing the Labour Party, Blair had removed the possibility that the Labour Party might change the country.

It felt like business as usual, and in many respects it was. But unlike the traditional rulers of Britain, the new élite of the 1990s presented themselves, and probably saw themselves, as meritocrats who had earned their money and power in the service of the people. Their privilege was justified because they gave the public what it wanted in the supermarkets, the media and government. What could be more democratic?

Michael Grade, a television executive, summed up their philosophy when he lauded a giant bubble the government and business had erected in Greenwich to match the bubble markets in the City a few miles upstream. 'The people are in charge,' Grade announced. 'They can make their own mistakes. They are not being told what to be or how to act. What the Dome is saying to them is: "Here you are, folks. Here are the choices. You decide."'

The new élite and its media loved the folks and were sure they could be made happier with tougher punishments for criminals and alien intruders. Attempts to produce both filled the parliaments of the time. As for the economy and the public services it funded, all serious contenders for power agreed that the raging bull market proved that privatisation and deregulation were the only ways to give the people the services they deserved. At the top of public life there were bitter culture wars about everything from the banning of fox hunting to the stig-matising of homosexuals. But with the exception of the peren-nial argument about Britain's place in the European Union, there was an agreement on the essentials. Inequalities between the rich and the poor – and the rich and the middle class – reached record levels. They might have led to discontent, but the boom years of the 1990s evolved a system to defuse poten-tial trouble. The masses were bought off with gestures on crime and race while their superiors were freed to enjoy their opu-lence.

The stock-market crash and the atrocities of 11 September made the previous decade appear a respite from crises, rather than the dawn of a new era. The savings of the thrifty were slashed as shares halved in value from the top of the market on New Year's Eve 1999. The Dome, which opened that night, pro-vided a preview of what was to come. Millions saw it as an insult to their intelligence, which revealed nothing but the emptiness of a meretricious meritocracy. The promise of a Net-driven revolution turned out to be a scam. Corporations which had paid the bills of political parties, and guided the policies of ministers, were exposed as criminal conspiracies. The new élite's playing to the gallery on race and crime was punished by the law of diminishing returns. It was eager to discard liberties the British had taken for granted for centuries in the interests of a few good headlines in the next morning's papers, but was too good for its own good at inciting fear. The public was persuad-ed that crime was out of control, and blamed politicians for an imaginary breakdown of order. All the attempts to pander to the people produced a people which despised politicians as never before.

What follows is a contemporary history which makes a stab at explaining how we got from the facile hopes of the Millenni-um to the sullen present. It's history because it goes back to the early 1990s to pick up the beginnings of the bubble world. It's contemporary because, whenever planes aren't crashing into skyscrapers or pension funds cutting their payments, the bubble world bounces back and reasserts itself with more attacks on liberties and more demands that dubious companies take over public services. It's also a chronicle of wasted time. Moments of peace and plenty are rare and should be seized. The implicit question behind the chapters on the New Labour government is, 'What was all that for?'

When you consider the opportunities . . .

As a believer in the basics of news journalism, I try to supply evidence to show how I've reached my conclusions. Even if you don't agree with them, my hope has been to give you grounds to think twice. I don't claim to be comprehensive any more than I claim to write in a neutral voice. Many important subjects aren't covered because I know too little about them. This is an argumentative book, and anyone who enjoys an argument knows that you can only argue about what interests and disturbs you.

Readers may object that I'm afflicted by a severe case of 'negativity'. I happily accept the charge; there has been, after all, plenty to be negative about. In mitigation I would add that most people can't choose most of the forces which shape their lives most of the time, all they can do is decide whether to accept them or fight them. More often than not change comes from a negative reaction rather than a positive programme. This isn't as consoling a thought as it sounds. The world we are stuck with won't last for ever, but, as I hope to show, there are elements in the opposition to the reigning order on both the right and the left which are frankly sinister. They can't be excused because their adherents presumptuously award themselves the labels of 'dissidents' or 'dissenters'. One day they may be in charge, and it's best to pick a fight with them before they get too big for their boots.

I have a final hope. We live in an age of manias, although few like to admit it. This book covers stock-market manias, crime manias, privatisation manias and religious manias. The pseudo-democratic cant of the times denies that we can swayed by delusions. 'The customer is always right,' bellow business leaders and politicians; 'People aren't stupid,' bellow talk-show hosts. The positive purpose of this book is to show that people can be very stupid and demonstrate how and why. If we accept our failings, we can then resolve that whatever cons we fall for in the future, at least we won't fall for the cons of a bubble world which should have been popped years ago.

PART I

Boom

'What is the alternative? What does the Right Honourable
Gentleman offer? Why was it that he made a policy-free speech,
apart from a load of nonsense from the Shadow
Home Secretary, most of which we are doing in any event?'

Tony Blair to William Hague and Ann Widdecombe,
House of Commons, 6 December 2000

ONE

Snobs and Mobs

What to talk about? How to pass the hours on the *Today* programme and fill the blank spaces between the ads on the newspaper comment pages? When nearly everyone in power agreed that history and the battle of ideas were at an end, what was there for politicians to debate as they wasted the boom years of the 1990s? On the afternoon of 12 February 1993 a Liverpool toddler provided an answer which kept Downing Street and Fleet Street happy for a decade. It shows no sign of losing its appeal.

The crime which began a political arms race wasn't hyped. James Bulger's murder was every bit as bad as the politicians and journalists said. The CCTV pictures of his mother, Denise, searching the Strand shopping centre in Bootle while his ten-year-old killers took her child away demanded a reaction. The police had few doubts that Jon Venables and Robert Thompson intended to murder. James Bulger didn't die at the end of a boyish game which had got out of hand. Weeks before, Thompson and Venables had boasted to schoolfriends that it was worth joining their gang 'because we are going to kill someone'. They took James from the Strand to a canal and joked about pushing him in the water. Under interrogation they said they had wanted to throw him in. When he wouldn't 'bend over the water', Venables talked for a while about getting ' him knocked over by a bus'. They picked him up and dropped him on his head, then covered the bruise with James's anorak hood and set off on a two-and-a-half mile tramp through Liverpool to the murder scene: railway sidings near Robert Thompson's home in Walton. Once they were sure no one was watching, they threw paint in James's eyes, stoned him and beat him with an iron bar. They dumped his bleeding body on the tracks and covered it with bricks. Then they climbed back to the street and went to look at the local shops.

The urge for a pat explanation was overwhelming. Liverpool was, and is, shockingly poor. Five hundred yards from where James was murdered stands the Saxon church of St Mary's, Walton, the city's oldest church. Small, irrational thoughts haunt people in extreme moments, and in the days after the killing the Reverend Peter Tilley regretted that he hadn't raised the funds to clean up his scruffy building. He would have liked James to have glimpsed something beautiful in his last minutes. 'I think my ideas about restoring the church have a strange relevance,' he said with a half-embarrassed sadness. 'I believe the aesthetic can raise people's hopes and aspirations.' As it was, his plans to illuminate the church with floodlights, fence off its grounds with neat iron railings, and clear away the rubbish, heroin needles, broken tombstones, old glue tubes and graffiti in its graveyard, which had seen many muggings and one rape, had remained plans. A glimpse of the church could neither comfort James nor inspire his murderers to think again. 'I am an optimist by temperament and calling,' Tilley said. 'But I have been shocked after coming back to Liverpool after ten years in the South. The great quality of Liverpudlians was that we had hope, however bad things got. But the hope has gone now and everyone seems dragged down by a general depression.'[1]

If the depression brought by poverty didn't suit as an easy answer, there was always family breakdown. Jon Venables' parents had split up, although they remained in touch. Robert Thompson's father had run off with another woman, leaving a wife to cope with the six children he had abandoned. She hit the bottle and her children hit each other. If that didn't work, rumours that the police may have minimised evidence that James had been sexually assaulted to spare the feelings of the Bulger family offered a third option. Everyone says that the abused become abusers, so perhaps a cycle of violence might explain the murder.[2] The trial judge and the press had another explanation. They were horrified that the boys had seen *Child's Play II* and implied that Hollywood should carry a part of the responsibility for turning children into monsters. Jon Venables' father had rented the horror film, but at least one officer on the investigation wasn't convinced the boys had seen it.[3]

So what if they had? Neither leftish arguments about poverty and abuse nor conservative condemnations of permissiveness and the collapse of families get near to explaining a terrible crime. The gap between understandable cause and inexplicable consequence is too great to jump – which is why people continue to rely on the concept of evil, despite the instructions of their betters to stop being judgemental. 'Hang him now!' cried a mob which gathered when a twelve-year-old boy was arrested a couple of days after the killing. Fortunately, the lynchers didn't get their hands on the entirely blameless child. Later, when detectives picked up Thompson and Venables, crowds smashed the windows in their homes and sprayed 'Amityville' on the walls. They tried to turn over the police van carrying the suspects and came close to succeeding.

In one sense, the flabbergasted anger was justified. The murder of James Bulger was an extraordinary crime. Prepubescents who kill are as rare as hurricanes in Hampshire. Children are too small and too weak to be murderers. They fret about getting into trouble. Their hormones haven't exploded and filled them with lusts and confusions. At the time of the Bulger murders about 70 children aged under five were being killed each year. The culprits were nearly always their parents. Nearly all juveniles convicted of murder or manslaughter were aged between fourteen and seventeen. In the decade before, there had been just six cases of children aged thirteen or under killing. There was no pattern to their crimes. The numbers of murderous children didn't rise with the divorce rate or fall with the inflation rate. They committed random and idiosyncratic crimes that didn't 'say' anything other than that a terrible loss had been inflicted.

Everything about the prosecution of Venables and Thomp-

son announced that children who killed were incomprehensible freaks. The system didn't know what to do with them. The
age of criminal responsibility in England was ten. If Thompson
and Venables had murdered before their last birthdays, the state
couldn't have put them on trial and would have had to hand
them over to social workers. In the Netherlands and Switzerland children were judged to be ignorant of the difference
between right and wrong until they were twelve. In France, thirteen. In Austria, Germany, Hungary, Italy, Latvia, Lithuania,
Romania and Slovenia, fourteen. In the Czech Republic, Den-
mark, Estonia, Finland, Norway, Slovakia and Sweden, fifteen.
In Poland, Portugal and Spain, sixteen, and in Luxembourg,
eighteen. Only Cyprus, Ireland, Malta, Northern Ireland and
Scotland asked more of their children than England and Wales,
and assumed that the under-tens had the moral strength to
carry criminal responsibility. Only a few redneck American
states would have done what England did to Thompson and
Venables, and put them on trial before press and public. The
dock had to be raised at Preston Crown Court so the boys could
meet the eyes of the jury. Before the jury could reach its verdict,
the prosecution had to prove beyond reasonable doubt that
they were guilty of the crime and that they knew that what they
had done was seriously wrong – and not naughtiness or child-
ish mischief.

The consensus in the developed world was that: (1) children
were different from adults; (2) it was difficult to prove that they
had criminal intent; and (3) they rarely killed. Tony Blair, home
affairs spokesman for the opposition Labour Party in 1993, disagreed. He decided that Thompson and Venables personified
the state of a feral nation. In a speech in Wellingborough on 19
February 1993, a week after the murder, he declared:

> The news bulletins of the past week have been like hammer blows
> struck against the sleeping conscience of the country, urging us to
> wake up and look unflinchingly at what we see. A solution to this
> disintegration doesn't simply lie in legislation. It must come from a
> rediscovery of a sense of direction as a country and most of all

from being unafraid to start talking once again about the values and principles we believe in and what they mean for us, not just as individuals but as a community. We cannot exist in a moral vacuum. If we do not learn and teach the value of what is right and what is wrong, then the result is simply moral chaos which engulfs us all.

The inexplicable motives of two aberrant boys were now symptoms of a British disease which Labour with its new morality would cure by . . . well, the remedy wasn't specified. What was clear was that a willingness to follow the hasty and violent opinions of the mobs on the street and in the newspaper offices was to be a selling point of a new-look Labour Party.[4]

The political world of the early 1990s which Blair destroyed now seems outlandish. Nothing is more foreign than the readiness of politicians from all parties to think carefully about how to handle crime. Labour blamed the explosion of crime on the explosion in unemployment during Margaret Thatcher's disastrous monetarist experiment. When it came to power, Labour would tackle both, while retaining a scrupulous regard for civil liberty. Roy Hattersley said in 1987 that 'the true object of socialism is the creation of a genuinely free society in which the protection and extension of individual liberty is the primary duty of the state.' Blair took over the brief in 1992, and appeared to agree. He told that year's party conference:

> When young men and women seek but do not find any reflection of their hopes in the society around them, when the Tories create a creed of acquisition and place it alongside a culture without opportunity, when communities disintegrate and people within them feel they have no chance to improve and nothing to strive for, then it takes not a degree in social science, merely a modicum of common sense, to see that, in the soil of alienation, crime will take root.

Such were the conventional leftish sentiments of the period. Nor were the Tories always as wicked as the left pretended. In 1990 they had to cope with a criminal justice system which had gone from its usual state of decrepitude into crisis. Respect for the English judiciary, which had been lazily called 'the best in the world,' was battered by the acquittals of the Birmingham Six and Guildford Four. What shocked public opinion wasn't just that the police had got the wrong men for the worst IRA atrocities in mainland Britain, but that it had taken the grudging courts years to correct the mistakes. For a few months miscarriages of justice were all the rage in media London. Previously obscure lawyers working from dusty offices in the basements of Camden were harassed by ambitious reporters who wanted a case of police brutality, and wanted it now. Gareth Peirce, the painfully shy solicitor for many of the acquitted Irish suspects, had to hide in her own bedroom while her children pushed open the letter box and shouted 'Go Away' at Emma Thompson, a Method-School actress who had been hired to play a crusading lawyer.

As the courts fell into disrepute, the jails were torn to pieces. The prison population stood at 50,000 in 1990. Britain had never seen anything like it. Back in the mid-1950s, 20,000 were in jail. The rise in crime and punishment in the decades since had produced an unmanageable and unconscionable system. Men were crammed in twos and threes into cells which stank of faeces and urine. In April 1990 riots hit twelve jails. At Strangeways, the violence escalated into the worst prison riot of the twentieth century. The Home Office didn't know how to retake the jail. The Greater Manchester Police tried the cruel and unusual tactic of erecting giant speakers and blasting out the greatest hits of Rod Stewart and Julio Iglesias. Even a sensory assault of this violence couldn't budge the convicts from the roof. The press claimed that the bodies of between eleven and twenty inmates would be found when the police eventually forced their way in. Although the reports turned out to be nonsense, the ferocity of the riot made them all too plausible on first reading.

There was no division between left and right on the need for reform. The *Daily Telegraph* was as liberal as the *Guardian*. On 7 April 1990 its leader writer asked, 'Why do we have to crowd more prisoners than any other European country into places like Strangeways . . . as everybody knows, most of our 50,000

prison population are not violent offenders.' David Waddington, the Tory Home Secretary, was a believer in hanging. His
death-wish didn't stop him introducing a Criminal Justice Act
in 1991 which aimed to divert vandals, thieves and burglars
from jail, even if they were persistent offenders. 'The object,'
Waddington said, 'is to have a more consistent sentencing policy. If the end result of all that is a continued fall in the prison
population, I will say I'm very glad to see that.'

Prison didn't work. The Tory government described it as 'an
expensive way of making bad people worse'. The most telling
statistic to come out of the Home Office in the 1990s was that
two-thirds of its prisoners had been so poorly educated they
weren't qualified to fill 95 per cent of vacancies advertised in job
centres. The jails couldn't try to succeed where the schools had
failed. They were too overcrowded to divert resources to the
education of their illiterate and innumerate charges. Inmates'
options on release were menial manual labour or crime. Most
chose crime. Half the men the Prison Service sent out were
back inside within two years. The government asked Lord
Woolf to conduct an inquiry into the gutting of Strangeways.
He recommended that prisoners should be kept in small jails
close to their wives or girlfriends. When it came to keeping men
on the straight and narrow, there was nothing like a dame, His
Lordship decided. Government should work to maintain the
emotional ties which gave men stability when they were
released. As for minor offenders, civil servants estimated that it
cost £25,000 per convict, per annum to keep them in jail. If you
locked up enough people, crime would fall. But you would have
to lock up hundreds of thousands before you had a fall the public would notice. The Home Office estimated that a 1 per cent
reduction in crime necessitated a 25 per cent increase in the
prison population. Money spent on crime prevention was 36
times more effective. After years of interviewing prisoners, Sir
Stephen Tumim, the Chief Inspector of Prisons, summed up
the official mood when he said: 'Two-thirds of prisoners should
be let out and the other third should never be let out.'

The government agreed. Serious offenders should have longer sentences and minor offenders should be punished in the community, it decided. As crime prevention was better than crime, ministers' advice boiled down to the practical if uninspiring slogan: 'Fit Better Locks!' Labour accused the government of being too timid. Maybe the charge was true. But by January 1993, the month before James Bulger's murder, the prison population had fallen to 41,000.

Although he was to become a demonic figure for liberals who didn't have the nerve to see Blair without illusion, Michael Howard didn't break with reforming conservatism when he became Home Secretary in 1993. Shortly after he took over, I was leaked the first draft of a tough speech his deputy, David Maclean, had planned to deliver. Maclean was an intransigent Thatcherite. He had already declared that 'there are no genuine beggars in London' and that ramblers should pay tolls if they wanted to tramp the fells. Criminals were next on his list. They should be driven from the streets like 'vermin', he had intended to say. Vigilantes deserved respect, and a justice system 'on the side of the criminal' deserved to be savaged. Howard's Home Office got hold of the draft and replaced every incendiary sentiment with platitudes, which the humbled minister duly delivered to MPs.

For no purpose other than to make mischief, the paper I worked for decided to run a piece comparing and contrasting what Maclean had wanted to say with what he had been allowed to say. Drive the Vermin from the Streets!/Fit Better Locks! The Police are the Thin-Blue Line Against Anarchy!/Fit Better Locks! The Law is on the Side of the Criminal!/Fit Better Locks! Fit Better Locks! Fit Better Locks! Just before we went to press, I phoned Blair and invited him to join the mockery of the minister. The shadow Home Secretary went quiet. He agreed to make a vague criticism of Maclean's 'wild talk', but was clearly uncomfortable. 'You see,' he muttered, 'a lot of *Daily Mail* readers would agree with him.'

I wondered why a Labour politician would care about the

reaction of a newspaper which hated all his party stood for. A disquieting thought about the direction Blair was taking flicked across my mind. I dismissed it as a laughable flight of fancy, and went away thinking that all I'd done was catch him in a wet patch.

It's a miracle I wasn't thrown out of journalism years ago.

The malign influence of Bill Clinton on British public life can't be overestimated. Because of his example children slashed their wrists in cells, the prison population all but doubled, ancient liberties disappeared, the incitement of fear became the favoured tactic of statesmen and the place of parliamentarians was usurped by newspaper editors and focus-groupies. By the end of the Clintonising process, millions had become so disgusted with the new élite's manipulation of their emotions, soldiers with fixed bayonets couldn't have forced them into polling booths.

To the Labour modernisers – Blair, Gordon Brown, Alastair Campbell, Peter Mandelson and an advertising executive called Philip Gould – Clinton was an inspiration. Old Labour had lost four elections. Its last defeat in May 1992 had shown that it couldn't win in the middle of a recession which could be fairly blamed on the Conservatives' ruinous decision to lock a high pound into the European Exchange Rate Mechanism. (Admittedly Labour had supported Thatcher's final blunder, but the detail is often overlooked by vengeful voters.) The gloom was pierced, in November 1992, when Bill Clinton succeeded where Neil Kinnock had failed and ousted a conservative administration. John Smith, the new Labour leader, wasn't impressed by Clinton's use of micro-policies crafted by political engineers to please a handful of people sipping bad wine in a focus group. 'I don't like the black art of public relations that has taken over politics,' he said. 'We're talking about the government of the country – not the entertainment industry.'[5]

The modernisers were enraptured, however, and regarded Smith as a living fossil. Gould joined the Clinton election team and bounded home like a star-dazzled schoolboy. 'Arriving at that campaign was like leaving the shadows and coming into sunlight,' he wrote in his autobiography. 'The campaign was not only friendly, it was also awesomely efficient.' He remembered every word of thanks his small services earned. The 'warm praise' of James Carville, Clinton's attack dog, was recorded for posterity; as was a toast the victorious Clinton campaign team made at Doe's Eat Place in Little Rock, Arkansas, to 'Philip Gould and the British Labour party for all their help'. Gould saw that Clinton was the future. 'Bill Clinton's election showed the world the left could win, and it showed how it could win.'[6] The death of John Smith on 12 May 1994 was the most important of the decade – far more significant than the death of Diana Spencer. It cleared the way for the Labour modernisers to do to Britain what Clinton was doing to America.

Playing on fears of crime was a lively and essential component of Clinton's snobmobbery. His strategist, Paul Begala, described it as the 'reality therapy of populism'. Clinton had 'worked for years on a set of ideas as a governor that put personal responsibility back at the centre of an activist communitarian philosophy, requiring responsibility in exchange for opportunity,' Begala explained.[7] Once the therapeutic and pseudo-philosophical language had been stripped away, what the New Democrats meant was that the mentally defective should be killed if their deaths would further the cause of activist communitarianism.

A short history explained their journey to the execution chamber. Clinton's 'reality therapy' began in 1980 when he was governor of Arkansas, a state in the old Confederacy. Cuban refugees being held in an Arkansas lock-up rioted, and the pictures of a racial struggle between white policemen and brown-skinned aliens helped lose Clinton the governorship. Bill and Hillary plotted what was to be a successful return to power and resolved 'never to be out-negatived again'. Christopher Hitchens, Clinton's best and least sympathetic biographer, says that the origins of the 'out-negatived' phrase were familiar to everyone who knew the politics of the South. When George Wallace lost the state of Alabama to a more nakedly racist opponent he swore in public that he would 'never be outniggered again'.[8]

If Clinton needed a reminder of the need to protect himself against the 'nigger-loving' charge, Michael Dukakis provided it in 1988. The Democrat's campaign for the presidency had been destroyed when George Bush Snr ran an advertising campaign which accused Dukakis of allowing a black rapist named Willie Horton to leave prison and rape again when Dukakis was governor of Massachusetts. Race and crime were running alongside Clinton when he ran for the Democratic presidential nomination in 1992. His campaign got off to a bad start. Gennifer Flowers, a nightclub singer of the type respectable mothers once warned their sons to stay away from, was telling journalists how Clinton couldn't stay away from her. The upholder of personal responsibility and activist communitarian values needed to prove he was a 'credible' candidate, and prove it quickly. He flew to Arkansas and covered his right flank by ordering the execution of Ricky Ray Rector, a black man with the mind of a child. Rector had been convicted of a double murder. Because he shot himself in the head when he was arrested, he was brain damaged and in no position to understand the charges and court proceedings. Judges in many jurisdictions would have considered him unfit to stand trial. When he was given his final meal, Rector pushed the pudding to the side of his tray – he was saving it 'for later', he explained to the guards. When he was strapped down, he helpfully directed his executioners to a vein into which they could inject the poison. A warder who witnessed the killing told *The New Yorker*, 'Ricky's a harmless guy. This is not something I want to do.'[9]

The 'pragmatic' defence of Clinton was that no hard-nosed American politician doubted that executing prisoners was something he had to do. If Clinton had shown mercy, Bush would have shown none and used Clinton's compassion against him.

*

No similar justification was available to the supporters of Tony Blair. The Tories had cut the prison population by 18 per cent between 1991 and 1993 and were in no position to accuse Labour of being 'soft on crime'. The war against civil liberty and rationality was begun by Blair without coercion. The responsibility was his alone. Blair attacked the Tories from the right for advocating policies Labour had agreed were essential only a few months earlier. Perhaps because he repeated the pious cant of Clinton's 'activist communitarian philosophy', or perhaps because nice manners and a public-school accent can still blind the British to the obvious, the sliminess of snatching a child's body wasn't seen for what it was. Gould was full of praise for the manoeuvre. The rightward shift after James Bulger's death was a 'repositioning [which] was classic Blair'.[10]

After the Bulger speech, there was to be no more bleeding-heart whining about the criminalising effects of poverty. In the *Sun* of 3 March 1993 all talk of alienation and deprivation was forgotten. Labour's new policy was simple. 'It's a bargain,' Blair wrote. 'We give opportunity, we demand responsibility. There is no excuse for crime. None.'

The Tories were bewildered. Kenneth Clarke correctly identified that 'Tony Blair has got the rhetoric of Bill Clinton off to perfection,' but predicted that Labour would soon retreat into 'vague stuff about how this is all really a social problem and it is all the result of economic success under Mrs Thatcher'. The next day Blair announced the first of what were to be dozens of 'crackdowns' on juvenile crime. As late as the autumn of 1994, John Maples, then a deputy chairman of the Conservative Party, was recommending that his government should invent ever more reactionary policies to test New Labour's machismo. He reasoned that 'either Blair will support our proposals and divide his party or oppose us and show he does not really mean what he says about crime'.[11] The silly man didn't realise what he was up against. New Labour would say or do anything. It had no last ditch or line in the sand. Abandoning principles wasn't an act its members performed with a grudging understanding that there was no other way to power. The passionate self-righteousness of New Labour, which Blair's religious belief may explain in part, distinguished it from cynical realism. The movement required its adherents to compromise with an ecstatic faith in the justness of compromise. You didn't get on in the political class of the 1990s if you gave up what you held dear with resignation, as a sad but necessary act in an inevitably imperfect world. You had to retreat with your eyes shining with the fire of belief. In these psychological circumstances, your former comrades – and sinful former self – were perverse heretics who rejected the true religion.

The Tories had to respond, had to show that they were as manly. They found the Bulger boys made useful punchbags. The trial judge took into account that Thompson and Venables had only shaved the age of criminal responsibility when he set their sentences. He recommended that they serve a minimum of eight years, a punishment which carried with it the hope that they would repent and be able to live honest lives in their twenties. The Lord Chief Justice, Lord Taylor, raised the minimum sentence to ten. Howard whacked it up to fifteen, nearly double the original minimum. The Law Lords were to hear in 1999 that Howard was closer to the views of *Sun* readers than those of the judges. The paper had persuaded 20,000 readers to send him coupons which demanded that 'Life should mean life.' The populist press and populist politicians began an ugly dance which stomps on to this day.

At the 1993 Conservative Party Conference, a strangely light-hearted Howard announced 27 measures to stamp out crime. After each one he paused, raised his arm and wiggled as the thunderous applause came in. Much of what was to become the 1994 Criminal Justice Act aimed to criminalise social misfits – New Age travellers, ravers, hunt saboteurs and demonstrators. They weren't breaking existing laws, but sight of them disturbed 'Middle England' – to use a pseudo-sociological label which was gaining in popularity. Howard told his party conference that he had also had second thoughts about prison and, what with one thing and another, discovered that it did work after all. He promised the jails would be filled when he took 'the handcuffs off the police and put them back on the criminals where they belong'. His language was now echoing unexpurgated David Maclean.

To make matters easier for the police, Howard said he would abolish the right to silence. The right not to say anything which might incriminate you came from deep in English history. Although defendants could refuse to answer questions before the Civil War, it was the crisis caused by Charles I's attempt to rule without Parliament which made the right to silence a fundamental liberty. The English common law didn't allow torture, even in cases of witchcraft. (The result was that England had far fewer witches than the other countries of Western Europe.) The ultimate means of persuading a suspect to break his silence could only be deployed by the King's prerogative courts, most notably the Court of Star Chamber. The repulsion the court aroused in Charles I's reign has ensured that 'Star-Chamber justice' has remained an insult to this day. The right to silence was secured when Parliament abolished Star Chamber in 1641. At times in the nineteenth century it was taken so seriously that the courts wouldn't let a defendant go into a dock and give evidence on his own behalf – even if he wanted to, even if giving evidence on his own behalf was the best means of saving himself from prison. The right survived Civil War, Restoration, industrial revolution, imperialism, decolonisation, the Irish troubles, two World Wars and one World Cup. It couldn't survive Howard and Blair.

A few years earlier the Birmingham and Guildford defendants had been acquitted because, in part, the courts had accepted that their confessions had been forced from them. The scandals should have led to greater protections for the innocent, but were quickly forgotten. Instead Howard proposed that a defendant's silence could be held against him in court. Blair worked hard to persuade John Smith and the rest of the shadow cabinet that Labour shouldn't oppose Howard's bill, but table 'reasoned amendments' instead. He later recalled with triumph that he'd caused Michael Howard's jaw to 'drop six inches' when he announced Labour's abandonment of liberty.[12] The inevitable final act was performed at the Labour Party Conference of 1996 by Jack Straw, who was given the Home Affairs brief when Blair became the Labour leader. 'Reasoned amendments' were forgotten. Labour had no intention of repealing any part of Howard's law, Straw told a fringe meeting.

With the Bulger boys rarely out of the papers, and new tales of 'rat boys' terrorising council estates and 'safari boys' being taken from custody to enjoy luxurious holidays at the expense of the long-suffering taxpayer, chastising children became a national obsession. In 1991, in the last years of the pre-Blair era, the Conservative government promised to end the grotesque practice of exposing fifteen- and sixteen-year-old boys to violence and rape by holding them in adult prisons. They were to be cared for in the secure local authority homes instead.

Ministers were prompted by the case of Philip Knight. Knight's suicide never achieved the notoriety of the murder of James Bulger, and I guess his name is forgotten now, but for a few weeks in 1990 he had a moment of posthumous fame. Knight was a fifteen-year-old adopted child who was sent to Swansea prison. His adoptive parents hadn't been able to cope with his petty crimes, and were advised to put him into care. The boy kept breaking out of the children's home and running back to them. After his death, his dismayed adoptive mother described how she had agreed with the professionals that the best way to help Philip was to tell him that she didn't love him. Breaking this to the boy was the worst day of her life, she said. 'He actually cried.' Knight was charged with, but never convicted of, the crime of stealing a handbag. He was held in the adult prison in Swansea because there was no local authority in all of England and Wales prepared to take him. Social workers warned the prison authorities that the boy might kill himself if he wasn't protected. Once inside, he tried to slash his wrists. The prison authorities held him in a bare cell for 23 hours a day. Although the absence of furniture was meant to prevent suicide, Philip managed to tear up a sheet and hang himself. 'The saddest fact is that there was just nowhere else for this boy to go,' said the West Glamorgan coroner Richard Morgan at the inquest.[13] Knight's death caused bishops and newspapers to fulminate and a 'distressed' Home Secretary to announce that he would make sure that boys were kept away from adult prisons.

As the war on crime hotted up, the number of boys in adult prisons increased, and humane sentiment evaporated. By 1996 there were 1,889 in adult prisons, a 72 per cent rise on 1992. The rise was accompanied by a fall in the number of secure places in local authority homes, where children might at least have a chance of changing their fortunes before it was too late.[14] In opposition, Labour condemned the government for breaking its word, and then adopted the Tory policy when it was in government. No one doubted that children were in danger in adult jails. Sir Stephen Tumim said that 'in many ways these youngsters have less in common with young men in their late teens than is generally realised. They are often despised by the older group. [They are] resented for their childishness and become victims of intimidation.'

Tumim's warnings were all very well, but as the 1990s progressed, politicians wondered where the advantage lay in saving a few prole boys, or adults for that matter. What headlines would they get for pursuing such an eccentric policy? The best they might hope for was that the papers and focus groups wouldn't notice. At worst, they would be accused of softness by the media and ridiculed as out-of-touch Hampstead liberals who cared nothing for the victims of crime. Why take the risk when the risk could be borne by others? There were 64 prison sucides by inmates of all ages in 1996, 68 in 1997, 83 in 1998 and 91 in 1999. The death penalty had been abolished for the British equivalents of Ricky Ray Rector decades before, but the mad, the young, the abused and the hopeless were free to dispose of themselves at Her Majesty's Pleasure.

Rather than get children out of prison, the Conservative government decided to gather together the most disturbed children in the country and hold them in private kiddy jails. New Labour opposed Howard on two grounds. Straw had said that he found the notion of profiting from human captivity – the business plan behind slavery – 'morally repugnant'. He was also committed to handing over the under-fourteens to local social services departments. Within two months of gaining power in May 1997, Straw broke his promises with a speed which was shocking then, but wouldn't raise an eyebrow now. Private jails for children and adults were the way forward, he said.

The cost of holding a twelve- to fourteen-year-old boy at Straw's new Medway secure training centre in Kent was £125,000 a year – ten times the price of a top-of-the-range private school. Disturbed child learned from disturbed child and, naturally, they rioted. In June 1998 they trashed the accommodation and education blocks and hurled pool balls at staff. Thirty police in full riot gear were needed to restore order. Group 4, the company running the jail, maintained control thereafter with a 'restraint squad'. According to the Social Services Inspectorate the team was set loose on children as often as 150 times a month. It relied on the use of unauthorised locks and holds, and 'on a number of recorded occasions this had led to injuries being incurred', the inspectors found. Teachers hurt children and children hurt teachers. In the Medway's first six months the Home Office recorded 100 assaults on staff by the tiny inmates. Many good teachers walked out of the graffiti-covered blocks to find less dangerous employment.[15]

Paul Boateng, Britain's first black minister, was the politician responsible for Medway. On his promotion to the Cabinet he rashly quoted Martin Luther King and said he hoped to be judged by the content of his character rather than the colour of his skin. Medway revealed Boateng's character. He described the children in the Medway as 'a menace' and refused to close the prison. Instead he gave Group 4 the money to open a second centre. What his government was doing made no sense by

the old standards of public administration. Rather than introduce violent children to each other, it would have been cheaper
and safer to teach them separately. Individual care would have
protected the public by diverting children from crime, rather
than teaching them how to be better criminals. But the politicians of the 1990s wanted to be tough on criminals, not tough
on crime.

The result was a deranged political world. Rumours, supposi-
tions and newspaper headlines which everyone in the know
knew to be false moved public policy. I provided one of the ear-
liest examples of the last item on that list when I phoned Jack
Straw just before the 1997 election. We chatted away and, for no
particular reason, I asserted that New Labour wouldn't want to
follow Bill Clinton's example and impose curfews on children
out after dark. I was mistaken. Straw burbled that the curfew
wheeze hadn't occurred to him before, but, on a second or so's
reflection, it seemed an excellent idea. 'There are a lot of complaints about youngsters out on the streets until late at night,'
he said. 'I see them when I'm driving back from the Commons
and wonder where their parents are.' He called back an hour
later and said that he hadn't meant to say what he had said and
New Labour had no plans to introduce curfews. He asked me to
forget the conversation and not to print my account of it. I
refused, not least because I'd told the editor he no longer had to
worry about the front-page lead. Because the *Observer* published his ramblings, New Labour was forced to save Straw's
face by drawing up a policy on the back of a fag packet. My
piece appeared on a Sunday morning. By Sunday lunchtime
New Labour had announced that it was convinced that children
under ten must be curfewed from 9 p.m. to 6 a.m.

I felt a guilty pang. Nothing should stand in the way of a good
story, as all journalists know, but martial law for tots seemed a
high price to pay, even for a front-page lead. Fortunately for what
passes for my conscience, not one local authority applied for a
child curfew order. Councillors reasoned that it was impossible
for the police to tell the difference between a nine-year-old and

an eleven-year-old and officers' energy would be better spent chasing criminals rather than going after children who had done nothing wrong. Rather than admit a mistake, Blair declared that curfews had been a success. The government extended the upper age-limit to fifteen. Not one local authority asked for the under-fifteens to be curfewed either.

Curfews were the appetiser. In 1999, at the height of Peter Mandelson's home-loan scandal, the order went out for ministers to come up with initiatives which would distract the press. Before they were thrown out, the Conservatives had tried to out-Blair Blair. If burglars were convicted of three offences, they were to receive automatic three-year sentences. New Labour opposed the plan at the time but, of course, that meant nothing. Straw looked around for something to do and decided that 'three strikes and you're out' was worth a go. Broadcasters and journalists responded to Straw's U-turn by giving the government enough favourable publicity to put a smile on Alastair Campbell's grim face. 'Three strikes and you're out', which once again was taken from Clinton's America, sounded tough, but there was a catch in the small print. If magistrates or judges found there were 'specific circumstances' in the defendant's favour, they could waive the mandatory sentence and impose a sentence of their own. Magistrates and judges loathe mandatory sentences. They take all the fun out of judging. There's no point in being a judge if the government stops you setting punishments which fit the crime. Every judge and magistrate found 'specific circumstances' which removed the need to give mandatory sentences. Not one was imposed.

'Night courts' delivering instant justice to yobs in pubs and clubs were launched with a fuss, but disappeared into quiet obscurity after lacklustre results from pilot projects. A Criminal Records Bureau was meant to examine 10 to 12 million citizens each year and tell their employers what crimes, if any, they had committed. Prison reformers said selective vetting might keep convicted paedophiles away from children, but mass vetting of the population would leave workers with a criminal record at a

distinct disadvantage if they wanted to find a job and go straight. They needn't have fretted. When, after many delays, the bureau opened in 2002, it couldn't manage to examine the pasts of 400,000 teachers, let alone the rest of the workforce.

From Jack Straw promising in 1995 to 'reclaim the streets' from 'aggressive begging of winos and addicts and the squeegee merchants', to Tony Blair promising in 2000 to allow police officers to march drunken yobs to cashpoints and hit them with a £100 fine for 'kicking in your gate, throwing traffic cones around your street or hurling abuse into the night sky',[16] government was reduced to a charade. Measures which could never work or should never work were hurled out of Whitehall by wanton ministers.

Without crime, Parliament would have been on part-time working. Between Blair's victory in May 1997 and the June 2001 election, 31 law-and-order bills were presented to Parliament. The Queen's Speech of 1999 presented nine for one parliamentary session. Another fourteen were enacted between June 2001 and March 2003. New Labour created 661 criminal offences between May 1997 and March 2003, with the Home Office coming up with 287 of them all on its own. The Tories worked out that in the eighteen months after the June 2001 election Downing Street and the Home Office launched 100 anti-crime initiatives.[17] At the 2002 Labour Party conference, just before another Queen's Speech filled with anti-crime bills, Blair talked as if no minister had looked at crime for years. He would put a stop to the neglect. It was time, he declared to an amnesiac audience, to 'rebalance the system emphatically and in favour of the victims of crime'.

The Tories were in a trap. Blair ensared each leader after Margaret Thatcher with the Clinton stratagem of 'triangulation'. Whenever they came up with an idea he liked – identity cards, the abolition of rights to jury trials – Blair would move to the right and steal it. He threatened to reduce the once-feared Conservative Party to the level of a new New Labour think-tank. To maintain the support of Conservative members, whose average

age of 65 left the party perilously exposed to the decimating effects of a bad winter, and of a Conservative press, which would rather see its friends stay out of power for a generation than re-examine one of its prejudices, the Tories were pushed further to the right.

The Canadian journalist Daniel Casse said of Clinton that 'he has learned how the Republicans can be at once a steady source of inspiration and a perfect foil'.[18] The same fate met the Tories. Blair was left holding the 'centre-ground' – a prize plot of land whose mortgage was paid by emptying the Labour Party of meaning. When he faced challenges from his miserable supporters, he could use the perfect foil of a Conservative revival to keep them in line. When the Conservatives looked as if they might revive, he could steal their ideas. Triangulation was a fantastically successful electoral tactic in the 1990s, although I suspect that when Labour loses power what's left of the party will be so drained and aimless no one will know how to revive it – or want to waste their time trying to revive it.

It's easy to forget that John Major began his premiership as a tolerant guy who welcomed the gay Ian McKellen into Downing Street and declared that he was breaking with Margaret Thatcher's martinet style. Triangulation pushed Major and Howard into ever-meaner postures. Not the smallest of New Labour's propaganda successes was to persuade the liberal majority in Britain that Michael Howard was a nastier politician than Tony Blair. To this day, the Conservatives are held responsible for a war New Labour started.

While Howard adopted the manners of a hanging judge, Major responded by announcing that he would go 'back to basics' by punishing promiscuous single mothers. Unfortunately, back to basics was an invitation to the press to examine the promiscuity of Conservative politicians. By the time the papers and New Labour had finished, 'a Conservative' had been redefined as a man who would pick your pocket and steal your wife (or husband in more exotic instances). When New Labour came to power, one of its first acts was to implement Conservative plans to impoverish single mothers it had denounced a mere year before. Its double standards didn't provoke uproar: the Conservatives were established as the fleshy hypocrites in the public mind.

William Hague tried to break out of the triangular trap when he became Conservative leader after the landslide defeat of 1997. Hague had noticed that the Tories no longer looked as if they understood or liked the country they were meant to love. He emphasised his willingness to lower the age of consent for homosexuals to sixteen and to allow gay marriages – 'When they're not causing harm to other people, why should we object?' He wanted a compassionate appreciation of single mothers – 'It is better for a child to have one happy parent who cares and loves him or her than to have two and suffer from domestic violence.' He went to the Notting Hill Carnival in a baseball cap, signalling a sincere if gauche acceptance of multiculturalism. He daringly slept in a hotel suite with Ffion Jenkins before a vicar had joined them in matrimony.

'Why do I share a party with those who advocate sodomite marriage?' howled Norman Tebbit. He was soon pacified. By the 2001 election Hague had been triangulated by New Labour and pushed into line by his supporters in the press. He ran on a manifesto of *Daily Mail* cuttings and the Tories went down to their second landslide defeat in succession.

Nothing like it had happened before. The Conservatives were Europe's most successful democratic party. They were hammered in 1906 and 1945, but were back as credible contenders for power by the elections of 1910 and 1950. Their opponents could be gratified by their descent into obscurity at the turn of the new century only for as long as they failed to grasp that what Blair had disabled was the Conservative Party, not conservatism.

The last thing Iain Duncan Smith, the new Tory leader, wanted to do was to repeat the mistakes of William Hague. Yet by 2003, the pressure from New Labour and the Conservative activists and press pushed him to the extreme. He, too, became a source of ideas and a perfect foil as he made a great show of snubbing those Tories who wanted to destroy their image as the 'nasty party'.

Knowing commentators shrugged when confronted with the posturing of gesture politicians. If the swinish multitude believed them, that was their problem. The sophisticated could comfort themselves with the thought that the curfews, mandatory penalties, night courts and the rest were just stunts. There was no reason to be alarmed because nothing really changed.

The affectation of superiority, which was endemic in broadcasting in my experience, missed the shift of power from the citizen to the state. Between the fall of the Berlin Wall and 11 September Britain had no foreign enemies. After the Good Friday Agreement, even the IRA gave up killing. Yet it was in this peaceful interlude that the political class came close to declaring a state of emergency. The Terrorism Act of 2000 designated as 'terrorists' those who damaged property for political reasons or planned to damage property for political reasons. (Hairy Greenpeace mystics who plotted to pull up genetically modified rape in an East Anglian field were on a par with Osama bin Laden.) Every few years first the Conservatives and then New Labour tried to order the population to return to the wartime expedient of carrying identity cards. New regulations on Internet use allowed the police and security services to read emails without going to the trouble of obtaining a warrant from a judge. Plans to force people the police didn't like to prove that their money had been obtained legally undermined the presumption that a suspect was innocent until the state proved he was guilty beyond reasonable doubt. As I write, the radio is saying the government is proposing to intern people it says have an untreatable personality disorder, and to make fair trials for the sane impossible by revealing their previous convictions to juries. Nothing special about that – I'd have heard much the same if I turned on the radio at any time in the decade after the Bulger case.

Nor was the refusal of the courts to implement all the zany ideas which fell from the incontinent minds in Westminster absolute. Judges weren't as independent as they liked to believe. If politicians and the media demanded sterner sentences, that was what they gave them. The legacy of Blair's crime war was a prison population which went from 41,000 to 73,000 in the decade after James Bulger's death. Rhetoric was as influential as legislation. When angry speeches were made and furious editorials written, the prison population went up. The legal system's susceptibility to an authoritarian climate explains why the incorporation of the European Human Rights Act into British law, New Labour's sole liberal achievement, had a negligible impact. Its supporters claimed it would revolutionise public life, while its opponents howled that the prison doors would be thrown open. As it was, change was minimal. A conservative and defensive judiciary rejected most claims that human rights were being abused.

The obsession with crime and the assault on liberty might have been justified if the country were falling into lawlessness. Yet the 1990s saw crime rates collapse. According to the British Crime Survey, the most authoritative guide, crime fell by a fifth between 1992 and 2001 and by a third between 1995 and 2001.[19]

Unemployment is one of many causes for crime; the decline in civilised culture, family breakdown and human wickedness play their part. But if Blair was an honest man, he might have looked at the figures and been struck by a bothersome thought. The crime figures showed that his grandstanding and assaults on liberty had been pointless as well as pernicious. Roy Hattersley had been right all along. Gordon Brown was a better Home Secretary than Jack Straw or David Blunkett. The evidence for these shocking conclusions would have been hard to dismiss. The punishment boom after James Bulger's death couldn't explain the fall in villainy – as the Home Office said, a 1 per cent reduction in crime necessitated a 25 per cent increase in the prison population. What worked was work for the unemployed. From 1981 to 1991, during the mass unemployment of the Thatcher regime, crime rose by 3 per cent a year on average. Between 1991 and 1993, when unemployment leapt up because of Thatcher's and Major's ERM debacle, crime rose by 11 per cent a year. The growth rate slowed to 2 per cent a year as the recession eased between 1993 and 1995, and fell by an extraordinary average of 6 per cent a year between 1995 and 2000 as the bubble market boomed and unemployment went back to pre-Thatcher levels. Few wanted to admit that full employment and lower crime went together – for where would our world be if we didn't have the fear of joblessness to keep workers in line?

Despite living through the first significant drop in crime since the Second World War, the public remained fearful. In 2002 the risk of being a victim of crime was at its lowest level since the researchers for the British Crime Survey began work in 1981. None the less, 71 per cent of the interviewees believed that crime was getting worse.

The new élite had proved it was on the side of the masses by terrifying the masses. There was a second paradox. The public was meant to be delighted by tough policies designed to assuage its fears and meet its desires. But at the 1997 general election turnout was 71.5 per cent – the lowest since 1935. In 2001 turnout fell to 59 per cent, the lowest in British democratic history. If the élite was populist, why wasn't it popular?

TWO

Elected Every Day

To get ahead in Britain it was essential for the ambitious to swear they were the enemies of élitism. Their power and wealth weren't privileges but the hard-won wages they earned from humble service for 'the People'. Peculiarly, politicians, businessmen, academics, culture managers and editors insisted that the true élite wasn't in power or close to being in power. The real élitists, the true enemies of the People, were men and women with no more hope of receiving a peerage from Downing Street than being made Director-General of the BBC.

Sceptics were élitist because they refused to share the People's authentic emotion at the election of Tony Blair or grief at the death of Princess Di. Critics of business were élitist because they presumed to know better than hundreds of millions of consumers. Fox-hunters were élitist because they wore fusty uniforms. The knowledgeable on any subject from flower-arranging to foreign policy were élitist because they knew more than the ignorant. Judges were élitist because they were judgemental. University courses which didn't have an immediate practical benefit were élitist because they offered education for education's sake. Broadsheet readers were élitist because they looked down their noses at tabloid readers. Tabloid readers were élitist because they looked down their noses at blacks and gays. The bookish were élitist because they thought that 'great' writers were 'better' than 'bad' writers. Authors who didn't put 'great', 'better' and 'bad' in inverted commas were élitist because they assumed that their subjective standards had a wider validity. To be in a minority was to be in the élite, and by definition those who disliked MTV or Classic FM or *Pop Idol* or Britart or piped music in restaurants or Andrew Lloyd Webber or the

National Lottery or cars or racist language or anti-racist language or sloppy grammar or ready-to-eat meals or America or
McDonald's or alcopops or homeopathic hocus-pocus or
chicklit or lad-mags or newspapers or television or advertising
or public nudity or stand-up comedy or football or attacks on
civil liberties were élitist because they disagreed with others
who did. If only for a moment, everyone was élitist. Except the
élite.

At the 1999 Labour Party Conference Blair promised to fight
'the forces of conservatism, the cynics, the élites, the establishment'. In New Labour's 2001 manifesto, he was at it again. For
too long, he declared, 'we have been undermined by weaknesses of élitism and snobbery'.

Like Margaret Thatcher before him, Blair was accused of being
presidential. He was far grander than that. Presidents in democracies were bound by written constitutions. In France and America, they often found that a rival party controlled the legislature
and did all that it could to limit their power. Britain didn't have a
written constitution, and the first-past-the-post system ensured
the Prime Minister could control the legislature with an enormous majority even if he had failed to win a majority of the vote.
'Presidential' was too tame a description. Like Thatcher, Blair was
monarchical. Yet here was the elected monarch, the fountain of
tens of thousands of quango jobs, peerages and favours,
announcing that he was the sworn enemy of the élite.

George Walden, the former Tory MP and cultural critic,
noted the absurdity and identified the cunning of an establishment which proclaimed it was prolier-than-thou:

> Machiavelli wrote that the only way the minority could rule the
> majority was by force or guile – the methods of the lion, or of the fox.
> Today we have the foxiest élite ever: one that rules in the people's
> name while preserving the lion's share of the power. For the first time
> in Western democratic history society is dominated by an élite of
> anti-élitists . . . [They are] prone to describing themselves as com-
> mitted egalitarians, but the problem with egalitarians is that they are
> so rarely on the level.'[1]

The new élite's hypocrisy was a pleasure to mock. Their opponents, however, had troubles of their own. The first and most dispiriting was that there weren't many who wanted to join the mockery. The 1990s were guided by a postmodern sensibility which provided a perfect justication for the few to pose as the comrades of the many. It may seem perverse to credit such wilful obscurantists as Jacques Derrida or Jacques Lacan with the wit to guide an old lady across the road. All I can say is that ideas matter, and that the dominant postmodern idea of wild subjectivity suited the powerful to a tee. In Britain, postmodernism suffocated what had once been a vibrant tradition. Anti-élitism had usually been associated with the left. The Chartists struggled against the aristocratic élite to secure the vote for working men. The Suffragettes struggled against the male élite to secure the vote for women. George Orwell, E. P. Thompson and Christopher Hill took working-class culture seriously, and defended it from the 'enormous condescension of posterity', in Thompson's words. In many university departments in the 1990s, anyone who used 'culture' without putting ironic inverted commas around it would be laughed out of the staff room. There was no culture, no truth and, in extreme cases, no reality. There were only subjective narratives which were all equally valid. Po-mo academics tied themselves in knots when they were asked how they would condemn the neo-Nazi narrative of Holocaust denial or the misogynist narrative of female inferiority. They couldn't, of course. Nonetheless, they clung to the dogma that it was élitist to 'privilege' Hamlet by saying it was 'better' than Confessions of a Handyman, and an insult to the intelligence of viewers and readers to suggest that advertising or the press could wash the smallest part of their brains when they were taking signs and symbols and building their own subjective and transgressive narratives.

If you don't believe that the reigning ideas of any age seep through society, and wonder how convoluted philosophers can influence people who have never read a word they've written, consider how often you hear 'judgemental' used as a stern rebuke. 'Judgemental' means using your judgement. It's impossible to be a half-way intelligent or quarter-way moral person without reaching judgements. But judging is élitist because it implies that you can appeal to standards which don't exist except as the constructs of oppressors.

Postmodernists presented themselves as radicals, but their theories made criticism of the market impossible. It was élitist to insist on standards other than making money and increasing market share. If you said there was no reason for the licence fee unless the BBC produced potentially unpopular programmes which commercial stations wouldn't touch, you were a paternalist. If you said most people didn't understand what happened to their money in the bubble market and were lambs waiting to be fleeced, you were accused of believing that people were stupid and needed top-down regulation to protect them. In a pseudo-democracy, it took aristocratic self-confidence to state that people could often be stupid and in need of protection. Such assertions didn't draw warm applause, particularly on daytime television.

The British plutocracy knew a bargain when it saw it. Murdoch's News International recognised its debt of gratitude to postmodern theorists who asserted that it was an élitist insult to smart and savvy consumers to worry about the concentration of power in the hands of propagandists. In 1993 Andrew Knight, the group's chairman, cried to a meeting at the Insitute of Directors:

> For heaven's sake, let's get over our hang-ups over who owns what. The future landscape of the media means that the perception (and it is only a perception – not a fact) of the mighty media mogul will belong to the past ... I am talking about the life-building dynamic of images and information where nobody is a sole provider, because the thinking, articulate, emancipated viewer is the only king in his or her sovereign individualist millions.'[2]

As Greg Philo of the Glasgow Media Group said, the logic of postmodernism would make it 'élitist' to complain if Rupert

Murdoch owned every newspaper and television station on earth. The 'sovereign individualistic millions' would still construct their equally valid and equally subjective semiotic narratives.

Other powerful men were as glad to discover that they were the People's chosen. Gerry Robinson, the chairman of Granada, who gave a tiny part of his fortune to New Labour – and received the chairmanship of the Arts Council – told artists that 'for too long performers have continued to ply their trade to the same white, middle-class audience. In the back of their minds lurks the vague hope that one day enlightenment might descend semi-miraculously upon the rest, that the masses might one day get wise to their brilliance.' The patronising cultural snobs he lectured would be lucky to make in a lifetime what Robinson pocketed in a year. Nevertheless Robinson was the working-class hero. Gavyn Davies, the friend of New Labour who received the chairmanship of the BBC's Board of Governors, denounced complaints about the Corporation's falling standards as a plot by the white, southern middle classes to 'hijack' the BBC. Gavyn Davies was white. He lived in London. To be strictly accurate, he wasn't middle-class. Estimates of the size of his stash hovered between £100 and £170 million. (I'm not going to bother trying to narrow that range: once you're in nine figures, what's the use of counting?) For all his advantages, when he looked in the mirror he saw a horny-handed and furnace-scarred defender of ethnic youth against the imperialism of the honky bourgeoisie.

If they were criticised, business leaders asked what was wrong with giving people what they wanted. The size of the piles of Davies and Robinson was neither here nor there, they argued. You could laugh all you wanted at their revolutionary pretensions, but their wealth didn't make them élitists because their performance was judged every day by customers in the direct democracy of the marketplace. Nor, they added, was it self-evidently wrong for politicians to follow the example of commerce. Successful corporations produced brands which had conquered the world. Business had shown it knew how to sell itself; Labour was a remaindered line gathering dust at the back of the stockroom.

Tony Blair was convinced and turned Labour into a convincing imitation of the anti-élitist corporation. He gave 'annual reports' as if he were chairman of the board. His MPs aped sales reps with no purpose other than to push head office's product. Shona McIsaac, the New Labour MP for Cleethorpes, was a prize-winning case in point. She exemplified the willing subservience of Blair's lower-middle managers when she said: 'We have to get real. I was voted in because I was a Labour candidate. Few people, if any, voted for me as a person. I have a sneaking suspicion that my husband voted for me because I was me, and I voted for me because I was me – but if I had not been the Labour Party candidate, I would not have voted for me either.' Philip Gould was as explicit. His job was to protect and promote the 'New Labour brand' with 'holistic' campaigns, which were 'a vast, multi-dimensional structure moving forwards and backwards, upwards and downwards, meshing abstraction and concreteness, policy with presentation, future to past. The art of campaigning is to take this complication and make it compellingly simple.'[3]

People like me found his gibberish insulting, but couldn't deny that it followed the gibberish from marketing departments with puppyish loyalty. Gould and his kind weren't insulted by the comparison. If a corporate Labour Party behaved like Sainsbury's and gave the public what it wanted, why should anyone but a snob wince at that? Wasn't pleasing the People the point of democracy? The exploitation of celebrated murders, the removal of liberties and the gestures on crime were justified by New Labour as a bending of the knee before the wishes of the sovereign people. They could no more be blamed for being responsive to the market-place than Sainsbury's could be blamed for selling Coca-Cola. Neither gesture politics nor sugary drinks were good for you, but if that's what the punters wanted that's what they must have.

The failure of the People to thank the political class by turning out for elections was an act of churlish ingratitude. The poor dears in Downing Street tried so hard to ingratiate themselves with the masses. They followed modern crowd-pleasing techniques to the letter, but were met with cynicism.

Since the 1970s, psychoanalysts and psychiatrists had served business by using focus groups to identify the subconscious desires of niche 'lifestyle' markets. Their organisers weren't interested in social class or gender – the traditional classifications of marketing departments. They wanted to know how to subliminally associate their products with the subconscious desires of potential consumers; how to direct advertising and products to people who saw themselves as free spirits or adventurous or unconventional or threatened. The typical focus-group question – 'If X plc was a car, what type of car would it be?' – wasn't as idiosyncratic as it sounded. Companies had to know if they were seen as fast, reliable, dashing or clapped out. In a developed world awash with goods which all but the poorest could afford, subliminal associations with sexy nonconformity helped a line shoot off the shelves. The brand's image mattered more than the product.

I don't want to pretend that Thatcher and Reagan were innocent parties in the debasement of public life that the transfer of advertising techniques to politics brought. Their aides knew all the modern tricks. Until the 1990s the Tories were always ahead of Labour in the race to bring the latest marketing gimmicks to politics. But gimmickry was taken to the extreme by Blair and his mentor, Bill Clinton.

In his campaign to be re-elected to the US Presidency in 1996 Clinton authorised the probing of the emotions of America. Under conditions of strict secrecy, hundreds of researchers were sent to hit the phones at offices in Manhattan and Denver. They were instructed to conduct a 'neuro-personality poll' which would map the electorate's psyche. Their questions had nothing to do with politics as it was conventionally understood. 'Do you go to parties?' asked the pollsters. 'Which spectator

sports do you prefer? Are you happy with your current situation? Are you spontaneous or organised? What would you do
on a romantic weekend?'

Voters were placed in niche categories – vaguely liberal types
in university towns, lovers of the outdoors. Clinton's Democrats
tended to be single. They liked rap, classical and Top 40 music.
Republicans preferred the golden oldies of the 1970s. Wavering
voters included a large number of anxious parents. Clinton
soothed them with neuro-policies which showed he felt their
fears. He declared his support for curfews, school uniforms and
for V-chips in televisions, which stopped children watching
porn. Like New Labour's growls at squeegee-merchants and
beggars, Clinton's stances meant little or nothing in practice. All
they did – all they were intended to do – was calm barely articu-
lated worries. Will my children's innocence be protected? Is that
hunched figure in the shadows staring at me? The distribution
of wealth and power, the old stuff of politics, didn't get a look-
in. Clinton was re-elected in 1996 with a landslide. Focus-group
politics appeared to work.4

By the early years of the new century, the trickery was being
seen through. Clinton was meant to have said that the most
powerful citizens in America were members of focus groups.
Philip Gould claimed that focus groups empowered the consumer by enabling 'politicians to hear directly the voters' voices'.5 Neither noticed that government wasn't a business.
Unless you are very unlucky, what you buy in a supermarket
won't kill a member of your family. If you have a son or brother in the army, the government can finish him off by declaring
war. A miscalculation by the Asda board shouldn't lose you
your job or home, unless you happen to work for Asda. The
Treasury could deprive you of both if it continued its blun-
dering tradition and took the pound into the Euro on the
wrong terms. Government is meant to be about what matters,
and most of what corporations sell doesn't matter in the least.
Focus-group politics was an attempt to reduce debate to commercial questions as banal as 'Do you prefer Pepsi to Coke?'

Millions refused to vote because they realised that the 'issues' and 'talking points' they were meant to choose between were ephemeral.

The anti-élitist élite was interested in distracting people, not empowering them. It proved its duplicity when it was confronted with focus groups with genuine power: juries. Authoritarian governments had always hated the idea that a random collection of citizens could gather together and reach verdicts which might contradict official policy. Lord Devlin, a Law Lord from the old establishment, warned in 1956 that: 'The first object of any tyrant in Whitehall would be to make Parliament utterly subservient to his will, and the next to overthrow or diminish trial by jury. [It] is more than an instrument of justice and more than one wheel of the constitution: it is the lamp that shows that freedom lives.'[6] His Lordship was prescient. The tyrants from the new establishment had little time for Parliament and no time for juries. The assault began in 1993 when the Royal Commission on Criminal Justice proposed removing rights to trial by jury for theft, burglary, dishonesty and minor sex and drug offences. The crimes weren't of the highest seriousness, but they carried prison sentences and could destroy careers and the good names of defendants. Michael Howard took up the Commission's proposal after the Bulger murder. Labour was scandalised by the dimming of the 'lamp of freedom'. Gareth Williams QC, a learned Labour lawyer, said: 'This would be madness. There are delays and inefficiencies at the moment, but the way to deal with them is to improve the mechanics not to erode a fundamental liberty.' Tony Blair said: 'Fundamental rights to justice cannot be determined by administrative convenience.' Jack Straw said: 'Surely cutting down the right to jury trial, making the system less fair, is not only wrong but short-sighted.'

New Labour won the 1997 election. Gareth Williams was elevated to the peerage and, as Lord Williams of Mostyn, became Attorney-General. Tony Blair became Prime Minister. Jack

Straw became Home Secretary. Together they tried to implement all the cuts to jury rights that Howard and the Royal Commission had proposed. In 2001, after an inquiry by Lord Justice Auld, a judge who would have been at home in Hanoverian England, the populists of New Labour went further. Not only would they abolish rights to trial by jury for alleged thieves, burglars and the rest, but for all defendants facing charges likely to attract a sentence of less than two years, for all alleged frauds and for all but a few defendants aged sixteen or seventeen. Auld also wanted to strip juries of the power to deliver 'perverse' verdicts when they felt sorry for a defendant or thought the law was dictatorial. No modern equivalents of the eighteenth-century jurors who refused to send poachers to the gallows or convict political activists were to be tolerated. Three-quarters of jury trials were threatened.[7] In America, Australia or any other common-law democracy, it would have taken a coup d'état to implement the government's programme.

None of the justifications for the removal of popular power stood up to one minute's scrutiny. The government said that professional criminals were exploiting the jury system. But hardened villains knew that if they opted for a jury trial and were found guilty, the judge would throw the book at them. The government said that jury trials were clogging the system. But the proportion of cases committed to crown courts by defendants who exercised their right to choose jury trial fell in the 1990s. One explanation remained: the populist élite despised the People, and was a little frightened of them.

Obviously, it couldn't come out and say that. So Jack Straw explained that by taking away the right of the People to decide whether a citizen was innocent or guilty New Labour was giving rights to the People. The true élite wasn't a government which threatened liberty, rather it was 'BMW-driving civil-liberties lawyers' who tried to protect juries. They subscribed to a 'woolly-minded liberalism' which took 'no account of the situation of those who are less favoured than they'. It remains a wonder of the age that this line of humbug can still be spouted after all these years.

Disillusioned New Labour idealists grew sick of it long ago. Derek Draper, who had been an aide to Peter Mandelson, looked back with contempt on the energy he wasted on the manipulation business. For all its flaws, the Labour movement was once 'a countervailing power' to the establishment, he said. To replace it with 'eight people drinking wine in a focus group in Kettering' and pretend that they could counter the influence of the big battalions was laughable. Focus-group politics 'suits big business, suits entrenched interests and suits the status quo'.[8]

No focus group instructed New Labour to part-privatise the NHS or fight Iraq. Blair was prepared to be unpopular when he wanted to be. Populism taught him how to keep the public sweet with trivial or savage policies. Gould admitted as much. His justification for the domination of politics by pollsters was that he and his colleagues were scientists who objectively examined the popular will and told politicians how to satisfy it. They had no agenda or interests of their own. Yet Gould was surprisingly picky about which scientific findings he accepted as objective. Just before the 1997 election when Conservatives were freely admitting that Britain had changed, Gould took the temperature at 'a vast polling meeting, stuffed with academic experts'. They told him that New Labour 'could safely put taxes up'. Was Gould, a man who lived and died by the messages the neutral polls deliver, relieved to hear that Blair might commit himself to combating inequality and improving public services? Not exactly. 'I couldn't stand it and left,' he said. 'I couldn't bear to watch.'

Power didn't reside in focus groups. More influential was a larger, more magnificent group whose pomp was matched only by its ubiquity. It believed it could determine the opinions of the polled, and expected to be treated with the respect it deserved.

*

On 25 February 2003 a balding man with a slight stoop and shy grin looked down on the members of the House of Commons' Culture, Media and Sport Committee. He was their superior in every respect. An MP had a salary of £55,118; the Prime Minister made £171,554; Paul Dacre, the editor of the *Daily Mail*, took £834,000 and had his employers' promise that he'd be free to cash share options worth £14 million in 2008 if the *Mail's* circulation continued to grow.

Although Dacre's paper attacked the 'politically correct' Islington mafia which was destroying old England, his London *pied-à-terre* was in an Islington cul-de-sac which combined the convenience of the capital with the charm of a village. On one side was a park. On the other, long herbaceous borders drifted down 60-foot gardens to creeper-covered cottages. Dacre's paper attacked restrictions on the freedom of motorists as 'political correctness gone mad!' But the residents of his terrace had no time for Mondeo men. Too many outsiders were parking in front of their houses, without so much as by your leave, and taking the places of Dacre's chauffeur and the neighbours' servants. Finding a space was 'dreadful', one cottage-dweller told the local paper. 'My gardener was forced to drop his ladders and mower off and park elsewhere.' Something had to be done. So the residents proposed buying their lane and turning it into a private road. If 'two-Jags' Prescott had matched this, he would have been exposed in the press and ridiculed by satirists. But while Prescott was a mere elected politician who deserved all the abuse he received, Dacre belonged to a more legitimate class of striving anti-élitist media managers. Dacre put MPs in their place as he explained his democratic superiority. 'Let me say first of all that unless you produce a newspaper that interests the public they are not going to buy you. I do not have a five-year term of office like you. I have to persuade the public every day to go out and buy my newspaper.'

Journalists liked to present themselves as the People's representatives in their battle with the élite. They were, on occasion. But journalists and politicians were both in the business of sell-

ing politics. To pretend, as postmodernists and Murdoch executives did, that the media didn't mould a society in which their
coverage filled every minute of every day was ludicrous. As
ludicrous, was the belief of New Labour's opponents that the
degrading of public life was all the fault of Tony Blair. The
struggles and alliances between the politicians and journalists
helped turn millions off politics and journalism.

Journalists appeared to have the upper hand. No editor on
Fleet Street and no attack-dog presenters on the BBC earned as
little as Tony Blair. Editors and star writers and broadcasters
were better dressed, better educated and much better paid than
most of the politicians they inspected and derided. The number
of Oxbridge graduates going into the press and television
tripled from 1971 to 1994.[9] The price of failure was high. At the
bottom, the newspapers and television companies relied on
low-paid, non-unionised labour. If you could crawl to the top,
however, a career in the media offered wealth, public recognition and a raffish freedom to defy the conventions the media
insisted on everyone else obeying.

If the picture of media grandees as aristocrats seems hyper-
bolic consider the following scenes. On Black Wednesday, when
the pound crashed out of the European Exchange Rate Mechanism, Kelvin MacKenzie, the editor of the *Sun*, rang John Major
and told him, 'John, I'm holding a bucket of shit in my hands
and tomorrow morning it's going to be emptied over your
head.' At the 1997 Labour Party conference Major's successor,
Tony Blair, was lunched by the *Mirror*. The conversation turned
to a recent decision by Gordon Brown to freeze the pay of his
Cabinet colleagues. Piers Morgan, the editor of the *Mirror*, was
probably earning three times as much as the PM. He had begun
his career as Piers Pugh Morgan, but had dropped the Pugh
because it was too élitist a name for a man making a career in
the masses. Plain Mr Morgan nevertheless relished his class
advantage over the PM. He threw a £20 note at the Prime Minister and bellowed: 'Hey, Tony, buy the kids some toys.' The note
landed on the table. A silence descended. It takes a man of

extraordinary vulgarity to bring out the hidden grace in Alastair Campbell. Piers Morgan was that man. Campbell picked up the crumpled note, straightened it out and handed it back. 'Why don't you give it to charity, Piers?' he said.[10]

Prime ministers didn't always find the media insolent. Senior politicians learned that television allowed them to appeal over the heads of their party members and their colleagues in Westminster and speak to the People in their homes. The rhetorical skills necessary to engage a large audience at a public meeting were a handicap on the intimate and domestic medium of television – as the career of Neil Kinnock, an inspiring politician born out of time, proved. But if leaders could modify their manners and delivery to suit television, they had a formidable new power. Yet they were weakened as they were strengthened. Because they no longer had to speak at mass meetings or produce speeches which would be printed in full for a mass readership, they were isolated by the medium which made them omnipresent. They could talk to the camera but had no way of feeling the reaction of the audience. All that came back was their own picture on the studio monitor. They had to rely on professional market researchers to find out what the viewers were thinking. Leaders could do without party members stuffing leaflets through letter boxes but they couldn't do without media manipulators.

In the words of Graham Allen, a Labour back-bencher: 'It is now the media not the parties which are crucial to securing electoral victory. They must therefore be kept onside and serviced at all times.' As the media wouldn't devote the necessary hours to covering debates in Parliament, Parliament was an irrelevance except in a crisis. What they require is 'one talking head that speaks for the whole of the Party and Government. Such a service must be virtually on demand and offer well crafted, pre-digested soundbites which minimise the need for effort from journalists – and even more important, from readers and listeners.' And, he might have gone on, the media also required instant emotion at moments of mass grief, egalitarian

bonhomie at moments of mass celebration and decisiveness at
all times. For television as much as the press, phrases such as
'It's a complicated issue and I need time to think it through' or
'Actually this isn't the government's business and we wouldn't
be able to do a thing about it even if it was' were at best
unbroadcastable and at worst laughable admissions of weak-
ness.[11]

Good stories were simple stories, as complexity might force
the viewer to switch channels. Thus disagreement within a
party was a 'split' or 'leadership bid'. To avoid charges of treason, politicians became clones in the Shona McIsaac mould,
and were duly lampooned for being clones by the media which
had helped make them clones in the first place. To please editors who would never broadcast or print a 30-minute speech,
politicians delivered 30-second soundbites and were duly lampooned by the media for being all spin and no substance. A
false move caught on camera – John Nott storming out of a
television studio or John Prescott punching a yob who had
thrown an egg at him – would be shown thousands of times. A
Freudian slip of the tongue was almost as lethal. Politicians
learned to be cautious about what they did and said and were
lampooned for their bland refusal to answer questions. Television and radio turned to pundits for lively comment. Pundits
could be entertainingly pungent and hurl themselves from one
position to another without worrying about charges of
hypocrisy from colleagues who didn't hold their own to
account.

Margaret Thatcher doled out knighthoods to editors because
she had more reliable allies in the Murdoch, *Mail* and *Telegraph*
groups than in her cabinets. They were let loose on her Tory
opponent,: the unions, Michael Foot and Neil Kinnock. John
Major's sporadic efforts in his first months in Downing Street
to run a collegiate administration were a disaster because they
ignored the media's *führerprinzip* that there must be a forceful
telegenic leader laying down the line. The 'ditherer' label never
left him, even though he was the most pig-headed of reac-

tionaries who ignored all sane advice when he ploughed ahead
with the privatisation of the railways.

After the destruction of Kinnock's and Major's reputations, it
was hard to blame New Labour for trying to tame the beast,
although inevitably the media wailed about the 'spin' they had
helped create. As influence shifted from the Commons to
Downing Street and Fleet Street, many other journalists could
follow Dacre and patronise MPs. Yet all the wealth and inso-
lence at the top could not hide the contradiction that while the
media were everywhere, their component parts were everywhere failing. National newspaper readership dropped by a
fifth between 1990 and 2002. The decline was merciless and no
Fleet Street manager believed it could be reversed when the
largest group abandoning newspapers were the young.[12]

Although there was a movement of readers from tabloids to
broadsheets, the overall temptation was to go for lurid and simple stories about crime, race and celebrity. Reading habits were
being destroyed by the audio-visual culture, but television executives were as insecure as newspaper managers and as willing to
grasp the lifelines of élite populism. There were oases of seriousness in television and radio, as there were in newspapers,
but the dominant cretinising trend was unmistakable. New
technology fragmented the television audience and the 1990
Broadcasting Act lightened the regulatory touch. The ideal current affairs programme in a falling market, explained one ITV
programme-maker, was now

> aimed entirely at the erogenous zones [of the] younger, more
> advertising-friendly audience . . . So there's lots of video of people
> doing bad things, even when there's no story to tell; there's one-
> sided sentimental interviews; and there is an obsession with crime
> and scary health stories. There's very limited range – very little for-
> eign, no political, nothing of real significance to the country like
> Northern Ireland because these are deemed to be unpopular.

A producer of BBC *Panorama* said: 'The encouragement from
management is that we become more tabloid, that we are
domestic, that we are human interest and that we disguise our

journalism to some extent and sugar the pill.' A colleague sounded close to despair when he added that because his bosses were obsessed with market share and saving money, current affairs journalism 'which used to be a power-house – the engine-room of different broadcasters – was being diminished. We are all becoming more ignorant because of it, and our children will become more ignorant.'

Between 1978 and 1998 the proportion of BBC current affairs programmes which dealt with foreign news fell from 29 to 18 per cent. Most of the few which were produced were shown on BBC2. The proportion of ITV documentaries which dealt with the world beyond the Channel went from 26 per cent in the 1970s to 7 per cent in the 1990s. In their place came documentaries on consumer grievances and crime, 'the biggest growth area in current affairs journalism'. Interestingly, crime came to dominate the drama schedules as well. 'The most noticeable trend over the twenty-year period is the growth of the police/detective genre which by 1997/98 dominated all channels except BBC2,' said the authors of a study of cultural decline in television.[13] There is an old criticism of newspapers that their pernicious effect lies not in what they think but how they think. In the 1960s Conor Cruise O'Brien said the British press exhibited 'cockiness, ignorance, carelessness, prurience, innuendo, and lip-service to the highest moral standards'.[14] By 2000, these vices had grown exponentially. Élite media managers had to follow Dacre's advice and 'persuade the public every day to go out and buy'. In a fragmented market, shouting louder and striking more aggressive poses were the sales pitches of last resort. For a few papers and channels, the tactic worked. But it didn't work for the media as a whole or the politicians who tagged along. The audiences for both shrunk. Cynicism grew as the screams grew noisier.

Diogenes of Sinope spread the ideas of the original school of cynical philosophers in the fourth-century BC. When Alexander the Great visited Corinth, Diogenes was the only leading citizen who refused to pay him homage. Intrigued, Alexander sought him out, and found Diogenes sitting in a tub. Was there anything he could do ot oblige him, asked the Conquerer of the World? Yes, replied Diogenes: get out of my space.

The conventional leftish view of politicians in the Blair mould was that they cackled in private about the ease with which the gormless multitude could be distracted by bogeymen. Conventional wisdom wasn't all wrong. Every now and again the mask slipped and the governors revealed their true appreciation of the intelligence of the governed. In December 2000, with a general election approaching, Blair stared across the Commons at William Hague and the shadow Home Secretary, Ann Widdecombe, as they tried to present themselves as the leaders of an alternative government. The PM was unimpressed and shouted, 'What is the alternative? What does the Right Honourable Gentleman offer? Why was it that he made a policy-free speech, apart from a load of nonsense from the shadow Home Secretary, most of which we are doing in any event?'[15]

The Prime Minister put the argument of this book in a sentence. His 'load of nonsense' had little to do with giving power to the People. But to draw evidence of a conspiracy from his frank admission would require us to imagine sinister men calmly plotting. I'm sure they do, but a lot of what we know about the modern élite shows it to be in a state of frenzy. Once you were in the old establishment, you were made; often the simple and involuntary act of being born into a good family was enough to deliver a lifetime of security. The modern élite was no less reliant on accidents of birth in its distribution of wealth and comfort. But its distribution of political and cultural power was closer to the vagaries of Hollywood. The celebrity system is never challenged, but individual celebrities are built up and torn down with a speed which makes it difficult to imagine a band now surviving for as long as the Rolling Stones or an actor being a star for as long as Paul Newman. Everyone at the top of the system can be replaced while the system remains the same. The recipients of transitory fame suffered from chronic sensitivity. The vapours could attack at any moment. Political élites followed Hollywood and were nervous to the point of hysteria.

Benji the Binman, the most effective champion of freedom of information at the turn of the century, brought the hysterics' secrets to the nation. Benjamin Pell, as he was properly known, was diagnosed as suffering from a 'very severe form of obsessive-compulsive disorder'.[16] It manifested itself in a deep hatred of lawyers. His loathing, which many wouldn't consider mad, began when his hopes of a career in the law were destroyed by an indifferent legal profession. He took his revenge by raiding the rubbish bins of the capital's barristers and law firms. Dressed in overalls and a fluorescent jacket, he toured the streets at night, identified promising bins, and tipped the bags into the back of his van. Benji's planning was meticulous. He had replacement sacks to put in the place of the stolen bags in case the lawyers noticed their rubbish had gone days before the council was due. His bedroom and garden were filled with discarded papers which he sifted to find a carelessly discarded bank statement or first draft of a confidential letter. Any scrap of paper which might embarrass a lawyer was gold to Benji.

It was only a matter of time before Fleet Street introduced itself to this enterprising if curious man. The matchmaker was Max Clifford, a publicist who brought together people who were dying to tell and sell their story with editors who were dying to pay for the pleasure of telling and selling it on. Benji began to accept commissions as newspapers pointed him towards bins worth a rummage, and promised to reward him if he struck gold. His friends insisted that he wasn't interested in getting rich. 'It's not about money for Benji,' said Clifford. 'It's about the thrill. In the past, I've had large cheques from News International [the Murdoch Press] for Benji and he's left them lying around the office for months.'[17]

The dustbins of Philip Gould were done over. Whether News International sent him to Gould's house, as the rest of Fleet

Street alleged, is an unanswerable question. The *Sun* and Benji denied any knowledge of Gould's rubbish. The bins were emptied nonetheless, and a series of first drafts of confidential memos went from Gould's refuse to the front page. One draft dug out in May 2000 revealed that the focus-groupie was close to a nervous breakdown. New Labour's 16-point lead in the polls wasn't a consolation. On the contrary, an unprecedented mid-term advantage for his party, or any other party, filled Gould with fear. 'Our current situation is serious,' he had written to the Prime Minister. 'We have got our political strategy wrong . . . We are not in tune with the people . . . the New Labour brand has been badly contaminated.' An earlier briefing from his rubbish bags had conveyed a similar impression of heedless and headless panic. 'TB is not believed to be real . . . TB is out of touch – he does not really care.'

Both memos showed Gould half-understood that the Clintonite methods he had championed had fostered cynicism. The government was presenting 'a whole raft of often confusing and abstract third way messages . . . We are suffering from disconnection. We have been assailed for spin.' Yet all he offered was more of the same: more spin and grandstanding stunts; more playing to the press gallery. The source of his worry was that: 'We are outflanked on patriotism and crime.' Blair must pick his Cabinet carefully and ask himself, 'How many ministers genuinely want to be tough on crime?'

A healthy culture would have enjoyed Gould's embarrassment and then moved on. When all is said and done, Gould and his kind were hired help. The Prime Minister was under no obligation to listen to them. But Blair listened and responded with one of the most demeaning orders ever issued by a British Prime Minister.

A copy of his memo, which appeared to have been another find from the bin of the careless Gould, was a new-élite manifesto. The Prime Minister instructed Alastair Campbell and Lord (Charlie) Falconer to impress upon the Whitehall apparatus that there are a clutch of issues – seemingly disparate – that are in fact linked. We need a strategy that is almost discrete, focussed on them. They are roughly combining 'on your side' issues with toughness and standing up for Britain. They range from: the family – where, partly due to MCA (married couples' tax allowance) and to gay issues, we are perceived as weak; asylum and crime where we are perceived as soft; and asserting the nation's interests where, because of the unpopularity of Europe, a constant barrage of small stories beginning to add up on defence and even issues like Zimbabwe, we are seen as insufficiently assertive.

The favourite verb was 'perceived', and the Prime Minister of Great Britain and Northern Ireland could see that the negative perceptions were nonsense. He continued:

All this, of course, is perception. It is bizarre that any government I lead should be seen as anti-family. We are, in fact, taking very tough measures on asylum and crime. Kosovo should have laid to rest any doubts about our strength in defence. But all these things add up to a sense that the government – and this even applies to me – are somehow out of touch with gut British instincts.

The shock that even he could be 'perceived' as weak disorientated him. New Labour politicians weren't going to explain to the public why its perceptions were mistaken. Instead, the first task of Blair's administration was to play along with illusion and perceived fear. Blair ordered 'a thoroughly worked out strategy, stretching over several months, to regain the initiative'.

He was particularly concerned about the furore which followed the conviction of Tony Martin, a farmer who was treated as a political prisoner by the Conservative press and the Conservative Party. Martin had interrupted a burglary of his home by Fred Barras, a waifish sixteen-year-old, and his older accomplice. Between them they had 114 previous convictions. Martin shot and killed Barras and was convicted of murder. The press and a large section of the public were furious that a householder had been jailed for life for protecting his property. The jury was more impressed by the bullet wounds in the boy's back and his final cry of 'I'm sorry . . . Please don't . . . Mum!' What worried Blair was 'the lack of any response from us that appeared to empathise with public concern and then channel it into the correct course'. On crime in general he wanted 'to highlight the tough measures: compulsory tests for drugs before bail; the PIU [Performance Innovation Unit] report on the confiscation of assets; the extra number of burglars jailed under "three strikes and you're out"'. (He didn't appear to know that no burglars had been jailed under 'three strikes and you're out'.) The government 'should think now of an initiative, e.g. locking up street muggers. Something tough, with immediate bite, which sends a message through the system.' He wasn't sure what the initiative should be – 'maybe, the driving licence penalty for young offenders'. But whatever it was it 'should be done soon, and I, personally, should be associated with it'. As with crime so with sexual morality. Whitehall was ordered to find 'two or three eye-catching initiatives that are entirely conventional in terms of their attitude to the family'.

A better insight into the élite's nervous relations with the masses has yet to be found in a Camden dustbin. Blair knew it was 'bizarre' to 'perceive' him as being soft on crime or asylum. But rather than make the case rationally, or explain that it was down to the courts to sentence Tony Martin, he would pander to popular sentiment and waste government time and public money with 'eye-catching initiatives'. He didn't know what the initiatives should be or whether they would work. The leader's aura of omnipotence had faded briefly because he had missed a few passing populist frenzies. His reputation had to be enhanced by being 'personally associated' with something – anything – 'eye-catching'.

This was a new type of government. It was hard to tell if Blair was responding to public opinion; if he was, the public didn't respond to him at the next election, when 40 per cent stayed at home. He was certainly responding to media opinion, particularly the opinion of Dacre's *Mail*, which made much of the family, crime, asylum, Martin and Zimbabwe. To a hack, his memo read like the fulminations of an editor whose paper has missed a story. Why didn't we get the Martin case? Why were our commentators so slow off the mark when I've told them before to 'empathise with public concern and then channel it into the correct course'? New Labour followed the media corporations in putting human interest before the public interest. It ran a permanent campaign to be elected every day; it chased stories, recycled 'eye-catching initiatives' and had a pundit's ear-catching opinions on all topics from Frank Sinatra's death to the fitness of Glenn Hoddle to remain manager of the England football team after he had made mildly distasteful remarks about the disabled.

Like many a gutter journalist, it knew that, when you needed to sell politics or papers, one emotion could still stir the jaded audience. Hate sold. Hate sold better than sex.

THREE

'They Hid Their Gold and Fawned and Whined'

The once dogmatic, leftist Labour Party and the Right-nationalist
FPO (Austrian Freedom Party) of old have both undergone an
ideological metamorphosis . . . As Tony Blair said: 'We have thrown
away the worst of our past and discovered the best.' The FPO, with a
new party programme, has done the same and adheres to a Christian, western tradition of thought . . . Are Blair and Labour on the
extreme Right because they advocate stricter rules on immigration?
If Blair is not extreme, then nor is Haider. (The latter is arguably less
tough on asylum-seekers and immigrants than Labour and Blair!)

Jorg Haider, writing about himself in the third person,
Daily Telegraph, 22 February 2000.

On 2 February 1900, at the start of a century which produced
more refugees from nationalist, ideological and religious terror
than any other, a British liner, the *Cheshire*, moored at
Southampton. A journalist from the *Daily Mail* was on the quay
to inspect the 600 passengers and file a report that would satisfy his readers and employers. 'There were Russian Jews, Polish
Jews, German Jews, Peruvian Jews: all kinds of Jews, all manner
of Jews,' he wrote.

> They fought and jostled for the foremost place at the gangways; they
> rushed and pushed into the troopshed, where the Mayor of
> Southampton had provided free refreshments. They had breakfast-
> ed well on board, but they rushed as though starving at the food.
> They brushed the attendant to one side, they cursed if they were not
> quickly served, they helped themselves at will, they thrust the chil-
> dren to the background, they pushed the women, they jostled and
> upset the weak, they spilled coffee on the ground in wanton waste.[1]

Readers who knew about the pogroms in Tsarist Russia –
the first of many ethnic cleansings the next hundred years

were to bring – might have suspected the report was rubbish.
Peruvian Jews?

Those who wanted to check out the story would have been frustrated, because the *Mail* relied on an anonymous officer to deliver the punchline. The exiles, the faceless officer said, had been 'so bad' on the voyage 'we had to arm'. I assume most readers wouldn't have been wary, and would have accepted the paper's message that the refugees were devoid of all human qualities save greed and cunning.

Fashion changes by repeating itself. On 2 February 2000, at the start of a century which hasn't been going swimmingly to date, the *Daily Mail* exposed the 'scandal' of refugees in detention centres whose comfortable cells made them almost as expensive as rooms at 'the Ritz'. Beyond the detention centre walls, the paper continued, 'police have recorded crime increases in many areas to which asylum-seekers have been dispersed'. An anonymous ayslum-seeker was said to have told the police that 'the great thing about Britain is that you join a queue and at the end of every queue you get money'. An anonymous police officer told the *Mail* that 'arresting them is one thing but whatever we do they are either already claiming asylum or promptly claim asylum so that there is no way we can deport them'.[2]

The *Mail* reporter of 1900 followed the *Cheshire*'s cargo from the harbour to Southampton station:

> Incredible as it may seem, the moment they were in the carriages they played all manner of games at cards, staking sovereigns on a single card. These were the penniless refugees, and when the Relief Committee passed by they hid their gold and fawned and whined [and] in broken English asked for money for their train fare.

In the spring of 2000 the *Mail* warned that

> something new and disturbing is intruding on everyday life in Britain. In towns and cities across the land, it is hardly possible to take a walk or go to the shops without being accosted by beggars, most of them healthy, able-bodied and capable of working. And behind every encounter with an outstretched hand there is the fear and sometimes the reality of violence. And then there is the prob-

lem of the new kind of asylum-seeker. Travellers on the London Tube, for example, are regularly confronted by women from Eastern Europe, often with babies in their arms demanding money. Not so long ago, begging was considered so demeaning that few would stoop to it except in desperate circumstance.[3]

Getting away with this line of invective requires a self-pitying inversion. Victims are turned into persecutors who dupe and rob the honest natives. In the winter of 1900 the *Mail* produced a 'quiet, sad-faced' Englishman 'with scarcely a rag of warm clothing' looking 'in silence' at the charity the Jews received. By the summer of 2000 asylum-seekers were pocketing more than money: they were taking the right to have children from the impotent British. 'Even in our increasingly surreal society, the disclosure that asylum-seekers from Eastern Europe are receiving costly fertility treatment free on the NHS takes one's breath away,' said the *Mail* editorial of 10 July.

> Inevitably, given the 'postcode lottery' for tightly rationed IVF treatment, allowing asylum-seeking couples access to it means that many infertile British couples must go without. They have every right to feel they are being betrayed by the system. How can it be right for hardworking British taxpayers to have no greater call on scarce resources than asylum-seekers?[4]

To be fair to the *Mail*, you could find similar commentary or worse in the *Sun* or the *Express*. The Association of Chief Police Officers was compelled to state that asylum-seekers were no more likely to be criminals than anyone else, and were more often than not the victims of crime.[5] (The officers might have added that asylum-seekers who had escaped to Britain from Saddam Hussein, Slobodan Milosevic, the Taliban or Robert Mugabe were already the victims of the world's greatest criminals.) The Kent police threatened several newspaper editors with charges of inciting racial hatred. Among the 'inflammatory and unacceptable' reports which alarmed its officers was the following from the friendly local *Dover Express*:

> Illegal immigrants, asylum-seekers, bootleggers and scum-of-the-

earth drug smugglers have targeted our beloved coastline ... We are left with the backdraft of a nation's human sewage and no cash to wash it down the drain.'

The editor protested that he was merely representing the views of his readers, and may have been telling the truth.[6] The constabulary's effort to impose restraint was one of the least successful police operations since the Great Train Robbery. The atrocities of 11 September fuelled fear of Islam and therefore the fears of minority Muslim communities in Europe, North America and India. Both were compounded when, in early 2003, the poison ricin was found at flats in north London, and Stephen Oake, a special branch officer, was murdered during a raid on an al-Qaeda suspect's home in Manchester. The press went over an edge it had been teetering on for years. 'Asylum-seeker', which once meant 'scrounger', now meant 'terrorist'. The *Sun* made the connection explicit in a mass petition from 400,000 readers to Downing Street. 'We campaign for a nation that lives in fear of Algerian terrorists who are allowed to roam free among us,' it told the Prime Minister. Before one al-Qaeda suspect had been charged, let alone convicted, *The Times* announced that 'terrorist leaders realise that one of the surest ways to plant agents successfully in Britain is to have them apply for asylum. At least three of the seven men being interrogated by Scotland Yard in connection with the north London ricin "laboratory" are understood to have made applications.' QED. What more proof did nit-pickers need?

If mass murderers being welcomed to Britain as refugees was not scary enough, 2003 saw the emergence of a new menace. Newspaper editors fell on a claim in the *Spectator* that 'Blair's epidemics' of Aids, TB and Hepatitis B were being spread by the Prime Minister's refusal to turn back disease-ridden asylum-seekers. The magazine said that New Labour was a party 'whose intellectual faculties are so crippled by political correctness that not offending would-be immigrants has become more important than saving the lives of British people'. Asylum-seekers weren't only scroungers and terrorists – but plague carriers, like the rats which brought the Black Death.[7]

Terrorist leaders who knew that the authorities were onto their scheme to use the asylum system to 'plant agents successfully in Britain' would, presumably, switch tactics and send their martyrs in as tourists or students or commercial travellers. The logical defence would be to ban everyone from the Muslim world from visiting Britain. Similarly, diseases don't discriminate between refugees and other travellers. The logical defence against foreigners with Aids was to screen or ban all visitors to Britain from Africa, Russia, Eastern Europe, India and China, or – why not go the whole hog? – all the 90 million foreigners who pass through the country each year. Logic led to the fantasy of a world without movement.

Asylum-seekers filled a gap. An inconvenient conjunction of circumstances had led to the demand for objects of hatred exceeding the supply. The breaking of trade-union power in the mid-1980s was followed by the collapse of the Soviet Union, which in turn was followed by the IRA ceasefire. The 1990s may be remembered as a soft period when the young were on gentle highs with ecstasy and adults were too absorbed by their iMacs or Nigella Lawson's recipes to waste their energy on conflict. Tony Blair's appeal was that he offered comfort. His image was of an unconfrontational, ordinary man who didn't look like a typical politician. But the market for hatred survived, as the fashion for public humiliation on TV shows proved in its small way. New enemies had to be found, and they didn't necessarily have to be truly ominous. It was enough for them to be guilty of 'inappropriate behaviour' – to use the favourite boo words of a decade which saw culture war replace class war.

The language of appropriateness came from liberal political correctness, but it was Margaret Thatcher's Tories who began the baiting of the inappropriately behaved. In 1988, as she was starting to flounder, her government began a small war against gays. The Conservatives didn't want to recriminalise homosexuality, merely to make sure that the country knew it was still a shameful activity. A 'message' was sent to homosexuals that they mustn't think of demanding equal treatment. The press had been running a campaign aginst 'loony left' councils which were allegedly subverting marriage by promoting homosexuality. The subverting process was never explained. If a couple's marriage could be driven onto the rocks by a councillor saying that homosexuals could be as happy as heterosexuals, wasn't it heading rockwards anyway? If a gay man was compelled by social stigma to con a woman he didn't love into marrying him, would the marriage be happy?

These quibbles didn't hold back a government which needed a useful smear. It banned local authorities from intentionally promoting homosexuality and local authority schools from teaching that homosexual partnerships were an 'acceptable' family relationship. From 1988 on, no suspects were prosecuted. Not one council officer was found ordering firemen to come to work in drag. Not one teacher was discovered turning red-blooded boys into mincing queens and the mothers of the future into lipstick lesbians by playing them Gloria Gaynor's greatest hits. Clause 28 was a unique achievement, unparalleled in the annals of jurisprudence. The crime it was devised to combat was vanquished as soon as it reached the statute book. There were two explanations: either it was the first prohibition since Hamurabi codified laws in 1800 BC to deter all potential offenders; or the Conservatives had invented a phantom menace to rally their supporters. The clause's sole effect, teachers complained, was to prevent them telling bullies beating the living daylights out of gay teenagers in the playground that there was nothing wrong with being homosexual. They feared they would be prosecuted if they did.

Huntsmen were the anti-Tory's gays. Their inappropriate behaviour was the unpardonable pleasure they got from chasing a fox across fields. Between the New Labour victory in 1997 and the Iraq war in 2003, most New Labour backbenchers accepted U-turns on all the policies they had once held dear, except one: the banning of hunting with dogs. If its true aim was to promote animal welfare, the proposed ban was a joke. The giveaway was the curious proviso that only hunting with dogs should be prohibited. Other means of culling were to remain legal. When a fox has the taste for blood, it slaughters lambs and chickens indiscriminately. The supporters of the ban accepted that farmers had to remain free to trap and shoot them. But if the farmer dressed in a silly costume and went after the fox with his dogs, he would be arrested – presumably by a British version of the Mounties. No one could say why it was crueller to wing a fox with a bullet and leave it to starve or bleed to death than to have dogs finish it off. But hatred of the hunters was deeper than concern for the hunted.[8]

It was tempting to dismiss the unused Clause 28 and the campaign against hunting foxes (but only with dogs) as meaningless gesture politics. Homosexuality went from the fringe to the mainstream in the 1990s, Clause 28 notwithstanding. So conclusive was the triumph of gay rights, Michael Portillo and the modernising Conservatives insisted that Tories must promote them if they ever wanted to be elected again. Outside Scotland, all bills to ban hunting (but only with dogs) were stopped by the House of Lords.

The inanity of both causes didn't prevent them appealing to solid constituencies. The anti-hunting protests were the most sustained of the late twentieth century – outside, as well as inside, Parliament. Every year thousands of saboteurs stalked the hunts. They were prepared to risk arrest as they shifted on the line between peaceful protest and civil disobedience. Many didn't share the casuistry of MPs. They would have banned hunting with or without dogs if they could. (Along with the livestock farmers who wanted foxes controlled and the butchers who sold the livestock farmers' meat.) Nonetheless, it was the hunters with red coats which drew the largest demonstrations and aroused the deepest anger. Millions, meanwhile, wouldn't give up on homosexuality. Brian Souter, the Stagecoach magnate, who had made £300 million out of the privatisation of the buses and trains, spent a few hundred thousand on a private referendum. He believed that a 'thirteen-year-old could be cultivated into almost any type of sexual activity, given the wrong

influence and circumstance'. He thought he could stop the arti-
ficial incubation of perversion in Scotland with a consumer survey. It looked a hopeless enterprise. The Scottish Executive had
already announced its intention to abolish Clause 28. Nothing a
freelance poll might produce would stop the inevitable repeal.

Souter sent ballot papers to Scotland's voters. Despite pleas
from the Scottish liberal establishment to bin them, about 1.2
million, or one-third of the electorate, voted. Of these 86 per
cent – just over one million people – wanted Clause 28 kept.

As we have seen, the majority of the population believed
crime was rocketing – even though it was falling faster than at
any time in a century. Heightening fears of crime was an
attractive card to play after the end of the Cold War. No one
likes criminals. Not even criminals like criminals when their
homes are burgled. But assaults on inappropriate behaviour
and villains couldn't begin to compare with the attractions of
going for asylum-seekers. It wasn't considered polite in the
1990s to go on about the niggers, micks, yids or pakis. Attacks
on asylum cheats were allowed – they were the racism of the
respectable. Asylum-seekers might have been designed by a
joint committee of the Conservative and New Labour parties,
the Civil Service and Fleet Street as the model scapegoat for
snobs to throw to the mob. They didn't vote. They didn't buy
newspapers. Because they weren't allowed to work, they were a
burden on the taxpayer (and, as despairing leftists knew, the
working and middle classes can always be made to feel greater
resentment for spongers on social security than billionaire tax
dodgers). Asylum-seekers were wary of antagonising the
Home Office or the authorities who would greet them in their
native lands if they were deported; most wouldn't make a fuss
to the few journalists who were prepared to give them a hearing. They were perfect: scapegoats who didn't bleat when they
were beaten. And on the rare occasions the new élite was challenged, it could produce the shred of a justification for its
palming the race card from the bottom of the deck.

*

'And I'll tell you what else I can't do. I know asylum is a problem, and we are trying to deal with it, but if people want me to go out and exploit the asylum issue for reasons of race that we all know about, then vote for the other man because I will not do it.'
Tony Blair to the 2000 Labour Party Conference

The fall of the Berlin Wall removed the communist enemy, but facilitated the supply of new enemies by opening up the Eurasian landmass. The trapped had the chance to move, and cheap flights and transcontinental haulage routes made moving easy. The end of the terrible stalemate had a further unforeseen consequence.

The Cold War had been anything but cold in a Third World where the United States and Soviet Union fought proxy wars. Without wishing to minimise the mountains of corpses they produced, the old superpowers needed the Third World and were prepared to make sacrifices for it. The US, to quote the most famous example, didn't only throw troops and bombs at countries from Korea to Indonesia to stop the advance of Asian communism, but money and trade privileges at the governments which remained on its side. In the 1990s, nations whose affairs had once concerned the foreign ministries of the great powers became superfluous to the new order of commerce. Much of Africa could have vanished from the map without global capitalism blinking an eyelid. Formerly strategic states didn't make profits for anyone but drug dealers and gun sellers. Afghanistan had a communist government in Kabul which was backed by the men and money of the Soviet Union and attacked by the fundamentalist proxies of Pakistan and the United States. After the Cold War no one in Washington or Moscow cared as millions fled from the warlords and the messianic Taliban. The purifying properties of slaughter and self-slaughter that the Taliban's guests from al-Qaeda preached might have been expected to alarm Western opinion. But the second most shocking news item of 11 September was the evident failure of intelligence agencies to appreciate what they

were up against. Liberal westerners were as careless as the
politicians they condemned for ignoring human rights. All but
a few feminists failed to protest about the barbarous patriarchy
of the Taliban. The life-work balance was more important.

It's not a competition, but in 2000 Sadako Ogata, the United
Nations High Commissioner for Refugees, surveyed her patch
and was almost nostalgic for the lost world of the Cold War.
'Twenty years ago, we dealt with 2.5 million refugees,' she said.
'Today we care for 21 million.' In one year – 1999 – her agency
had to cope with one million Kosovans fleeing from Milosevic's
Yugoslavia, 200,000 East Timorese runnning from militias
backed by the Indonesian military, and 200,000 Chechens displaced by Russia's war against their autonomous republic.[9]

You would never have guessed it from the wails of indigna-
tion in Europe, but the asylum crisis was a Third World crisis.
Ninety-five per cent of refugees were dirt poor and couldn't
afford to reach the developed world – they were lucky if they
could make it across the nearest border. In 2000, Australia had
one refugee for every 1,138 citizens and Germany one for every
456. Pakistan, which bordered the failed Taliban theocracy of
Afghanistan, had one refugee for every 75 citizens. Iran, which
bordered both Afghanistan and the all-too successful tyranny of
Iraq, had one for every 36.[10] A tiny minority of refugees sought
sanctuary in a Europe which was trumpeting that globalisation
was the path to a capitalist Utopia. They tended to be better off
and better educated, and ought to have been welcomed as
promising recruits to the global labour market.

The extent of globalisation remains the subject of dispute.
Critics of the concept said that local cultures and identities
remain strong, for all the money and American culture which
whizzes round the planet. Global migration, like global trade, is
neither new nor spectacular and is only now reaching the levels
of the nineteenth century.[11] The critics didn't, however, deny
that there was global migration in the 1990s and that the pattern of the nineteenth century was reversed. Europeans once
went to other people's lands, now other peoples came to

Europe. Pure capitalist theory had no problem with migration. It held that there should be free movement of people as well as goods. Potential workers needed to be able to move to where businesses had work waiting for them, otherwise they would be idle and the businesses would fail. As unemployment fell, Britain had plenty of skivvy work for migrants – booming London would have collapsed without their labour. Meanwhile the government quietly admitted that it needed skilled migrants when it allowed the NHS to scour the globe for doctors and nurses. But although Britain, Europe, Japan and Australia approved of freedom of trade they couldn't bring themselves to embrace freedom of movement, even when they were quietly poaching poorer nations' doctors.

A second poisonous consequence of the end of the Cold War helped explain their caution. Again, I don't wish to appear nostalgic for the decades of Mutually Assured Destruction, but ethnicity and ancient religions did matter more when the certainties of the old ideological conflict vanished. A school of apocalyptic writers took the case of the break-up of Yugoslavia as typical and held that murderous nationalism was the wave of the future. Fortunately, they proved to be over-pessimistic. The former Soviet empire had hundreds of nationalities. Outside Chechnya, they found ways of living together. (People who have experienced the worst that men can offer occasionally do.) Still, there were new pulls on loyalty, and religious manias proved far harder to contain than nationalism.

Britain wasn't immune to the politics of ethnic and religous hatred – Northern Ireland had known nothing else. Nor had it ever been straightforward for Britain to assimilate immigrants or for immigrants to assimilate. Until the 1990s, however, the old multinational and multiracial notion of Britishness offered new citizens a partial protection against racism. When being British could mean anything from being a Pict to a Pole, an immigrant had a diverse national myth which gave a limited protection. Devolution chipped away at it. Englishness, Scottishness, Welshness were more exclusive concepts than British-

ness and had the faint potential to send their roots down into
blood and soil. It's as easy to overestimate as underestimate
racism in Britain. But when the right was emphasising national
identity, and the left was emphasising the paramouncy of racial
and religious identities, the reception for immigrants was
unlikely to be warm. Who was 'really' British or English or Scottish or Welsh came to matter more.

Successive British governments were unanimous in how to
respond to the change in circumstance and the shift in mood.
They promised to welcome genuine refugees and uphold the
finest traditions of the country by offering them a haven. Their
scorn was reserved for 'bogus asylum-seekers', 'economic
migrants' and 'illegal immigrants', who would be exposed and
expelled.

It was an enormous lie: the lie of the decade. The truth was
the precise opposite. Before I give the lie a seeing-to, I should
say that the government was entitled to sympathy. It had to
cope with an influx of asylum-seekers unparalleled in the twentieth century. In the mid-1980s, before the Iron Curtain fell,
about 4,000 people a year applied for asylum. In 1989 the figure
jumped to 20,000. Between 1991 and 2001, just under 500,000
people sought asylum in Britain.[12] In 2001 Britain received
more asylum applications than any other European country. It
had a liberal reputation, which wasn't altogether unwarranted
when the British were put alongside the French. (A well-
informed refugee looking for a new home would notice, for
example, that Britain didn't have a mass neo-fascist party, if it's
not Europhobic to harp on this.) There were other attractions.
Britain had settled refugee communities which could support
new arrivals, and newcomers could make themselves understood when the world was learning to speak English.

From another angle, the influx into Britain wasn't as great as
the raw numbers implied. Every year in the 1990s Britain came
ninth or tenth in the European league table of number of asylum applications per thousand of population. Liberals liked to
look from that angle, but you needed a bleeding heart of stone

not to feel a smidgen of compassion for the Home Office. It had to find the means to cope with hundreds of thousands of wretched and determined people from a standing start.

The 'fact' that 80 per cent of them were rejected was quoted everywhere. Only one in five was a genuine refugee, said the media and government; the other four were either scroungers cadging benefits or economic migrants looking for work. The argument was convincing until the boring detail was examined. It was true that about 20 per cent of applicants were initially accepted as refugees. But the Home Office's examination of their cases was perfunctory and civil servants showed a predisposition to reject as many claims as possible. Asylum-seekers appealed. And once the system had been forced to pay attention to their stories, the proportion of refugees accepted as genuine rose to about 40 per cent in most years. On top of that was another 10 per cent or so who were given exceptional leave to remain in Britain because it was unsafe or impractical to send them home. All in all about half were allowed to stay.[13]

The other half were dismissed as cheats. The anonymous police officer the *Mail* quoted was right to say that their number included foreign criminals seeking to avoid deportation by shouting 'asylum'. He forgot to mention that most were just disconsolate people looking for better lives. They were pigeon-holed as economic migrants, and there were claimants from Eastern Europe and elsewhere who were just that. But it was hard to believe that all the rejected claims were from migrants using the asylum system to sneak into Britain when there was no correlation between poverty and asylum-seeking.

In 1993 pre-Taliban Afghanistan was a poor, war-ravaged country. Anyone who could afford to migrate to Britain to seek economic security had a strong incentive to do so. In 1993 there were 315 asylum applications from Afghans. In 2001, the last year of the Taliban's theocracy, there were 9,000. You could play the same game with any nation which was assaulted and battered by oppressive rulers. In 1993, Zimbabwe was prosperous by African standards but most of the population weren't living like kings. In 2001 Robert Mugabe's torturers were working overtime. In 1993, there were 40 applications for asylum in Britain from Zimbabweans. In 2001 there were 2,115.

Between the clear refugees willing to become full citizens of a new country and the migrants looking for work, there were fuzzy claims from people who didn't fit. The Home Office rejected Kurds from the safe haven in Northern Iraq which was protected from Saddam Hussein by the Royal Air Force and US airforce. The Kurds were secure, but lived with the plausible fear that Saddam would hurl poison gas at their villages again if he got the chance. Did their apprehension justify their claims to be refugees? Or did they have to wait until poison seeped under the door before they could flee and be accepted as victims of persecution?

And what to make of the Islamist asylum-seekers from Algeria who exercised the press after 11 September? Their stories of being persecuted by the Algerian state were likely to be true. But to be accepted as a refugee is to be accepted as a citizen. Given that 3,000 people were murdered in one morning in New York – as many as were murdered in the 30 years of war in Northern Ireland – should the government be careful about liberally extending citizenship to people who hated liberalism? In 1850 the Austrian ambassador to London complained to the Home Secretary, Sir George Grey, that the refugee Karl Marx and fellow members of the Communist League were discussing killing kings and emperors. He received a fine lecture on the principles of Victorian liberalism. 'Under our laws,' replied Grey, 'mere discussion of regicide, so long as it does not concern the Queen of England and so long as there is no definite plan, does not constitute sufficient grounds for the arrest of the conspirators.' Marx didn't believe in terrorism, so Grey's insouciance was more justified then he realised. But how was a modern Home Secretary meant to come to terms with the possibility that a handful of genuine refugees might commit an atrocity beyond the imagination of his Victorian predecessors?

The bureaucratic burden was heavy. In the mid-1990s, as the

first roars from the stock market could be heard on the limitless blessings of computing power, the government turned to the suppliers of information technology and asked them to lighten its load. In April 1996, during Michael Howard's watch, the Home Office signed a Private Finance Initiative contract with the computer conglomerate Siemens. New Labour took it over. The party was inspired by the dream of the computer revolution. It was 'committed to achieving leadership for the UK in the global digital economy' because, as Tony Blair explained at the launch of UK Online, the government's project for an e-future, 'there is no new economy. There is one economy, all of it being transformed by information technology.'

Seimens promised to deliver a system which would allow immigration officers to process asylum applications in a fair, firm and fast manner. Its reward depended on its mastery of the technology. 'Siemens Business Services will bear the risk of the project running into delays or for the project failing,' the Home Office pledged. 'No payment will be made until the computer system is working satisfactorily.' This seemed a wise precaution when Siemens took charge, and the Immigration Service collapsed. The system Siemens promised couldn't be made to work on time. Mounds of mouldy paper files, whose contents couldn't be transferred to disks, piled up in warehouses and had to be fumigated by pest-control specialists. Jack Straw fell for the patter of management consultants. He decreed that immigration officers must become 'multi-skilled team workers' who pulled together to reach their verdict. But team members weren't housed in the same room or, often, the same building. Exhausted Home Office postboys lugged papers from one team player to the next. Not that there were many players left on the field: the unworkable system was being paid for by sacking trained immigration officers.

The strain of coping with a wrecked service was too much for the remaining officers: 363 resigned in 1998 compared to 106 in 1995. As they walked out, the lease on Immigration and Nationality Directorate headquarters ran out. The inevitable confusions of relocation were added to the chaos. The average time it took to decide a case went from fourteen months when Labour came to power in 1997 to 28 months in 2000. Mike O'Brien, the immigration minister, admitted in the Commons that his department received a daily average of 56,223 calls in June 1999. Just 1,707 were answered. The backlog of undecided cases was 98,000 at the begining of 2000.

Siemens' attempt to solve the problems of globalisation by throwing computers at them was abandoned in 2001. Despite assurances to the contrary, Siemens didn't accept the costs of failure as a brave private-sector risk-taker should: it was paid from public funds until 2003 to help clear up the mess it had made.[14] The paralysis extended beyond the IT department. Immigration officers were unable to pick up the majority of asylum-seekers whose claims had been rejected and throw them out of the country. When an applicant lost his appeal he wasn't detained but allowed to go home while the Home Office applied for an order from a magistrate to deport him. The paperwork took weeks. By the time it was completed the appellant had often vanished. To the rather touching reasons for an asylum-seeker choosing Britain – its liberal reputation, the spread of the English language – a more basic motivation must be added: once you were here, you were in. Judges handling asylum appeals reckoned that seven out of ten found a legal or illegal way to stay.

The crumpling of the Immigration and Nationality Department at the moment when the wars in the former Yugoslavia were sending refugees flooding across Europe must rank with foot-and-mouth and the Child Support Agency as one of the great Civil Service disasters. Although the Commons Public Accounts Committee and the specialist computer press dissected Siemens, the fiasco didn't receive wide coverage. When Siemens brought its expertise to the Passport Office, by contrast, there was a media screaming fit and Home Office panic as the service fell apart and a backlog of 565,000 passport applications piled up. Middle England needed passports and bureaucratic incompetence became a national issue. No one, not even Jack Straw, shifted the blame to 'bogus holidaymakers' who had no intention of leaving their back gardens but maliciously pretended they needed passports to holiday in Florida. Straw apologised in person to citizens queuing at Petty France in the summer of 1999. With asylum-seekers, it was better, far better, to imply that the emergency was due solely to the hordes of illegal immigrants, who proved they were frauds by paying people-trafficking gangsters to smuggle them into the country.

*

There was only one catch and that was Catch-22, which specified that a concern for one's safety in the face of dangers that were real and immediate was the process of a rational mind. Orr was crazy and could be grounded. All he had to do was ask; and as soon as he did, he would no longer be crazy and would have to fly more missions. Orr would be crazy to fly more missions and sane if he didn't, but if he was sane he had to fly them. If he flew them he was crazy and didn't have to; but if he didn't want to he was sane and had to.

Yossarian was moved very deeply by the absolute simplicity of this clause of Catch-22, and let out a respectful whistle.

'That's some catch, that Catch-22,' he observed.

'It's the best there is,' Doc Daneeka agreed.

Joseph Heller, *Catch-22*, 1961

In the lazy way of clichés, Catch-22 has come to mean a fix. It's shorthand for such profound insights as 'The bookies always win' or 'You can't beat City Hall'. The modern usage might have disappointed Joseph Heller, whose trap was far subtler. The catch with Catch-22 was that your authenticity proved your fraudulence: a genuine attempt to save your life marked you as a charlatan.

In 1999, when refugees were struggling out of Kosovo, New Labour introduced an immigration and asylum bill. The unstated aim was to make it impossible for a refugee from

Milosevic or any other psychotic goon to reach Britain legally. In all but rare circumstances, they would be forced to turn to criminal gangs and therefore, by definition, become 'illegal immigrants', who were no better than criminals. Only by putting yourself in the shoes of a refugee can you appreciate the elegance of the trap and admire the art which went into the trapmaker's arrangement of guillotines and bolts. This was some catch.

From Bosnia to Zimbabwe, as soon as war or internal persecution produced refugees, Britain imposed visa restrictions on the afflicted country. Assuming your enemies allowed you to stroll unmolested through your capital, you would need to reach the British embassy. Once inside you would tell the staff that you wished to fly to Heathrow to escape persecution, and would be grateful for a visa. They would show you the door. The immigration rules do not include a desire to claim asylum as a valid reason for visiting Britain.

Forewarned, you lie and pass yourself off as a business traveller. Your bedraggled appearance and nervous eyes betray you. If you are suspected of being an asylum-seeker, you will be ejected.

The policy was as harsh as the measures adopted by Whitehall when Hitler was sweeping through Europe. No modern politician, however, imitated the agonising of Sir Samuel Hoare, who was Home Secretary in Neville Chamberlain's government when the Nazis moved into Austria in 1938. 'Many persons were expected to seek refuge,' Sir Samuel told the Cabinet. 'I feel a great reluctance in putting another obstacle in the way of these unfortunate people.' The hand-wringing didn't stop Chamberlain introducing visa restrictions. His government didn't want the unplanned accumulation of more Jewish refugees. MI5 warned that the Germans wanted to create a 'Jewish problem' in Britain. British Jewish leaders agreed, saying that Austrians of the 'shopkeeper and small trader class' wouldn't move on to new countries once they reached Dover, but stay for good.[15]

Very well, you reason, if Straw and Blair are going to be more authoritarian than Hoare and Chamberlain, you can skip the British embassy and head off without a visa. Should you carry your passport? You certainly should not, as a standard letter of refusal from the Home Office to asylum-seekers with passports made clear: 'The Secretary of State noted that you were able to obtain a properly issued passport which you then used to leave [insert country] through normal immigration channels without difficulty on [insert date]. He concluded that this indicates that the authorities have no further interest in your activities.'

OK, if having a 'properly issued passport' was to be taken as a sign that your country's regime didn't intend to shoot you, should you travel without a passport? You certainly should not. The standard letter of refusal for 'undocumented passengers' made clear that your claim for asylum would be rejected 'owing to your failure to produce a passport when requested to do so on arrival'.

Forging, borrowing or stealing a passport is often a necessity. Milosevic destroyed the passports and property deeds of ethnically cleansed Muslims so they would never be able to seek restitution. As far as the record showed they had never lived in their homes, never existed. Saddam Hussein made 120,000 Kurds and Turks disappear from the files when he drove them out of Northern Iraq between 1991 and 2003.[16] The potential victims of other dictators have ditched their old identities and got new ones sharpish to protect themselves from the secret police. In opposition, Tony Blair condemned the Tories for believing that a false passport was the mark of a fraudulent refugee. 'The Secretary of State spoke about those who destroy documents . . . That is not necessarily evidence of fraud. There may be good reasons why that has happened.'[17]

You certainly should not take him at his word now he is Prime Minister. His Home Office's standard letters to the holders of forged documents read: 'In considering your application the secretary of state has noted that you sought/gained leave to enter the United Kingdom using false documents . . . Your actions in doing so have seriously undermined the credibility of your claim to be a genuine asylum-seeker in need of international protection.'[18]

Can't get in with real passports, can't get in with forged passports, can't get in with no passports. Asylum-seekers still got in because the visa catch was tough but not unbeatable, for the basic and under-appreciated reason that asylum-seekers weren't immigrants. Immigrants were admitted on the whim of the government. Their rights to be British citizens depended on whether the government decided that, say, marriage to a British citizen conferred British nationality. Asylum-seekers were protected by international treaty. The 1951 United Nations Convention on Refugees was an idealistic response to the victims of Hitler and Stalin being denied an escape from their torturers. The Convention said that a refugee was anyone who 'owing to a well-founded fear of being persecuted for reasons of race, religion, nationality, membership of a particular social group, or political opinion, is outside the country of his nationality, and is unable to or, owing to such fear, is unwilling to avail himself of the protection of that country.' If your country was trying to kill you, you had the right to ask for safety in a new country. The right was an individual right. Governments couldn't impose quotas on genuine refugees or say that they wanted genuine rocket scientist refugees but not genuine refugees from the 'shopkeeper and small trader class'.

The combination of internationally guaranteed rights and judicial supervision of their treatment caught out ministers. Their catch had a snag. The British courts decided that whether or not asylum-seekers had a visa or passport when they arrived at Heathrow had nothing to do with whether or not they had well-founded fears of persecution. If they could cross the Channel, their claims for asylum had to be considered. If they needed protection from persecution, they couldn't be sent back.

And there was nothing the government could do about it. Except stop them crossing the Channel. Which is what it tried to do.

New Labour began fortifying the white cliffs of Dover by building on foundations dug by the Conservatives. The Thatcher government imposed what was known as 'carriers' liability' on airlines and ferry owners. Flight attendants had to check passports and turn away asylum-seekers travelling without a visa. There was a financial incentive. The government fined airlines for each asylum-seeking passenger who disembarked without a visa. Crews became unpaid immigration officers who turfed out anyone without the correct papers. Stopping in Britain became a costly business for airlines. In 1991 a flight from Toronto to Copenhagen was forced by bad weather to land at Glasgow. The airline put passengers in a hotel overnight as it waited for the storms to clear, and was fined for every unauthorised visitor.

Carriers' liability was costing British Airways £2.5 million a year in the 1990s, and its managers complained about being forced to do the Immigration Service's work for nothing.[19] A stronger complaint was that carriers' liability was a transparent attempt to get round the 1951 Convention. The opposition Labour Party was disgusted by the double-dealing. Gerald Kaufman said the Conservative Party had 'abandoned any standards of decency'. In 1992 Labour's then home affairs spokesman, one Tony Blair, pinpointed the rather obvious moral flaw in carriers' liability when he said: 'Many people find it objectionable that no distinction is drawn between bogus and genuine claims. The liability remains regardless of whether the claim is bogus or genuine.'[20]

In office, Blair extended the 'objectionable' measure to cover all means of transport. The 1999 Act imposed fines of £2,000 per asylum-seeking passenger on the owners of lorries, cars, vans, caravans, camper vans and people carriers, as well as planes and ships. Owners risked the confiscation of their vehicles if they didn't pay up. The only way in was through the Channel Tunnel – and that was closed in 2001. Legal entry became impossible. All the ports were closed. Genuine refugees needed a visa, but they couldn't get a visa even if the government knew they were genuine refugees. New Labour would have turned Anne Frank into an illegal immigrant.

It's a measure of its rush to reaction that principled opposition didn't come only from the Liberal Democrats and a small group of Labour backbenchers, but from the Conservatives. For those who clung to the illusion that Straw and Blair may have to do dirty work, as all politicians must, but remained decent sorts at heart, the debates on the 1999 asylum bill were an unsentimental education.

David Maclean, the Conservative minister whose blusterings about sweeping criminal 'vermin' from the streets I'd put to a nervous Blair six years before, was a big softie in comparison with New Labour. He was concerned that the bishops were saying that the bill would 'cause great hardship and injustice'. Answering Maclean was Mike O'Brien, Labour's immigration minister. 'It comes rich from the Right Honourable Member – who, when he was a Home Office minister in the previous government, proposed several bills on immigration and asylum – now to complain that the government are introducing draconian provisions,' he sneered. The Conservatives couldn't criticise because they had introduced draconian legislation; Labour was simply twisting the knife and making it more draconian. Thousands of 'balanced debates' inside Parliament and on the BBC went this way. New Labour adopted Tory policies, or on occasion went to the right of the Tories. The Tories attacked the government as an opposition should. New Labour said, 'Well, you did the same thing when you were in power so yah, boo and sucks to you!' There was balance, but no debate.

James Clappison, the Tories' home affairs spokesman, wondered whether the government wanted to kill refugees. There had been reports of asylum-seekers suffocating in airtight containers or being thrown overboard by European crews anxious to escape punishment for bringing in illegals, he said without exaggeration. Faced with the virtually impossible demand that they obtain visas, refugees became stowaways. It was hard to breach the controls at airport security desks and there were few places to hide in safety on a plane. Docks and ships were open areas in comparison. As accessible were container lorries, which were often loaded without their cargoes being checked. If you could sneak inside, you had a chance. The disadvantage with climbing into containers was the high risk of suffocation. Little stories of grim deaths made it into the news sections. In 1994, the bodies of four Romanians were found when a sealed container was opened at Felixstowe. A toxic cleaning solution, used to keep the container pristine, had poisoned them. In 1997, seven bodies docked in Humberside ports – again, the dead had been asphyxiated by the fumes in the deep holds. The alternative to suffocation was to scramble out and surrender to the crew. It was a risky tactic. Carrier liability cost the international shipping industry $20m a year in fines from Western governments, according to the insurers at P&I Clubs. Clappison quoted the legal reform group Justice, which estimated that about 1,000 stowaways were thrown into European waters in 1998 by crews who were determined to avoid punishment.

The figure was impossible to confirm because stowaway murder could be the perfect crime – no body, no clues, no way of the police knowing that a victim had been on board and that there had been a murder they needed to investigate. Every now and again, a witness survived to tell the story. In 1992, Kingsley Ofusu described the deaths of seven Ghanaians who crept on board the MC *Ruby* bound for Le Havre. Sailors spotted them, and in the ensuing struggle one smashed Ofusu's skull with an iron bar. As he staggered to a hiding place, he heard his brother cry: 'Kojo! Kojo! They are killing me!' His brother was picked up and dropped over the side. The Ukrainian sailors told the police that their owner had been fined when they had handed over stowaways in Rotterdam at the end of an earlier trip. He was furious and docked their pay. They preferred killing to the risk of losing more money. In 1996, Filipino crew members told how their Taiwanese shipmates on the *Maersk Dubai* hurled three Romanians into the sea after leaving Spain for Canada. Frightened of reprisals, they demanded asylum from the Canadian authorities before agreeing to give evidence.[21]

The practicalities of bringing the law of the sea to the road also worried the Tories. Had the government seen a curtain-sided lorry, loaded from above with sealed containers? Was a driver meant to climb in and search before heading for Calais? What was he supposed to do if he found a desperate man with his family cowering in the dark? Throw them out? Beat them up if they resisted? Take a beating if the refugees proved to be determined to travel at any cost? New Labour's response was to accuse the Tories of being soft on immigration. Undeterred, the Conservatives asked if drivers would be fined if the asylum-seeker on board was a baby? They would. What if the baby had died en route? The police would have to investigate whether he or she had died in British territory before deciding if a fine was necessary.

The bill, Clappison said, was a manifest injustice to lorry owners as well as asylum-seekers. If a driver was found carrying asylum-seekers, he would avoid fines of £2,000 a head only if he could prove that he had been forced to bring them to Britain. The driver might have no idea refugees were hiding in his container, but ignorance was no defence. The government was dropping the requirement that a citizen was innocent until the state proved he was guilty beyond reasonable doubt.

Answering Clappison was Geoff Hoon, a junior minister who was to go on to take the Ministry of Defence through several wars. He faced three charges: of fixing the law so that it was all but impossible for the most authentic refugee to reach the country legally; of extending a murderous system; and of turning the first principle of British justice on its head.

An honourable man would have defended his reputation and the reputation of his party with angry vigour. Hoon was bored. Although he 'had listened to a great number of very tedious speeches in this place, I doubt whether anyone has ever plumbed so deeply the depths of dullness achieved by the Hon. Member for Hertsmere [Clappison].'[22]

New Labour's impatience with criticism went from weariness to exasperation. When Clappison's arguments hit home, Mike O'Brien protested to Norman Fowler, the shadow Home Secretary and Clappison's boss. Clappison's indecent concern for the refugees was excessive, 'clear evidence that the Conservative Party is trying to wreck the Government's attempts to clamp down on illegal immigration,' O'Brien wrote. The Tories were 'filibustering' and forcing the parliamentary Labour Party to miss the beauty sleep even its best friends conceded it needed. The asylum committee had been made to 'sit through the night' for eight long and dark hours because Clappison had insisted it discuss 'just one clause'.

That the clause in question was the one that tore up the right to sanctuary by pronouncing it unlawful for any refugee to cross Fortress Europe by any means of transport didn't bother O'Brien. The Opposition must be condemned for opposing. He appeared to expect Fowler to discipline his deputy for making life difficult for the government. Hard interrogation from Parliament, charities, the media and citizens was no longer the normal business of politics, but an unthinkable assault on a Third Way consensus. There was also a clear threat in O'Brien's letter. The Tories were obstructing the clampdown on 'illegal immigration'. How would it play with their supporters if New Labour outflanked them on the right on race as well as crime? The Tory leadership was alert to the danger. Clappison and Fowler were pushed out of their jobs, and a competition between the parties on who could be toughest ensued.

*

MIKE O'BRIEN (New Labour Home Office Minister): Many asylum-seekers come from communities where wealth may be stored in jewellery or other financial bonds – and it is right for us to take account of that wealth ...
DIANE ABBOTT (Old Labour MP): Is the Minister suggesting that asylum-seekers should sell their jewellery, perhaps their wedding rings, as an alternative to the Government meeting its moral and international responsibilities to provide a reasonable level of support?

o'brien: I certainly am suggesting that . . .
unidentified tory: You'll be wanting the gold fillings out of their teeth next.
abbott: Is the Minister going to strip the rings from their fingers?
o'brien: If the Hon. Lady will listen for a moment, I will explain. I personally met an asylum-seeker who had bought large amounts of gold so that she could enter and stay in the UK and have a substantial sum amounting to several thousand pounds. The gold could be exchanged easily. No one is suggesting that asylum-seekers should sell their wedding rings. That would be complete nonsense. However some communities decide to store their wealth in the form of jewellery. When people possess jewellery that is worth thousands of pounds, they are clearly not destitute.[23]

The hatred of refugees in 2000 was as great as the hatred of refugees in the 1930s in all respects but one. The millennium was a comfortable time for the majority of the British. Unemployment was back below the levels of the Thatcher years. Across London and the Home Counties and in the gin-and-Jag belts of Warwickshire, Cheshire and Yorkshire employers were begging the jobless to fill vacancies. The standard depressed conditions for hatred of outsiders stealing jobs and benefits weren't there. But the hatred burnt brightly for all the booming markets – in Whitehall ministries as well as council estates.

The Devil, like God, dwells in the detail, and I'd like to meet the civil servant who worked out how to give the screw the final twist. He or she served a New Labour Relief Committee which wasn't about to be fooled by refugees who 'hid their gold and fawned and whined'. As surely as the *Daily Mail* of 1900, the party knew that these schemers were in Britain to fleece the taxpayer. Jack Straw was emphatic: 'They come in principally to claim cash benefits,' he said. Asylum-seekers weren't allowed to work, so claiming benefits was all they could do unless they were prepared to beg or join the black economy. Straw cut their dole to £36.54 a week for a single adult. Under the Tories asylum-seekers lived at 10 per cent below the poverty line; New Labour pushed

30,000 people 30 per cent below the poverty line. As with crime, pollsters found that the public hugely overestimated the benefits asylum-seekers received along with, inevitably, the real number of asylum-seekers in Britain. The majority believed that each got £116 a week. In reality most experienced hunger and couldn't afford shoes and clothes.

Their penury was caused by how they were paid as well as how little they were paid. A government which couldn't pluck up the nerve to take Britain into the Euro created a new currency for the stateless and destitute. Its printing and distribution was to be the responsibility of Sodexho Pass International, a conglomerate that profited from the 'outsourcing' of public services. Britain made Sodexho a mini Royal Mint: the privatised producer of the ghetto currency of asylum vouchers. Vouchers turned out to be three times as expensive as giving cash benefits. But the government never pretended it was trying to save public money. Its aim was to deter thieving foreigners.[24]

Most of the paltry sum asylum-seekers were given – £25 of the £36.54 – was in vouchers, not cash. And in a moment of inspiration, the unknown civil servant came up with the final twist. The fawning cheats were clearly here to get their hands on coins and notes. The supermarkets must therefore keep the change from vouchers rather than hand it to their grasping customers. Sodexho Pass explained the policy to the stores in the voucher scheme. 'If goods to the value of £4.50 are purchased with a £5 voucher, the 50p change should not be handed back, but you as a trading partner will receive the full £5 value for that voucher.' Trade unions and churches protested. Sainsbury's said, 'We do not want to keep the change and profit at the expense of asylum-seekers'. The Home Office refused to budge. The law didn't specifically state it was illegal to give change, explained a spokeswoman. But ministers had made a decision and the shops had to obey it.[25] To strengthen the deterrent, the babies of asylum-seekers were stripped of the statutory protection the Children's Act had guaranteed.

Little stories crept into the papers. I came across a man in

Dover who went to the Co-op and tried to buy a razor and shaving foam. The staff refused. They were under instructions only to allow asylum-seekers to buy 'essentials.' He walked a mile to a Kent social services office to complain. Social workers said he must have made a mistake. He trudged back. The shop again refused to serve him. He went back to the council office. A social worker returned with him and, after an argument, secured his right to have a shave. There were thousands of similar humiliations. People begged because the vouchers didn't arrive on time. They couldn't afford to buy cheap food in street markets because stall-holders couldn't accept vouchers. They were marked as aliens each time they opened their wallets and purses in supermarket queues.

After this performance, you might have expected that the suffering would have been worth it in official terms and that asylum claims would have fallen. The press and politicians said asylum-seekers were drawn to Britain by the lure of cash benefits. Cash benefits were reduced to a pittance. Every legal route to reach Britain was shut down, and airline stewardesses and lorry drivers were ordered on pain of punishment to stop visa-less refugees boarding.

All for nothing.[26] In 2002 there were 110,000 applications – an all-time record. Apparently asylum-seekers weren't coming to Britain to scrounge. They were either genuine refugees or else migrants willing to disappear into the black economy. There was, however, one difference between the newcomers and their predecessors. Where once they could travel legally, now, thanks to New Labour, the majority could arrive only by availing themselves of people-smugglers. Desperate people take desperate measures, and putting themselves in the hands of criminals was the only option for most. Ocassionally they paid with their lives. On 18 June 2000, one of the hottest days of that summer, a lorry with 60 Chinese migrants hidden behind boxes of tomatoes boarded the ferry from Zeebrugge to Dover. The driver worked for a Turkish gang based in Rotterdam. He closed the air vent on the side of the lorry to stop the illegals being overheard by port officials. He forgot to reopen it. On the ship, he had a meal and watched a video while they tore off their clothes and sucked at the tomatoes for moisture. The hot, stagnant air turned to carbon dioxide. When Customs officers opened up the lorry at Dover they saw a mound of bodies. Two of the 60 survived.[27]

Most smuggling operations don't end in disaster. The gangs provided transport and false visas for those who could afford them. Once in Britain, the old escape from Catch-22 still applied. The UN Convention on Refugees and the British courts ensured that claims had to heard. The futility of the repression didn't deter politicians from noticing the propaganda value of refugees being pushed into the care of criminals. Tony Blair thundered against 'the horrors illegal immigrants endure at the hands of the people-traffickers'. He forgot to add that he and his European partners created human-trafficking as surely as the Prohibitionists created bootlegging.

There was a hard-headed defence of the broken promises and relentless persecution. When you put its cruelties to the political class, you were treated to a bluff lecture on pragmatism. We agree with much of what you say, you were told, but live in the real world, son. There's only so much immigration society can take. We're civilised people, but you should see our Neanderthal constituents. If we aren't harsh, there will be a racist backlash.

The argument had a brutal plausibility until other political voices piped up. Strange press releases trickled out of the Home Office stating that with an ageing population and a declining birth rate, Britain would need about 150,000 immigrant workers a year every year for twenty years if pensions were to be paid and prosperity maintained. Very quietly, the *Mail* and *Sun* agreed. At the Treasury, Gordon Brown was impressed by America and wondered whether its success had anything to do with the welcome it gave to immigrants. He introduced a highly skilled migrant programme to divert a few to Britain. The press didn't go wild.

Asylum-seekers, who included doctors and nurses and engineers, remained loathed. Every trick and bureaucratic strategem to keep them away had fallen at the final hurdle. The government responded with its last shot. It lobbied the European Union in 2003 to abandon a UN convention which allowed refugees to claim sanctuary once they were on British soil. In future asylum-seekers should be accepted as refugees only if they didn't make their claims on British or European soil. Russia, the Ukraine and other poor countries on the peripheries of the EU should be paid to house them in 'transit processing centres' beyond the borders of Fortress Europe. EU governments would decide who they wanted, and the rest would be sent packing. There would be no more appeals to the courts and international law.

All the talk of welcoming genuine refugees while despising economic migrants was admitted to be as bogus as the most fraudulent asylum-seeker. In 2003 Beverley Hughes, the immigration minister, was unblushing and refreshingly straightforward. 'We have introduced tough reforms to reduce asylum claims,' she said. 'Alongside this we continue to welcome legal migrants to benefit our economy and improve productivity, growth and social cohesion.'[28]

New Labour understood people who moved to make money. What it found intolerable, almost incomprehensible, were those who ran for their lives because they had made a stand on – of all things! – political principle.

FOUR

Have a Nice Holocaust Day

Forgive me for impugning your sobriety, but I imagine you may have been caught in a pub row once or twice and know how the bickering goes. As the company gets drunker, polite difference degenerates into screaming dispute. Arms are waved and fingers wagged (simultaneously on heavy nights). Drinkers repeat the same point with increasing ardour – unaware that they've made it ten times before. The next morning, or afternoon, the participants wake up and try to remember whose view prevailed. An unfailing method for the recovery of fuzzy memories was offered by Zoe Williams of the *Guardian*. 'Whoever mentioned the Nazis first lost,' she ruled. What they meant was: '"I have just likened you to an evil so pure as to be unarguable. So you'd jolly well better shut up!" It's an egregious, dozy, meaningless, emotive catch-all.'[1]

By the exacting Williams standard everyone lost. The further the Nazis receded into history the larger they loomed. It was thought to be a good argument against vegetarianism that 'Hitler was a vegetarian', and a good argument against the European Union that 'Hitler wanted a united Europe'. Tony Blair remembered the Finest Hour when he flew to New York after 11 September and told Rudy Giuliani that Britain would stand with the United States because 'my father's generation knew what it was like. They went through the Blitz . . . There was one country and one people that stood by us at that time. That country was America, and the people was the American people. As you stood side by side with us then, we stand side by side with you now.' The Blitz began in the summer of 1940. The United States entered the Second World War in December 1941. It was bad taste to dwell on the chronology.

Churchill was voted the 'greatest Briton' in a BBC poll whose popularity surprised the corporation. Channel 4 producers reckoned that inserting the word 'Nazi' in the title of a history documentary doubled the audience. 'The Nazis are business,' said Ian Kershaw, one of hundreds of biographers of Hitler. 'Stick a swastika on a magazine or book cover and it will sell.'

There was no sign of interest in Nazism fading with the passing of generations. A survey of schoolchildren by *History Today* found that about the only history the young knew was the history of Hitler. Thomas Matussek, the new German ambassador to Britain in 2002, was 'very much surprised when I learned that at A-level one of the three most chosen subjects was the Nazis'. His confusion turned to disgust when he read an anti-German press whose 'We want to beat you Fritz' headlines on the sports pages created a climate in which 'totally innocent young German schoolchildren get beaten up'. The children he had in mind were in a party from the small town of Harsewinkel who went on an exchange visit to south London. Two joined a park football match. The local boys set on them when they discovered they were Germans. One had his glasses broken and the second was shoved into a bush. Other German pupils heard chants of 'Nazis' as they walked to school. Boys fight all the time. But it was morbid that 'Nazi' was being used as an insult by English fifteen-year-olds who hadn't been conceived until after the 40th anniversary of the end of the war. 'Would Russian schoolchildren be described as communists?' asked the Germans' teacher. It was a better question than she knew.[2]

Kershaw explained the past which will not pass away by the magnitude of the calamity Hitler produced. Lenin and Stalin murdered more people over 36 years, but only Hitler started a world war and ordered the greatest single act of genocide. Whereas the Russian and Chinese revolutions happened in backward empires, Nazism retained its fascination because it showed that a 'devastating doctrine of inhumanity and regime of breathtaking brutality and destruction could arise in a modern, economically advanced, and culturally sophisticated country such as Germany'. If there, why not anywhere?3 To Kershaw's reasons should be added the astonishment of the generation of the 1990s when it looked back at what their parents and grandparents had been through and done, and the appeal of the Finest Hour to those suspicious of a treacherous continent which was seeking to bind Britain into the European Union. These were rational, or at least half-rational, reasons for the Hitler craze. What, however, was the half-way rational British citizen meant to make of the events on the evening of 27 January 2001?

Prince Charles, Tony Blair, William Hague, Charles Kennedy and Jack Straw joined Sir Ian McKellen, Sir Bob Geldof and Sir Trevor McDonald at Westminster Central Hall to inaugurate Britain's first annual Holocaust Memorial Day. Two hundred survivors of the Nazi extermination camps were present, and heard the Prime Minister speak well:

> The Holocaust was the greatest act of collective evil the world has ever known . . . It is to reaffirm the triumph of good over that evil that we remember it. We remember it so as we do not forget what the human race at its worst can do. We also remember it so as we learn how it happened and never believe, in our folly, that it could not happen again.

Holocaust Day was a national event. The BBC broadcast highlights from the Westminster memorial. Large services were held in Edinburgh, Gloucester, Bristol, Plymouth and Cardiff. Across the country there were hundreds of smaller exhibitions and workshops in hundreds of schools, libraries and town halls. Britain was paying homage to Hitler's victims, and the spectacle could set teeth on edge.

To begin with, the ceremonies were a bit late – 56 years late, in fact. Then there was the question of whose history was being confronted. There were no Dachaus on the outskirts of Edinburgh, or Treblinkas in the Peak District valleys. With the exception of the Channel Islands, Britain wasn't invaded and had no history of collaboration with the Nazis to confront. Coming to terms with the evil of foreigners isn't a traumatic task – it's more of a pleasure than a duty. A day dedicated to the victims of the Irish famine or of slavery or colonialism would have been more bracing. In any case, if we had to have a Holocaust Day, why on 27 January, when Auschwitz was liberated by a Red Army that went on to subjugate half of Europe? What about 15 April when the British Army reached 40,000 inmates in Belsen – a moment which, whenever it is recalled, can make even my unpatriotic eyes prick? (Admittedly Belsen wasn't an extermination camp, but it was 'part of the process', as they say.) A Home Office spokeswoman explained that a 15 April commemoration wasn't possible for the banal reason that there would be years when it clashed with the Easter holiday.

Holocaust Day came after lobbying from British Jewry, but its concern for official remembrance of the dead begged the question: why had the Holocaust become central to Jewry? Wasn't it a posthumous victory for Hitler? If these questions were unsettling, they couldn't match the toughest question of all: why the Holocaust?

Until the 1960s, there was no Holocaust with a capital aitch. Hitler's attempt to destroy the Jews wasn't separated from the attempted destruction of gypsies, homosexuals and the disabled, or the mass murder of millions of Russians, Poles, socialists, communists and anyone else who got in the way. Jews were one group among many victims. The leaders of post-war Judaism didn't emphasise the camps either. Their silence wasn't as peculiar as it now seems. It takes time for horrors to become established in the popular imagination. It wasn't until the late 1920s that the trenches of the First World War were seen as death traps rather than glorious battlefields. In the case of the Holocaust, the religious turned away from a crime which subverted faith in a benign god. The few survivors of the extermination camps were displaced people far from the centres of cultural power. Most wanted to forget what they had been through and try to build a new life. Many were in Soviet-occupied Europe and weren't free to speak if they had wanted to, particularly when Stalin developed Nazi tendencies in his later years. On the other side of the Cold War divide, American Jews were wary of being branded communist sympathisers by going on about the final solution at a time when the West was turning Germany from an enemy into a bastion of democracy overnight. Their wariness was increased by the knowledge that a large number of American communists were Jews. Jewish organisations were determined to prove their loyalty. A US Jewish leader complained to a colleague that American Jews were 'not taking anywhere near the measures or using the efforts in combating Communism as they do against Nazism. I know they'll bring up the question of the two world wars and 6,000,000 Jews exterminated. But that is the past, and we must deal with the facts today.' In 1951 one member of the American Jewish Committee complained that 'for most Jews reasoning about Germany and Germans is still beclouded by strong emotion.' A second said that Jews needed a 'realistic attitude rather than a punitive and recriminatory one', for upon Germany 'rested the future of Western democratic civilisation'.[4]

By the end of the century, Holocaust museums had sprung up across America and Europe. The death camps were depicted in Oscar-winning films and their inmates were remembered in memorials by fashionable sculptors. The 1998 Annual Survey of American Jewish Opinion rated 'remembrance of the Holocaust' as the most important Jewish activity.[5] On the Jewish side the urge to forget and get on with life had passed, along with traditional Judaism. As religious belief declined, being a man or woman Hitler would have murdered defined what it was to be Jewish. For other Europeans and North Americans, not being someone who would have murdered for Hitler defined what it was to be a liberal democratic Westerner.

It had to be the Nazis. The Soviet Union wouldn't have done as a symbol of evil because totalitarian Bolshevism was followed by decades of autocracy which kept most survivors silent and kept historians from the archives. (The same difficulties attended a reckoning with Mao's China.) Going on about the

Soviet Union embarrassed the left, just as going on about the millions killed, directly or indirectly, by the United States in the Cold War embarrassed the right. The world could unite against Nazism, and the Holocaust Day service in Westminster tried to draw universal lessons. 'I believe that, as we enter a new millennium, it is essential that the Holocaust is never forgotten,' Jack Straw, the then Home Secretary, told readers of the *Jewish Chronicle*. 'Recent events in Rwanda, the Balkans and East Timor show that ethnic cleansing and mass murder are still affecting the world today.'

But the confusions brought by having a day dedicated to one genocide couldn't be contained. The Holocaust was commemorated because Hitler's extermination of the Jews was meant to be 'unique'; not in the sense that each historical event is unique, but because it was an incomparable attempt to kill every man, woman and child from one group. But if it was unique, what 'lessons' could be drawn from it for the present and future? How could studying its history avert similar catastrophes when, by definition, there couldn't be similar catastrophes? If it wasn't unique, why should there be a Holocaust Day which concentrated on the Jewish victims of Nazism? Shouldn't it be a Human Rights Day or an Anti-Genocide Day which included all the victims of mass murder? Many took the latter view, and a victimhood competition began as the day of the British ceremony drew near.

The Home Office had banned all mention of the Turkish slaughter of 1,500,000 Armenians in 1915. It was the first twentieth-century genocide, but it retained too many impolitic resonances. Turkey, Britain's Nato ally, denied the slaughter had happened. It referred to 'the events of 1915', on the rare occasions it mentioned them at all. Turkey didn't want to be reminded of the parallels between its treatment of the Armenians 85 years before and its persecution of the modern Kurdish minority. Its government was prepared to fight to ensure its version of history prevailed. In 2000 it threatened to deny the Americans use of bases on Turkish territory if Bill Clinton for-

mally accepted the massacre of Armenians as genocide. American Jews and Israel took the Turkish side in the interests of
chauvinism and realpolitik. One American Jewish leader
explained that he couldn't support recognition being given to
Armenians because

> many contend the Holocaust was simply a terrible event, neither
> unique, nor particular. To compare Armenians [in 1915] to the situ-
> ation of Jews in Europe in 1933 or 1939 is a dangerous invitation to
> revisionism about the Holocaust. If Jews say every terrible event is
> genocide, why should the world believe the Holocaust is distinctive?

The designers of the Washington Holocaust Museum promised
to give space to the Armenian genocide, but were overruled by
the museum's governing council. The Holocaust's 'unprecedented character' couldn't be diluted, the designers were told.
The council was backed by Israel, which didn't want to offend
Turkey, its only friend in the Middle East.[6]

Proportionately as many gypsies were slaughtered by Hitler
as Jews, but Holocaust Day didn't mourn them (the papers
were full of outrage about gypsy beggars from Eastern Europe
getting into Britain as bogus asylum-seekers at the time). There
wasn't much of a market for remembering that Hitler also
gassed homosexuals. In 2000 Jonathan Sacks, the Chief Rabbi,
who must have known that gays and Jews died together in
Auschwitz, berated the government for trying to lift the ban on
councils 'promoting homosexuality'. (No one asked him how
he would have reacted if fundamentalists from a rival creed had
demanded a ban of the promotion of Judaism in schools.)

The BBC team preparing the coverage for Holocaust Day
became fractious as it struggled with the casuistries. Fergal
Keane, a foreign correspondent, sent a memo to his bosses
complaining about the apparent pressure to commemorate
only approved oppressions. 'Wasn't it Hitler who said "Who
remembers the Armenians?" when he laid the groundwork for
the slaughter of the Jews?' he asked.[7] Indeed it was – the Turks
inspired the Nazis. As the row grew noisier, the government
relented. Armenian groups were assured that the first twentieth-

century genocide would be mentioned in the ceremony. The concession did the government no good at all. Tony and Cherie Blair walked out of Westminster Central Hall to be confronted by jeering Turkish demonstrators in full denial about 'the events' of 1915. Upholding universal standards was a thankless enterprise.

The far-left had a superficially plausible explanation, as it invariably does. Holocaust commemoration was a fraud and an assertion of brute power, the argument went. The Jewish élite in America and the rest of the West weren't interested in the Holocaust when Israel was a weak and anti-American state. They discovered it only after Israel's defeat of the Arabs in 1967, when the alliance with the United States was forged. The Holocaust was used to dismiss the sufferings of the Palestinians at Israeli hands as trivial when compared against the attempted extermination of the Jews, and to slander legitimate critics of Israel as anti-semites. In the West, most Jews had escaped from poverty by the 1960s. Their leaders invented the threat of anti-semitism – which was nearly always described as 'virulent' anti-semitism – for two reasons: it got Jews behind Israel, the refuge of last resort if the ubiquitous 'virulent anti-semites' were to seize power in Washington or London; and it allowed the comfortably-off to pretend that they were greater victims than, say, blacks. Much was made by the left of the condemnations in the US of affirmative-action programmes which gave blacks preferred access to universities. American Jewish organisation likened these programmes to the anti-semitic laws of old Europe which limited Jewish access to higher education. The Holocaust, in the words of Norman Finkelstein, allowed 'American Jewish élites [to] strike heroic poses as they indulged in cowardly bullying.'[8] Anti-semitism was the cry of the powerful who raised a demon from the dead to justify their oppression of the Palestinians and the poor. More grievously, he continued, by demanding compensation for Holocaust victims and the return of stolen property 'the Holocaust Industry' actually cre-

ated racism. 'Pursuing this end with reckless and ruthless abandon, it has become the main fermenter of anti-Semitism in
Europe.'[9]

The charge that supporters of Israel used the Holocaust to
counter criticism of the occupation of the West Bank was unde-
niable. In 1998, the then Foreign Secretary Robin Cook toured
Israel. He was denounced as a man who didn't care about
Hitler's victims by the Israeli government when he visited a
memorial for Palestinians massacred by the Israelis, but not the
Holocaust Museum in Jerusalem. The charge was proven
beyond reasonable doubt. However, the claim that racism wasn't
the fault of racists but 'fermented' by the victims of racism was
quite a follow-up accusation, but a perennially popular one for
all that.

As the fury with Israel grew, resentment of Holocaust commemoration produced curious species of cant. Israel's opponents had to pass over real racism in Europe and the Middle
East to maintain the purity of their rage. They couldn't, for
instance, look at the Baath parties which ran Iraq and Syria.
Baathism was founded in 1943 in Damascus when Hitler
seemed certain to win the war. Sami al-Jundi, one of its early
leaders said: 'We were racists, admiring Nazism, reading its
books and the source of its thoughts.' Other Baathists were
inspired by Stalinism. Saddam Hussein had a keen admiration
for both, and created a recognisably totalitarian state. There was
a cult of the Great Leader, which gave Iraqis thousands of Saddam statues to pull down after the war of 2003. His enjoyment
of show trials and his murders of his closest associates were
recognisably Stalinist. The Baathist drive for racial purity was
authentically Hitlerian. In its early years, Baathist Iraq was bap-
tised with the execution of Jews before screaming crowds in
Baghdad. The persecution of Freemasons, another favourite
target of fascist and reactionary Europe, and of communists
and trade unionists followed.[10] The Kurds were ethnically
cleansed or massacred because they weren't Arabs. Saddam's
cousin, Ali Hassan al-Majid, aka 'Chemical Ali', who directed

the annihilation of at least 100,000 Kurds between 1987 and 1989, was thoroughly Nazi when he discussed the extermination of the inhabitants of the Kurdish town of Halabja. Hitler had let out a contemptuous 'Who remembers the Armenians?' when he planned the gassing of the Jews. When Ali planned the gassing of the Kurds, he was caught on video telling Baath officials, 'Who will say anything? The international community? Fuck them.'

Outside the Baathist states, Egyptian television ran a month-long serialisation of *The Protocols of the Elders of Zion*, featuring 400 actors. The *Protocols* were invented by Serge Nilus, a secret policeman working for the Russian Tsar. He pretended they were the minutes of secret meetings of a Jewish conspiracy which was seeking absolute power. (The resourceful Nilus stole the idea from a French satire of Napoleon III which didn't even mention Jews.) The classic paranoid racist fantasy was useful to the Tsarist autocracy, which, like the tyrannies, monarchies and theocracies of the Middle East, had an urgent need to find scapegoats. The Israeli-Palestinian conflict was a comfort to those regimes. If it were to be settled, it wouldn't change the lot of oppressed Syrians or Libyans, and they might start to wonder about local reasons for their misery. Islamists were as interested in fascism. Hassan al-Banna, the founder of the Muslim Brotherhood, admired Mussolini's blackshirts and divided his organisation into phalanges in the Franco style. Muslim fundamentalism, like Jewish fundamentalism, Christian fundamentalism, Hindu fundamentalism and, for all I know, Moonie and Mormon fundamentalism, has implicit totalitarian potential; it's the nature of the fundamentalist to wish to annihilate rival creeds and heresies and enforce conformity on the faithful. Muslim fundamentalists didn't need outside help to become anti-semitic, any more than Jewish fundamentalists needed prompting from others to become anti-Muslim. They could manage that by themselves. Nonetheless, the condemnations of Western 'Orientalist' prejudices about Islam, which were delivered by many intellectuals in the 1990s, missed the point that the Middle East had imported the worst of Europe: Israel was inspired by colonialism; Israel's enemies found inspiration in fascism and communism.

A noisy section of the European intelligentsia wasn't satisfied with saying that Israel occupied the West Bank, Gaza Strip and East Jerusalem in defiance of United Nations resolutions, and that Palestinians were destitute and living in fear of assassination. To explain away the Palestinian suicide bombings and the retreat of Arab militants into brutish religion, they had to conjure up the worst image of Israel imaginable. And, inevitably, Jews became the Nazi organisers of a new Holocaust. Tom Paulin, a minor poet and major media don, wrote of Palestinian boys being 'gunned down by the Zionist SS'. He told the Egyptian newspaper *al-Ahram Weekly* that American-born Jewish settlers in the occupied territories 'should be shot dead. I think they are Nazis, racists, I feel nothing but hatred for them.'[11] In the spring of 2002, at the height of the suicide bombing campaign, the International Parliament of Writers sent a delegation to the West Bank. José Saramago, a Portuguese novelist, said Ariel Sharon's siege of Yasser Arafat's compound in Ramallah was 'a crime comparable to Auschwitz'.

No one died during the siege.

'Where are the gas chambers?' a journalist asked.

'Not here yet,' Saramago replied – darkly.

After he escaped, somehow, from the new Nazi state, Saramago wrote of how vengeful Jews built absolute power by exploiting the gullible gentile world's sympathy:

> The Jews endlessly scratch their own wound to keep it bleeding, to make it incurable, and they show it to the world as if it were a banner . . . Israel wants all of us to feel guilty, directly or indirectly, for the horrors of Holocaust; Israel wants us to renounce the most elemental critical judgement and for us to transform ourselves into a docile echo of its will; Israel wants us to recognise *de jure* what, in its eyes, is a *de facto* reality; absolute impunity. From the point of view of the Jews, Israel cannot ever be brought to judgment because it was tortured, gassed and incinerated in Auschwitz.

Saramago wasn't considered a noxious oaf by the discerning. He was awarded the Nobel Prize for Literature in 1998.[12]

Israel used the Holocaust to defend the occupation of the West Bank. Arabs and Europeans used the Holocaust to attack Jews as a genocidal master race.

Peter Novick, an American historian who examined the strange history of Holocaust commemoration, had little faith in the claim that it taught lessons on how to avoid future genocides:

> The principal lesson of the Holocaust, it is frequently said, [is that] it sensitises us to oppression and atrocity. In principle it might, and I don't doubt that sometimes it does. But making it the benchmark of oppression and atrocity works in precisely the opposite direction, trivialising crimes of lesser magnitude . . . The United States is, by a wide margin, the wealthiest country in the world. In the humanitarian assistance it offers to the poorest nations, as a percentage of gross national product, it ranks, also by a wide margin, last among the industrial countries. Every American president in recent years has had moving words to say about how shameful it was that the United States stood by as millions died [at the hands of the Nazis]. If one president has been moved by, or has noticed, America's standing on the list just mentioned, if he has expressed shame and mortification at that standing, it's escaped my research.'[13]

When the Bosnians begged Europe and America to save them from Milosevic's rapists and murderers in 1992, Warren Christopher, Clinton's Secretary of State, said the fate of the Bosnian Muslims couldn't be compared to that of the Jews. Because the Serbs weren't actually seeking to gas every Muslim, Nato shouldn't intervene. When the European Union imposed diplomatic sanctions on Austria for allowing Jorg Haider a voice in government, Euro-sceptic pundits screamed that Haider wasn't a Nazi. He wasn't; he was a racist mob-rouser. Wasn't that enough? The not-a-Nazi gambit is played daily. I once had a go at the government's assault on civil liberties while sharing a platform with a New Labour cheerleader. His instant response was 'Nick Cohen thinks Blair's Hitler.' I thought nothing of the sort and wondered whether the Holocaust card was played to render criticism of New Labour's record illegitimate until the moment the Cabinet dressed in black leather and invaded Poland.

The Holocaust was a minefield but it was also a theme park. No cause was too trite to appropriate the Holocaust. Like Elvis or Diana, it became an 'icon' in the mass-media market. Consider the fate of the ringing and historically accurate description of the rise of Hitler from the anti-Nazi pastor, Martin Niemöller:

> First they came for the Communists, but I was not a Communist – so I said nothing. Then they came for the Social Democrats, but I was not a Social Democrat – so I did nothing. Then they came for the trade unionists, but I was not a trade unionist. And then they came for the Jews, but I was not a Jew – so I did little. Then when they came for me, there was no one left who could stand up for me.

Al Gore and *The Encyclopaedia of the Holocaust* moved the Jews from last to first place. The Holocaust Museum in Washington cut Communists from the list. Gore cut Communists, socialists and trade unionists, and added Catholics. The Catholic Cathedral in Boston also added Catholics. Gay rights activists added homosexuals. Versions of Niemöller's words have been quoted by Hugh Hefner when he was fighting the banning of *Playboy* by 7-Eleven stores, anti-abortionists and the Massachusetts Association of Underwriters when it was protesting against regulation of the insurance industry ('They came first for the disability market.').[14] Just before the Iraq war, a London publisher issued a book of 101 anti-war poems and included Pastor Niemöller's text.[15] It wasn't a poem. Nor was it a particularly good rallying cry for the peace movement when it could be recast as 'First they came for the Kurds, but I was not a Kurd – so I said nothing. Then they came for the Marsh Arabs but I was not a Marsh Arab – so I did nothing . . .'

Britart was the new élite's official culture in the 1990s. The critic Julian Stallabrass dissected its popularity as a mixture of the appeals of tabloid newspapers, tabloid television and the lifestyle sections of broadsheets:

In its content, violence, sex, child abuse, the British character, celebrity, gossip and an obsession with itself; in its style, the speedy delivery of messages, leading to the prevalence of one-liner art, jokes, clichés, the use of advertising strategies, glossy surfaces but equally the appeal of grunge and anti-intellectual posturing.[16]

With the Holocaust everywhere, and thus nowhere, it was inevitable that it should attract the artists who gathered at the Groucho Club, the coke-raddled heart of media London. Gordon Burn, a gushing critic, told *Guardian* readers how Damien Hirst ordered the club's luckless cleaners to collect the 'cigarette butts, champagne corks, matchbooks, cocaine wraps' left after a rough night in the West End. The installation Hirst created in a giant plastic ashtray was 'like a horrible record of a Srebrenica, of an Auschwitz or Belsen'. Not to be outdone, the Chapman Brothers hit back with 'Hell' in the 2000 *Apocalypse* exhibition at the Royal Academy. Jake and Dinos spent two years moulding and painting 5,000 models of Nazi soldiers, and placed them in a landscape dotted with models of concentration camps. The result of their labours was a room of glass cases filled with tiny Nazis mutilating each other in toyland Treblinkas. The Chapmans struck me as no more profound than the men who used to retire to their sheds, construct scale models of St Paul's from match-sticks and send them to *Blue Peter*. The concentration camp reference, however, was enough to convince the Academicians that they were the heirs of Goya.

The French synchronised swimming team wanted to perform a routine based on the theme of Auschwitz at the Olympics and was taken aback by accusations of tastelessness. (As they had every right to be. Why should swimmers be singled out?) Reputable sources reported that Taiwan had a restaurant with pictures of camp inmates on the walls to delight the diners. When Arnold Schwarzenegger told Californians he was considering running for governor of their state, he floored those who suggested that a beefcake might not be up to the job by revealing that he'd received an award from the Simon Wiesenthal Centre for Holocaust Studies.

The only way out of the crassness and special pleading was to bellow 'Enough already!' Worthwhile politics doesn't rest on robbing the graves of the dead but on principled consistency. You can't mourn the victims of the gas chambers and then exploit their memory to deny rights and land to living Palestinians. You can't weep tears of pity for the Palestinians while ignoring the monsters of the Arab world. You have to have universal principles. Left-wing politics is meant to rest on the ideals of Liberty, Equality and Fraternity. Of these fraternity is the virtue most needed in international affairs, but is the trickiest concept to define. It involves feeling camaraderie for strangers who share your ideals. You must be willing to make sacrifices for them when circumstances aren't ideal or of your choosing – which they never are. The effort involves imaginative sympathy: the ability to put yourself in the place of the others and recognise friends and, conversely, enemies. Fraternity is a tough ideal. Its first requirement is that you know yourself. Its second is that you know your comrades, and stick by them in hard times.

How, by these standards, did New Labour fare when it offered fraternal sympathy to the concentration camp inmates of Hitler's Germany? Blair's eyes were moist in Westminster Hall as he mourned the victims of a dead tyrant. When the 'grieving process' was at an end, he carried on authorising the use of every low trick to stop the victims of modern tyrants finding sanctuary. The racism his campaign against asylum-seekers generated had a predictable effect. Determined not to be attacked from the right by New Labour, William Hague began to attack aliens who enjoyed a luxurious life courtesy of 'local councils [which] spend more money looking after bogus asylum-seekers than after old people in homes'. The Tories went into the 2001 election promising to send every asylum-seeker to purpose-built prisons, or 'reception centres' as they called them with a nice Orwellian touch. (They couldn't say where the jails would be built or how much they would cost, but detail was never their strong point.) The racist climate respectable politi-

cians helped foster encouraged the growth of the neo-Nazi
British National Party. 'The asylum-seeker issue has been great
for us,' said Nick Griffin, its leader and wannabe British führer.
'This issue legitimates us.' 'Nazi' was an accurate description of
the BNP programme. Griffin was animated by the national
socialist belief that a Jewish conspiracy controlled the media
(among much else) and provided 'us with an endless diet of
pro-multicultural, pro-homosexual trash.'

New Labour fought fascists in local elections, but was more
docile when it took the Blairite message overseas. Blair stunned
Italian socialists when he formed an alliance with Silvio Berlusconi, the media monopolist whose administration included
Italy's 'post-fascist' parties. The aim of the Blair–Berlusconi
pact was to slash the rights of European workers. The Prime
Minister overruled Robin Cook and insisted that British companies should carry on selling arms to the genocidal Indonesian
dictator, whose invasion of East Timor in 1975 resulted in the
extermination of somewhere between one sixth and one third
of the local population.

Blair aided mass murderers and denied shelter to their victims. But he still thought he could get away with using anti-
fascist history as therapy, death camps as a life-affirming
experience. Holocaust Day made him feel good about himself
and the liberal-minded feel good about him. What a brass-
necked, two-faced waste of DNA. Who could sink lower than
this treacherous jerk?

Tony Benn's determination to bring undemocratic power to
book can't be shaken. If he were to bump into the Permanent
Secretary at the Department for Work and Pensions or the
Chief Executive of Carphone Warehouse he would expose their
autocracy like a surgeon cutting through flab to reveal a cancer.
As the great democrat said: 'If I meet a powerful man, I ask five
questions: What power have you got? Where did you get it
from? In whose interests do you exercise it? To whom are you
accountable? And how can I get rid of you?'[17] On 2 February

2003, just before the start of the war against Iraq, Benn flew to Baghdad to meet Saddam Hussein in a televised interview. If the interviewee had been honest, the answers to Benn's questions would have been:

(1) 'My friend, I have the absolute power of life and death over 25 million Iraqis.'
(2) 'What else but my control of the instruments of torture and death?'
(3) 'Mine.'
(4) 'No one.'
(5) 'As you are an honoured guest in my country and a comrade of the glorious Iraqi people, I will give your final question the frank answer it deserves. Within a few weeks of formally taking power in 1979, I tortured about one third of the senior national and regional leaders of the Baath Party until they were prepared to sign confessions I had prepared earlier. (I told them their families would die if they refused.) They were executed, but in a touch I'm sure you will appreciate as a fellow politician, the firing squads were composed of Baath Party members. Guilt was spread and the executioners knew that they must sink or swim with me. Please don't wince, I understand collective Cabinet responsibility follows the same principle, if rather less bloodily. In 1980 I launched a preemptive strike, as you say, against Iran. Ayatollah Khomeini sent human waves of martyrs to certain death. I met them with poison gas. The body count had reached one million by 1988, when we had to stop. We'd run out of young men. The West, of course, supported me against the Ayatollah, as did the Soviet Union and my brothers in the Arab capitals. The whole world did what you as a just and merciful man now call on it to do now and 'engaged' with Iraq. Encouraged by the ways of international cooperation and free trade I ordered the killing of between 100,000 and 200,000 Kurds and Assyrian Christians your Archbishop of Canterbury doesn't seem to have heard about. Gas again, of course, always my favourite, and I think one thousand villages were destroyed – or was it two? or three? Your memory's going too? Yes, I can see that. But I do distinctly remember signing the order for "random bombardments using artillery, helicopters and aircraft at all times of day or night in order to kill the largest number of persons present in those prohibited areas". Long before the sanctions you so rightly blame for all my poor country's troubles, Iraq's economy had collapsed under the human

and financial costs of the war against Iran and my rule. In 1990 I devised an alternative economic policy. I ordered another preemptive war, against Kuwait this time. My troops seized its oilfields within a day. They deployed torture, rape, electric shocks, mutilations and executions to convince Kuwaitis of the benefits of becoming citizens of a greater Iraq. The imperialist warmongers attacked me and my peace-loving countrymen and drove us out of Kuwait in 1991. Another 100,000 went in the heroic struggle against aggression. What was left of my peace-loving countrymen were led astray by degenerate Zionist Crusaders who tricked them with their rat-like wiles into abandoning their father and protector and staging a revolution. I lost control of fourteen of the eighteen provinces of Iraq. Fortunately the Kuwait war really was "all about oil" for both sides and sagacious politicians in your country and others said no one should help the rebel dogs. I killed another 40,000 – or was it 80,000? – by driving them into canals and minefields or firing on them from helicopter gunships in the heavens. The United Nations imposed sanctions, which was the response of cowards, not men. Sanctions might have broken the puny Afrikaaners, but they were merchants who preferred democracy to South Africa being cut off from the world economy. Your Western money grubbers didn't understand my warrior's mind. My tyranny exists to preserve the power of the tyrant. That's all there is to it. If sanctions cause 500,000 Iraqis to die of malnutrition but my rule is not shaken, why should I care? If what's left of the middle class join the four million Iraqis in exile, professors have to sell their books to buy food and the only businessmen to make money are black marketeers, how does their suffering hurt me? As you can see from my palace, the United Nations hasn't forced me to cut the costs of the show all leaders must make to keep up the people's morale. There were still dangers, despite the failure of sanctions. Alas, I found that those I trusted most were the most dangerous. You, I know, learned the same bitter lesson when you were a mighty leader in Britain. For the news reached the banks of the Tigris of the perfidy of the she-devil Patricia Hewitt. I, too, have had my trust betrayed and seen my closest allies join the enemy. You will weep with me when I tell you that my own sons-in-law conspired against me, although they never got close enough to take a shot – no one gets that close. They fled to Jordan. Knowing that magnanimity is the ruler's duty, I forgave them for my daughters' sake and allowed them a safe return home. Unfortunately I couldn't prevent my hotheaded supporters from delivering just punishments, but the young must be allowed to make their own mistakes. My Republican Guard was infiltrated by the CIA. I found out about the satanic plot only when officers gladly confessed their treason with their dying breaths. It is for this reason that Iraq's secret police forces have secret police forces inside them to spy on the spies. Everyone in Iraq must know that someone is watching them. I am an old man and will die one day. But my sons Uday and Qusay have listened and learned at their father's knee and are ready to inherit the family business. Fools say that we kill without purpose. They can't grasp that fear works. Gassing works. Torture works. All the economic and social movements that the womanly intellectuals you allow to live in your country believe will change societies will be stopped if the men with the guns say they should stop. And not only guns. Here in Iraq all industrial implements have a dual purpose. When we imported a machine for shredding plastic, we didn't let it stand idle when its work was done. We dropped prisoners in head first, if they were minor criminals, or feet first if they deserved a slower death. If men won't talk, their wives are suspended from their hair or raped to encourage their husbands to help the police with their inquiries. If men or women talk against me, their tongues are cut out. If . . . Please forgive me, your eyes are glazing over and I can see I've lost your interest. What was your question again?'

'Ah yes, Mr President, here it is. My last question was: How can I get rid of you?'

'I would say that if engagement, disengagement, sanctions, revolution, palace revolution, assassination, mutiny, CIA coup and my own natural death are likely to be ineffective, all that's left is a foreign invasion. Unless the Americans are criminally incompetent, far fewer people will die than if I stay on. More tea?'[18]

But Benn didn't ask how he could get rid of the most powerful man he'd met. Nor did he raise awkward questions on the tricky subjects of democratic legitimacy and accountability. Presented with a despot who had started two wars and waged a one-sided civil war against the peoples of Iraq for decades, he preferred to ask : 'I wonder whether you could say something yourself directly through this interview to the peace movement of the world that might help to advance the cause they have in mind?'

To which Saddam replied:

We admire the development of the peace movement around the
world in the last few years. We pray to God to empower all those
working against war and for the cause of peace and security based
on just peace for all . . . Tell the British people if the Iraqis are sub-
jected to aggression or humiliation they would fight bravely. Just as
the British people did in the Second World War.

The next two months were to prove that Saddam wasn't the
most accurate of forecasters. But Benn didn't follow up and ask
why the majority of Iraqis would want to fight for him.

His powder-puff interview over, Benn returned to Britain.
On 15 February 2003 he was a star speaker at the anti-war march
which brought about 750,000 to the streets of London, according to the police, and two million according to the organisers.
An anomalous figure stood alone in the crowd. Sama Hadad
was a refugee from Iraq and was demonstrating against the
demonstrators. 'Everyone here is wrong,' she told Benn. 'Everyone here has a moral and humanitarian duty to call for the
removal of Saddam Hussein and to create a just and democratic Iraq . . . Hundreds of thousands of Iraqis are dying.'

'I know,' interrupted Benn. 'Because of sanctions.'

'No, not because of sanctions, because of Saddam,' she
cried.[19]

She should have saved her breath. The British centre-left had
its hands over its ears and was screaming. Benn didn't want to
know. Nothing she could say could shake his conviction that
the effects of tyranny weren't the fault of the tyrant. The shame
brought by what he didn't say to Saddam was compounded by
the shamelessness of what he did say to Saddam's victims.

A stale whiff of Stalinism was in the February air, and I
thought, 'Oh no, not again.'

FIVE

The Second Battle of Stalingrad

This book might just as well have been called 'How the Left Loses'. It looks at the deftness with which fears of crime and foreigners can be used to befuddle the voters, the difficulty of taking on an élite which poses as the friend of the people, the appeal of getting rich quick, the conviction fostered by the long bull market that privatisation and deregulation were the only ways and the alliances between political and corporate power. Those left-wingers who weren't rabbiting on about fox hunting (but only with dogs) resisted. They fought and lost honourably. But reluctant though it was to admit it had faults, the left wasn't defeated for years solely because of the cunning of its enemies. The Iraq war showed that it could match Blair's opportunism. If he could try to beguile the public with spin, so could his opponents. If he looked a hypocrite when he tried to come to terms with the legacy of Hitler, his opponents feigned ignorance of the legacy of Stalin. A tiny minority still yearned for dictatorship. They were willing to strike alliances with the fundamentalist enemies of the Enlightenment and salute a tyrant with the blood of hundreds of thousands on his hands. No one could explain why, but the tiny minority led the opposition to the war outside Parliament.

For six weeks in the spring of 2003 it was possible to believe that the left wouldn't lose. The anti-war demonstration was largest in living memory. It had a fair claim to be the largest in British history. The revolt of Labour MPs against the motion authorising war against Iraq was definitely the greatest Commons rebellion by members of a governing party. It was bigger than the revolt on Irish Home Rule which split the Liberal party in the nineteenth century, bigger than anyone could have imag-

ined when the 'clones' of New Labour took office in 1997. Robin
Cook resigned. His explanation for quitting the government
was delivered in devastatingly plain language. 'Britain is not a
superpower,' the former Foreign Secretary told the Commons.

> Our interests are best protected, not by unilateral action, but by
> multilateral agreement and a world order governed by rules. Yet
> tonight the international partnerships most important to us are
> weakened. The European Union is divided. The security council is
> in stalemate. Those are heavy casualties of war without a single
> shot yet being fired.

Labour and Liberal Democrat MPs broke into spontaneous
applause. 'Hear-hears', stomps and thumps had been the only
forms of approbation the Speaker had allowed. But it was a
time of precedent breaking, and MPs gave Cook an appreciative
hand. Until Iraq, Blair had been lucky in his enemies on the left
as well as the right. Chief among the left's many weaknesses was
that it had no intelligent leadership. By forcing Cook to resign,
the Prime Minister had sent the most effective opposition
speaker in Parliament to the back benches from where he might
eviscerate what remained of the government.

To add to his troubles was the knowledge that among the
other leaders of the revolt were Peter Kilfoyle, Chris Smith, Mo
Mowlam, Frank Dobson and Graham Allan: serious politicians
who had accepted jobs from Blair. They had worked with him
because they believed that a little good might come from New
Labour. Iraq pushed them to their tipping point. The half-full
glass emptied into the desert sands.

The capriciousness of the policy staggered practical men and
women. Cook spoke for most of his party when he looked with
shock and awe at the Bush administration. 'Only a year ago, we
and the United States were part of a coalition against terrorism
that was wider and more diverse than I would ever have imagined possible. History will be astonished at the diplomatic mis-
calculations that led so quickly to the disintegration of that
powerful coalition.' Kilfoyle, a former defence minister who
had once counted Blair as a friend, warned the government that

its 'impatience will reap a whirlwind, a whirlwind which will affect us and ours for generations to come'.

Saddam wasn't a pressing menace. His wars and the UN sanctions had enfeebled his country. Why Iraq? Why poke a snake when you can leave it alone? Why should Britain always be at America's beck and call? There was a half answer to the first question. Iraq was in breach of a sheaf of UN resolutions – but so was Israel. The answer to the second came from a Bush administration which made the hair of every European social democrat stand on end. The war wasn't 'all about oil', it was all about power, the argument from Washington went. The attacks on the World Trade Center and Pentagon showed the danger of the proliferation of weapons of mass destruction. Saddam had used chemical weapons twice: on the battlefields of the Iran-Iraq war and against the Guernicas of Kurdistan. To eliminate the faint possibility that they might be used again he had to be overthrown. Only the threat of invasion had forced Iraq to re-admit United Nations weapons inspectors, but they couldn't be trusted. Saddam had shown before that he could run rings round them. The world should have supported the Iraqi revolutionaries in 1991, and finished off the tyrant there and then. America had the power to do it now and would begin the process of democratising a Middle East whose tyrannies nurtured terrorists. It was the one region left where the US followed the Cold War policy of supporting dictatorship as a matter of course. A fat lot of good that had done. The repression and religious extremism of the Saudi Arabian monarchy had produced Osama bin Laden and most of the hijackers of 11 September.

The American answer was no answer at all to centre-left opinion in Europe and every other continent. Europeans believed in Cook's world of rules. The United States had ignored the rules by refusing to ratify the International Criminal Court and the Kyoto Treaty. Admittedly Saddam had defied sixteen UN resolutions, but the rule-bound insisted that a seventeenth was essential. Meanwhile, evidence of Iraqi links to al-Qaeda was slight, to put it at its mildest. MI6 told the Prime

Minister it hadn't found one lead which could stand up to scrutiny. The likelihood of Islamic fanatics attacking Britain wasn't going to be lessened by taking on Iraq. It would push Muslims into the arms of murderous fundamentalists. Talk of bringing democracy to the Middle East on the back of an American tank sounded crackers, a recipe for mayhem. The bulk of the Labour Party wanted no part of it, but at this critical moment they were stuck with Blair. The nominally left-of-centre leader was prepared to destroy his internationalist foreign policy, ignore his colleagues and risk a conflagration, for what? For George W. Bush. For a Bible-bashing know-nothing whose strings were pulled by Big Pharma, Big Oil and the Big Guy in the Sky. The Bush administration laughed at the deepest beliefs of progressive Europeans. Blair was widening its grin and widening the gap between Britain and her natural allies in Europe.

Previously obscure loyalists said they could no longer serve as junior ministers. Charles Kennedy saw an opportunity and repositioned the Liberal Democrats as an anti-war party. Clare Short went on the radio and repeatedly condemned the Prime Minister as 'reckless'. She didn't give a coded warning the crypt-analysts in the Westminster lobby could decipher and explain to the public. She went for Blair as if she were the leader of the opposition. The rules of collective Cabinet responsibility said that she must resign or be fired. The once mighty Prime Minister didn't sack her. He couldn't afford to lose Short as well as Cook. Blair and Gordon Brown begged her to stay on. She relented, but she looked wretched: a broken woman in a broken government.

On 26 February, 121 Labour MPs rebelled against the government. Downing Street and the Foreign Office thought they could contain further rebellions by securing a United Nations resolution specifically authorising an invasion. On 10 March Jacques Chirac said France would veto it 'regardless of the circumstances'. The Americans said that they would push ahead regardless of the circumstances. Britain's attempt to create international agreement had come to nothing. It didn't feel extravagant to compare the Foreign Office's failure to Suez.

Irreconcilable left-wingers in the Campaign Group said that now was the moment when the Labour Party might rid itself of Blair. Cabinet ministers derisively replied that they had over-played their hand and inadvertently rallied waverers to the Prime Minister's side. After the war was over, ministers admit-ted that the left had been right. Blair was safe in theory. The government would survive the vote on 18 March authorising war because he had the support of the Conservatives. But tech-nicalities don't matter in a crisis. Jack Straw looked at the Neville Chamberlain example. He had resigned and allowed Churchill to become Prime Minister, despite winning a major-ity in the 1940 Norway debate on his conduct of the Second World War. What mattered was 'sentiment', Straw said. Perhaps it would need 206 Labour MPs to vote against the government – a majority of the parliamentary Labour Party – perhaps fewer than that. 'It would have been one of those things that would have been obvious had we arrived at that point.' Straw told his wife he 'might well' have to resign and spend more time with his family. Her response wasn't recorded.

Geoff Hoon, the Defence Secretary, warned Donald Rums-feld, his counterpart in Washington, that if the vote 'went wrong' Blair would go. 'The US came to understand it was about us gambling just about everything on getting it right.' To the despair of a Downing Street which was puffing Britain's vital role in the conflict, Rumsfeld told the press that if Britain pulled out America could and would fight alone.

On 18 March, 139 Labour MPs voted against the government. The 'sentiment' was that Blair could stay on. It was a remarkably generous sentiment. The contrast between the two sides was between whipped yes-men and their passionate opponents. The Labour MPs who supported Blair included ministers who were more convinced of the need to hold onto their jobs than of the judgement of their leader. 'Either Tony knows something the rest of us don't know, or he's insane,' one muttered to the *Guardian*'s political correspondent. Every dodge was tried to win Labour members' backing. Cherie Blair begged MPs to support her husband. Straw acknowledged that he couldn't win the argument on its merits. He warned his colleagues the issue wasn't Iraq but 'whether you want to keep this government in business'. At both debates, fear kept most of the loyalists in line: fear of losing their places in government or a leader who had brought them to Westminster. His opponents had all the best tunes.

There were two exceptions. Blair spoke of uniting Iraq's 'disparate groups on a democratic basis'. He hoped that British troops would be fighting to create a country which accepted human rights and basic freedoms. He had an unlikely ally. Ann Clwyd was a left-wing Labour backbencher. She was no friend of the Prime Minister, but she was one of the few friends of the Iraqis left in Parliament. She spoke at the 26 February debate a few days after coming back from the only free part of Iraq, the Kurdish enclave in the north. Saddam's forces had been held off ever since the end of the 1991 Gulf War by guerrilla fighters and the no-fly zone enforced by the RAF and USAF.

While in Kurdistan she had accepted the grim honour of opening a 'genocide museum' in what had been a Baathist jail until Saddam's forces were driven out. As she went in, a widow handed her pictures of her husband and two sons who had died in the prison's torture chambers. Clwyd inspected the walls and saw they were covered with graffiti written in blood. She spoke to refugees from the Iraq beyond the no-fly zone who said that prisoners were being executed every day in the jails under Saddam's control. A former inmate of the Abu Ghraib prison in Baghdad told her that 2,000 were killed after an attempt on Uday Hussein's life. The prisoners couldn't have been the assassins, but the regime wanted to 'send a message'.

Clwyd ran Indict, a pressure group which had the Quixotic dream of bringing the leaders of the Baath Party to justice. She turned lawyer and carefully recorded the witnesses' statements. The story that got to her was about a university professor who had given birth in Abu Ghraib. The academic subsisted on a diet of thin soup and bread. She begged the guards for milk for the child. The guards shrugged and the baby died. 'She held that baby in her arms for three days and would not give up the body,' Clwyd told the Commons. 'At the end of the three days, because the temperature in the prison was very hot – some 60° C – the body began to smell. They took the woman and her dead baby away. I asked the former prisoner what happened to her and he said that she was killed.'

Blair sacked Clwyd from the shadow cabinet when New Labour was in opposition – for speaking out about Iraq, naturally. But she believed it was a higher priority to get rid of one of the worst dictators in the world than get rid of Tony Blair. She turned to the Labour benches and said: 'When I hear people calling for more time [for weapons inspections], I say who will speak up for the victims? I say to my colleagues, please, who is to help the victims of Saddam Hussein's regime unless we do? I believe in regime change. I say that without hesitation, and I will support the government tonight because I think that they are doing a brave thing.'[1]

Blair's hopes for a better future and Clwyd's descriptions of a monstrous present changed few minds. Blair was dismissed as a transparent fraud whose excuses for war switched by the day. First Britain was fighting to remove weapons of mass destruction and then to break up the alliance between Saddam and al-Qaeda and finally for freedom. When one justification went, he found another. He was a straw man twisting in the wind. Clwyd could be written off as an obsessive. She was a well-meaning woman, but she did have a thing about Kurds. Once she got going, you couldn't shut her up. The smart interviewers had a ready put-down for her sort. If we're going to overthrow this ghastly regime, they asked, 'Where do we stop? Burma, China, North Korea, Zimbabwe, Libya . . .?' Nonetheless, Clwyd offered solid reasons for thinking Iraq wouldn't be a new Vietnam whatever the left claimed. Deserters from the army who made it into the Kurdish safe haven were saying their comrades weren't so different from Europeans as the anti-war movement assumed. They didn't want to risk their lives to keep themselves in a despot's custody. 'Where do you start?' was the best reply to 'Where do you stop?' If the capricious Americans could overthrow the regime with a minimum of civilian casualties, why not start in Iraq?

Britain's relations with the European Union divided the political class while boring the public. Iraq was a national issue. The majority was against Blair. His approval rating – the gap between those who said they were satisfied or dissatisfied with his conduct – went from plus 42 in November 2001 to minus 20 in February 2003. Two-thirds of the population opposed war without UN approval.[2] Again, nothing like these figures had been seen before. British troops had always gone into combat with overwhelming public support. Alastair Campbell complained to Whitehall information officers that he couldn't persuade broadcasters to interview Iraqi refugees who were telling Downing Street that they supported an invasion. After years of being spun, the consensus among Westminster journalists was that all news from Number 10 was contaminated, and it was their job to pick apart the lies. The public concurred.

Even if Campbell had been revered as the George Washington of PR, Blair's middle-class constituency would have shut its eyes to the scars of Iraqi refugees. The intellectual leaders of the liberal-left didn't want to know. Pundits who had either made excuses for Blair, or had found more interesting subjects to concern them, went wild. BBC presenters battled unsuccessfully to preserve their neutrality. The letters pages of the *Guardian* and *Independent* became wailing walls for despairing Labour Party members. Britain's best novelists and playwrights joined the opposition. Their rhetoric had the venom of betrayed lovers as they cried that Blair had made them ashamed to be British. (It was a feature of the Iraq debate that no one was as belligerent as the peace campaigners.) At London Fashion Week Katherine Hamnett sent her models down the catwalk in T-shirts bearing the slogan 'Stop War Blair Out.' Her anti-war chic was all the rage for at least a fortnight. Royal Shakespeare Company actors announced that their forthcoming production of *The Merry Wives of Windsor* in Michigan in no way implied that they supported the American overthrow of a dictator who was the spit of Macbeth. A wise society would make it an imprisonable offence for actors to use their own words in public instead of other people's. Few laughed at the thesps at the time.

The opposition was joined by a significant minority of conservatives who put the hard question of how war was in Britain's best interests. Patriots couldn't see why Britain had to be at America's side. They could acknowledge what the believers in the 'special relationship' couldn't bring themselves to admit: an America which spent as much as the rest of the world put together on its armed forces didn't care about Britain or need its support.[3] The Prime Minister was ignoring Britain's oldest foreign policy tradition, and getting precious little in return. From the Spanish Armada of 1588, first England and then Britain had fought the Habsburgs, Louis XIV, Napoleon, the Kaiser and Hitler. Until the 1990s, Britain had always opposed any nation which threatened to dominate the world – unless that nation was Britain.

Dissident Tories joined artists, intellectuals, the churches, British Islam, and Labour and Liberal Democrat supporters to form a giant centre-left coalition against Blair. It opened fire with everything it had – and failed to kill.

The forlorn editor of the anti-war *Daily Mirror* said he had never seen public opinion move so quickly. War switched the debate from complex questions to simple ones: who do you want to win and why? On the one hand the public was presented with the affecting sight of British servicemen and women risking their lives by throwing away their hard hats and putting on berets so they could assure the people of Basra that they were members of a force which didn't torture, loot and rape. On the other were Saddam's goons who did little else. What did it say about you if you preferred the latter to the former?

Blair's approval ratings shot back up as a majority of voters decided that they supported the war after all. Blair was applauded for ignoring the 'appeasers' and bringing down a dictator who could be compared to Hitler. The comparison was apt in all respects except one: if Saddam had been in possession of a world-threatening or region-threatening military arsenal, he would have had to have been appeased. The Americans would have backed off for fear of a huge counterattack. The old policy of keeping in place sanctions which had led to the deaths of countless thousands might have been maintained. Iraq might have remained a private prison of the Baath Party. As it was, Saddam's threat could be neutralised in 2003 only because he didn't threaten anyone, except Iraqis.

The British government tried to spin its way out the conundrum. No one doubted that Saddam was making a mockery of international arms-control efforts, but London and Washington went further. In September 2002 Blair said that Saddam was 'continuing to develop weapons of mass destruction and with them the ability to inflict real damage upon the region, and the stability of the world.' In January 2003, Downing Street released a hair-raising dossier on how Iraq hid its arsenal. The information came from intelligence sources, we were assured. Downing Street said that Iraq had attempted to procure uranium from Africa for its nuclear programme. Its evidence was cited by a grateful Bush administration. Downing Street terrified servicemen's families by saying that Iraq had chemical and biological weapons that could be ready for the order to fire in 45 minutes.

Anyone who believed the government must have expected an apocalyptic conflict. The war came and went. A regime facing extinction didn't fire chemical or biological weapons at the agents of its destruction. Baghdad surrendered and months passed. Next to nothing was found.

Even before the fighting began, there were doubts. The 'intelligence sources' account of Saddam's hidden arsenal was discredited when a bright surfer on the Net noticed that it had been cobbled together by a Downing Street minion who had put 'Iraq' and 'weapons of mass destruction' into a search engine and cut and pasted together what he found. The International Atomic Energy Authority said it had no evidence to support Britain's claim that Iraq was looking to import uranium. After the fighting, even Bush White House apologised for repeating the British claim that Iraq was trying to restart its nuclear programme. The uranium report was either invention or based on a scrap of uncorroborated intelligence.

Meanwhile Andrew Gilligan, the BBC's defence correspondent, announced that Alastair Campbell had ignored the wishes of the intelligence services when he went public with the assertion that Iraq could deploy weapons of mass destruction in 45 minutes. Campbell denounced the 'lie' and demanded an apology from the BBC. The government and state broadcaster went for each other.

The BBC didn't say it had the evidence to prove that Campbell had exaggerated a tentative report from MI6, merely that an anonymous high-level source had alleged to Andrew Gilligan that the 'sexing up' had taken place. The hunt for the source consumed Whitehall for weeks. In early July, Dr David Kelly, an official from the Ministry of Defence who had spent the past decade overseeing the disarming of Saddam, told his superiors that he had briefed Gilligan, but hadn't accused Campbell of wrongdoing. The government was delighted. It leaked Kelly's name and his repudiation of the BBC story to the press. It sent Kelly to the Commons Foreign Affairs Committee where he looked miserable as he faced the jeers of MPs. Maybe the experience tipped him over the edge. Maybe Gilligan's account of their conversation was accurate and Kelly feared being discovered. Maybe he hated being thrown into the preening, screaming world of Westminster politics and journalism. It was hard to be sure what drove him to suicide, but on 18 July Kelly's body was found in low hills near his Oxfordshire home.

Britain felt like a filthy country where public servants were driven to their deaths by bickering politicians and journalists. Tony Blair's approval ratings, which had bounced up after the war, bounced back down again. Whatever the truth of the Gilligan accusations, Blair had appealed to the public to trust his claim that Iraq had world-threatening weapons of mass destruction, and it didn't. His left-wing opponents had failed to stop Britain's participation in the war or bring down Blair, but they could claim that they had discredited him in the eyes of the electorate for good. Never again would be he be trusted. But local elections results and polls showed that it wasn't the left which benefited from the Prime Minister's discomfort. The far-left parties which organised the gigantic demonstrations managed to win just one council seat while the Tories took hundreds from Labour. The Conservatives could say that they supported British troops as they overthrew a tyrant, but deplored Blair's deceit. Iain Duncan Smith, who was closer to Bush and the Washington neo-conservatives than Blair, was secure in his job for the first time since he became party leader. He presented himself as a dull but honest man who didn't look so bad when set against the flashy, insincere PM. The supposed renaissance of the British left had led to a modest advance for the British right.

Here was the rub. The opposition was meant to be principled, but what principle was it following? There appeared to be a surfeit of principles. Pro-Europeanism, opposition to American corporate power, opposition to Blair's monarchical rule, patriotism, a yearning for honest government and a prudent fear of terrorist attack. Strong cases could be made for them, but they all had the ineluctable conclusion that Iraqis must continue to live under a pitiless dictatorship. Stopping the war meant saving Saddam. The left in Europe, Australia and America had nothing to offer Iraqi liberation movements. If Blair's opponents had admitted the obvious, they would have been able to expose his failings without being undercut by events. When Iraqis showed a natural inclination to prefer the invader to a tyrant, the left had nothing to say to them.

Britain is a moralising country, if not always a moral one, and the left needs to feel self-righteous more than most. Those who opposed the war thought they were better people than Blair and far better people than Bush. That was their problem. They couldn't bring themselves to accept that when they cried 'Stop the War!' they were liberals against liberation or Muslims for the oppression of Muslims or revolutionaries for the status quo. Working out who was the friend of the four million refugees from Saddam wasn't as easy as it once was. New Labour tried to keep them out of Britain, but helped remove their persecutor. The left deplored Blair's treatment of asylum-seekers but the logic of its argument was that the dictator who forced them to flee must stay in power. Perhaps the subconscious realisation that they were in a morally ambiguous position explains why the most fantastic predictions of disaster gained mass credence. For whatever reason, Blair's opponents tried to spin their way out of their conundrum. They had to believe that the violent overthrow of Saddam would be worse in its means and ends for Iraqis than letting him be.

The war on the home front opened with an army of Mystic Megs pounding the government with crystal balls. The public was told that there would be race riots in Britain (there weren't); and that the Arab 'street' would rise up (it didn't). Israel was going to use the cover of war to ethnically cleanse the West Bank (America wouldn't let it). Turkey was going to invade Iraqi Kurdistan (ditto). Iraqi cities were going to be carpet bombed (they weren't because there had been a revolution in military technology since Vietnam which rendered carpet bombing unnecessary).

Tony Benn said he'd been gentle with Saddam 'for one purpose only: namely to hear what he had to say before the massive attack upon Iraq takes place in which half a million casualties are expected.' Amnesty International predicted 50,000 deaths, 500,000 casualties and two million refugees. It's hard to be precise but there were about 2,500 civilian deaths and hardly any refugees.[4] Pacifists or semi-pacifists were unimpressed by the utilitarian argument that fewer innocents died in the war than would have died if the tyrant had been allowed to remain in place. (Although to be frank, utilitarianism loses much of its logical power when you are on the wrong end of a cluster bomb.) Others were left to judge for themselves as the graves in which the Baathists had dumped the bodies of tens of thousands of Shia and Kurds were uncovered after the fighting was over.

Caroline Lucas of the Green Party remembered that Saddam had begun fires which burned for nine months when he ignited the oil wells in Kuwait during the Gulf War of 1991. 'This time we are likely to see environmental destruction on a much greater scale,' she said. We didn't, because British and American special forces got to the fields before most of the bombs on the wells could be detonated. They weren't thanked. Instead, the prevention of environmental destruction was taken as proof that the war was 'all about oil' and that the Americans were more concerned with protecting oil fields and ministries than hospitals. If they had listened to their critics, they wouldn't have had troops to spare for either mission. Their soldiers would have been too busy protecting themselves. Attacks by the Fedayeen, Saddam's fascistic militia, were meant to presage a popular uprising against the invasion. (It didn't. The brave militia earned its spurs by killing unarmed opponents and ran from an enemy who shot back.) When the Fedayeen evaporated and the Americans reached the outskirts of Baghdad, politicians, professors and pundits agreed that the world was about to witness a second battle of Stalingrad. Anthony Beevor, author of a best-selling history of Stalingrad, complained that he couldn't get a moment's peace from journalists demanding that he give viewers and readers a preview of the coming catastrophe.

The left, the BBC, the Royal United Services Institute and the liberal press were adamant on this point. America's technological advantage would count for little in the merciless street-by-street fighting of urban warfare. Just as Stalin's miserable subjects had borne unimaginable privations to defend Russia from the Nazis, so Saddam's would put country before government and die in the last ditch. As soon as it mentioned the Nazis, the left lost. Bush wasn't Hitler and nor was Blair. Soviet citizens fought because they knew they would get a bullet in the back of the head if they were captured. Iraqi soldiers were more likely to get a Big Mac.

Prediction is an attempt to silence debate. The prophet tries to convince the audience that he has been to the future and is reporting back impartially on what it will be like. Passive listeners are meant to accept the inevitable outcome and understand that they can't change destiny. If the prophet is proved wrong, however, his authority vanishes. To keep changing the subject, to return unabashed with fresh predictions of calamity, may sound like a flexible opposition strategy which keeps the establishment on the back foot. But it leads to a sort of madness. During the conflict Blair had no difficulty in seeing off detractors who appeared in the end to be unhinged.

For the politically committed, a descent into clairvoyancy is fatal. They are meant to be guided by a morality which creates consistent principles and an intelligence which shows how their principles explain the world. When they make false prediction after false prediction they appear either shameless or foolish. Behind the many warnings of calamity in the Iraq crisis lay desire rather than understanding: the barely concealed desire to see a disaster rather than admit a mistake.[5] The Cassandras posed as radicals, but there was nothing left-wing about the hope that the oppressed would sacrifice their lives for their oppressors.

The inability to face up to the admittedly difficult circumstances which forced a choice between Bush and Blair on one side and Saddam on the other was a symptom of a wider malaise. It was associated with the far-left but could be found everywhere.

The twentieth century hadn't been kind to revolutionary socialism. It was difficult to know what did greater damage: the 'victories' of Lenin's and Stalin's Russia, Mao's China and Pol Pot's Cambodia or the 'defeats' of the fall of the Berlin Wall and

China's switch to a sort of capitalism. With no prospect of an
Anglo-Saxon revolution, British and American revolutionaries
lived vicariously for generations. They found a confirmation of
their faith in the backward world, where, starting with Russia in
1917, Marxist revolutions actually happened. (It took hard the-
oretical work to explain them. Karl Marx believed that communism was possible only in the advanced economies.) By the
1980s, the consolation offered by tumult in remote corners had
faded. Revolutions continued, but they weren't communist.
The masses revolted in the Philippines because they wanted
clean government, in Eastern Europe because they wanted the
chance to join the boring European Union bourgeoisie and in
Iran because they wanted an Islamic state. Communist parties
either converted to social democracy and survived, or stayed as
they were and withered away. Trotskyist parties did as well as
they had ever done, which is to say terribly. The successful revolution of the twentieth century, and the most likely source for
revolutionary change in the twenty-first, was the emancipation
of women. Colonial subjects enjoyed the partial success of freeing themselves from European rule, but hundreds of millions
continued to live on next to nothing. They needed an idea
which placed them at the centre of the world's affairs. Marxist-
Leninism wasn't it.

As its failures grew, and the movements they could commit
themselves to vanished, the far-left ought to have vanished too.
But the crushing inequalities of capitalism were greater after
the Berlin Wall went than before, and an anti-capitalist movement grew to oppose them. It was as impossible to generalise
about the new opposition as it was about 'the left.' There was no
coherent anti-capitalist ideology any more than there was a
coherent left. Good and brave people marched alongside thugs
and raving mystics. The best were ashamed of the indifference
of the privileged North to the suffering of the South. The worst
dreamed of a one-party state.

But among a section of the anti-capitalists and in the Stalinist and Trotskyist parties which survived the twentieth century

there was a kind of unity in a critique which expressed absolute scepticism about everything from the West – except themselves. Unlike communists in the Cold War or the supporters of Third World revolutionaries, they had no Soviet Union or Nicaragua. The absence freed them because they didn't have to argue for any policy or defend any action. Their opposition could be pure, and no one could throw the record of 'their side' in their faces and require them to jusfify it. They didn't have a side and had nothing to justify.

Pure opposition suffocated doubt. Purists didn't feel bad when they took to the streets to demand that other people continue to suffer in prison states. Noam Chomsky was the most influential advocate of the view that the West and capitalist corporations were behind all human suffering. But although Chomsky was the most-read left-wing intellectual in the world, he wasn't read by millions and you couldn't call pure opposition 'Chomskian'. 'Anti-Americanism' was a part of it – but the term didn't cover the territory. I was going to call the purist critique a 'party line'. But most of its adherents frowned on parties as vehicles for sell-out politicians. The purists weren't 'left wing' in the old meaning of the words. Many of their assumptions were conservative, and a few degenerated into racism. Wealthy journalists and comedians aped the mannerisms of pure opposition. Reactionary Muslims who had to shift the blame for their problems shared a belief in purist anti-American tenets as thoroughly as pseudo-Marxists. Purism was as much a sensibility or style as a political position.

God knows, it was easy enough to fall for its seductions. You hate the government of your country and the reigning global order of which it is a part. Words such as 'democracy' and 'freedom' on the lips of its leaders sound like 'love' on the lips of a whore. When the time for war comes the great powers demonise enemies who could have been picked at random from a world heaving with misery. Dictators half the public has never heard of, and with whom the West once did business, are turned into monsters overnight by the state and the corporate media. Suddenly they are 'tyrants' or 'terrorists'; suddenly they are 'evil'. What about the governments who armed Saddam, or the CIA agents who helped the young bin Laden? Aha! You have caught them. You at least have seen through the old, old story of hypocritical politicians whipping up jingoism in the name of justice. You know better than to fall for that. What about Palestine? What about Rwanda? What about the millions who die every day for want of clean water? There is a double standard at work, a falsity which the wised-up have seen through. You understand who pulls the levers of power and are revolted by their manipulation of honest good feeling.

In any case, you wonder, how free is Britain? Look at the spin and the corporate influence. How dare Blair force other countries to change their governments when his own is so debased. What arrogance! What presumption! Actually, as a true sophisticate you know that Blair doesn't have the independence to be truly arrogant. He's the poodle of the White House. And when you hear Bush's America claim to be the land of the free you can't keep your breakfast down. Bush didn't really win the election – well, sort of didn't anyway. His country can't afford a health service but can find the money to keep two million people in prison (a disproportionately large number of them black). Prisoners are executed (and the hangmen are also overfond of practising their craft on black men). The American political system guarantees corruption. It's impossible to get to Congress without tens of millions of dollars to buy ad slots on television; reaching the White House requires hundreds of millions. The money comes from corporations as often as not. The bought politicians do favours for their paymasters. For reasons you don't understand, rotten America has acquired a successful economy. (It must be something to do with imperialism.) The rest of the world has no choice but to go along with what its government and corporations want. American corruption isn't a local affair but a global pandemic which is seen at its most malign when the military-industrial complex funds the politicians who authorise the wars which boost its profits. What could be sicker?

All the steps you take can be justified with libraries full of supporting evidence. Your arguments and your ideals are noble. But you are heading towards the edge of a cliff if your favourite words are 'What about?' If, when you are presented with a crime you don't want to face, you change the subject and say 'What about Rwanda?' without admitting to yourself that had the West intervened you wouldn't have been mollified. You would either have fallen silent or denounced an 'imperialist' war. 'The language of priorities is the religion of socialism,' said Nye Bevan. But with hope of revolutionary socialism gone – and Bevan's democratic socialism nullified by Blair – you cannot see a greater priority than opposition. Like a supporter of Israel who uses the Holocaust to justify the treatment of Palestinians, you fight oppression as long as it can be blamed on the West. Oppressors must be fought, but only if they are the right type of oppressors.

The next step takes you over the cliff's edge. You muse that your enemy's enemy may not be so oppressive. Perhaps people only think they are oppressive because of the propaganda of the corporate lackeys in the media. Even if most Afghans don't actually like the Taliban, and most Iraqis don't support Saddam, they will have found ways of coping. Perhaps they realise they need a strong man to prevent anarchy. Perhaps demands for universal standards of human rights are themselves racist. Isn't it élitist for outsiders to assert that one form of government is 'better' than another? Anti-racism used to mean freeing people from oppression. But 'freedom' means joining the capitalist system, and that, you know from your experience of life in Britain, is as bad or worse than life in Iraq.

Pure opposition was at its purest in the opposition to Blair's wars. He fought four before Iraq. The smallest was the intervention in Sierra Leone. It was an act of altruism. A rebel movement was killing thousands. Its punishment of choice was to lop the arms off babies. The British army moved in and the killing subsided. Try as they might, no one could find an ulterior motive. Sierra Leone was an embarrassment. People didn't like to talk about it.

The Kosovo campaign of 1999 was provoked by the clear determination of Slobodan Milosevic to ethnically cleanse the Albanian population in the south of the old Yugoslavia. There were many legitimate criticisms of Nato's response. It was tardy, to put it mildly. Since 1991 Serb and Croat death squads had used nationalism and religion to update fascism and rampaged across the Balkans. The Yugoslav massacres exposed the emptiness of the European Union. Its justification was that it would never again allow Europe to sink back into the disgrace of the 1930s. But the EU sat on its hands while Bosnia was devastated. The most determined opponents of intervention were John Major and Douglas Hurd, his Foreign Secretary. 'Any time there was a likelihood of effective action,' said Tadeusz Mazowiecki, the Polish Prime Minister, '[Hurd] intervened to prevent it.' Blair's war to stop the Kosovo Muslims sharing the fate of Bosnian Muslims was conducted with rank cowardice. Allied forces just bombed from the air. ('Don't worry, we can bomb forever,' Bill Clinton told Blair.) At one point it looked as if Kosovo would be the first European war in which only civilians died. Then there was the unsavouriness of the likely benefactors. The Kosovo Liberation Army didn't share the democratic aspirations of the Bosnian government. Everyone knew that the Serb minority in Kosovo would have to protected from its fighters once the war was over.

As Labour Foreign Secretary, Robin Cook led the defence of the operation. The absence of UN authorisation didn't matter because he had two advantages over his successors in the Iraq war. Journalists could work in the Balkans. There were pictures of the Muslims fleeing from Kosovo. Most of Saddam's crimes, as with the genocide in Rwanda or the destruction of Grozny, took place off camera. Iraqi totalitarianism ensured that crews couldn't move without permission from their minders. The coalition against the war in Iraq included nearly every actor and artist in Britain. They prided themselves on their 'empathy', but the majority couldn't imagine the sufferings of Saddam's victims without prompts from the box in the corner.

Cook's second advantage during the Kosovo campaign was that Bill Clinton was America's president. Clinton authorised the aimless bombing of Iraq for years. The sanctions he enforced brought disease and the premature deaths of several hundred thousand – while doing nothing to disrupt the luxurious lives of the Baathist élite. The European centre-left loved him nevertheless because he was on its side in the culture war between liberals and conservatives. His good manners helped. Clinton was at his best as a politician when he gave the convivial impression of agreeing with every word of his conversational partners. Bush, by contrast, was on the wrong side of the culture divide and didn't flatter progressive opinion in other countries. The style of the Bush administration was abrasive and if conversational partners raised objections it usually ignored them. But a hard look at the consequences of both men's policies doesn't always flatter Clinton. Clinton, with Cook's support, imposed terrible sanctions on Iraqis while insisting they continue to live under a merciless tyranny. The Clinton/Cook strategy was to keep Iraq on the rack. They prolonged Saddam's rule, Bush stopped it. Meanwhile the same corporations which funded Bush funded Clinton. Clinton talked a good game on the International Criminal Court and Kyoto, although he never delivered American ratification of either.[6]

The self-interest in the Kosovo campaign was that the European Union countries couldn't handle more refugees, while Nato feared the conflict would spread into Macedonia and across the southern Balkans. For purists there had to be a more to it than that. It had to be 'all about oil'. Kosovo had no oil. Never mind. With the energy of Texan prospectors, the comrades set out on the search for the Lost Oilfields of Kosovo. After travelling thousands of miles east they struck black gold by the Caspian Sea. The oil was half a continent away. No problem. The Nato plan had to be to detach Kosovo from Yugoslavia and turn it into a client statelet which would be a secure terminus for a pipeline from the Caspian to the Adriatic. War came and went. To the disgust of Muslims, Kosovo wasn't detached from Yugoslavia. Nor was a pipeline run across a country where there was barely enough flat land to lay a football pitch. The comrades weren't disheartened. In 2001, a plan to build a pipeline from the Caspian to the Adriatic was unearthed by a diligent researcher. It wouldn't, unfortunately, go into Kosovo. But it would go into neighbouring Albania, if it was built. That was close enough to raise the most profound suspicions. 'I can't tell you that the war in the former Yugoslavia was fought solely in order to secure access to oil from new and biddable states in central Asia,' said George Monbiot of the *Guardian*. 'But in the light of these findings, can anyone now claim that it was not?'[7]

Explaining away the intervention in East Timor was as tough a proposition. The cause of the East Timorese had once been dear to the left. For Noam Chomsky, his British disciple John Pilger and many others from the Vietnam generation, East Timor had been lost in a hole in the memory of the second half of the twentieth century. Hitler was abominated. Stalin was castigated. But where was the remembrance of the crimes of the West in the Cold War? Vietnam hadn't been forgotten. But Hollywood had turned it from the destruction of a peasant people into a war which exemplified American self-sacrifice and victimhood. What America did to Chile, Bangladesh, central America, Laos, Cambodia and East Timor – either directly or by proxy – was barely a blip on the popular radar. Subliminal bad conscience about opposing the overthrow of tyranny wasn't the only reason the left kept making false predictions of huge casualties from the interventions in Yugoslavia onwards. Many of the speakers at the great demonstration were old men from the Vietnam generation – Tony Benn, Tariq Ali and Tam Dalyell, the 'father of the House of Commons'. The Vietnam generation had seen America kill hundreds of thousands and get away with it. America's cures were always worse than the disease. They couldn't bring themselves to acknowledge that war had changed and the world had changed. After the collapse of communism, democracy flourished. South American countries elected leftish leaders who would have attracted CIA-sponsored assassins in the Cold War. They were left alone because the great powers no longer had an incentive to invade.

East Timor infuriated everyone who knew its history. In 1975 General Suharto, the Indonesian dictator, who had himself come to power in a fantastically violent coup, secured permission from Henry Kissinger and President Ford to invade the island. East Timor was a colony of the collapsing Portuguese empire and had a local left-wing leadership which had fought off rivals and was ready to take power. Cold War America wouldn't tolerate leftism. No one knows how many died after the Indonesians landed: the highest estimate was 200,000. Western governments did nothing to restrain Indonesia. They honoured its leaders and sold them arms. Britain remained Indonesia's quartermaster under Blair, who refused to allow mimsy ethical objections to prevent the flow of weapons.

Everything fitted. In the interests of pleasing the military-industrial complex, Western governments became the handmaidens of genocide. But in 1999 Western policy began to disconcert right-thinking people. The Suharto regime was overthrown and the new democratic government of Indonesia allowed the East Timorese to vote for the independence they had been denied for a quarter of a century. Militias backed by the Indonesian army went on the rampage. They were stopped by the intervention of British and Australian troops.

You might have expected the friends of the East Timorese to be delighted that more of their comrades weren't going to be killed (while not forgetting one bit of the West's perfidious treatment of the islanders). Most welcomed the intervention, but Pilger couldn't. It was done in the interests of the capitalist order, he insisted. 'The country risked being slotted neatly into the globalised system of exploitation, debt and poverty, known as "stability".[8] Pure opposition meant he could say no other. His friends would have denounced him if he had faltered.

The island had further unpleasant surprises. Its population was Roman Catholic. No one gave religion a second's thought until November 2002, when a tape of what sounded like the voice of Osama bin Laden was played on Al-Jazeera. Among his anathemas was a passing reference to the murder of Australian tourists in a Bali disco. Australia had been punished for helping Roman Catholics leave a Muslim country. 'They ignored our warning and woke up to the sound of explosions in Bali.'

In a sentence the explanatory power of pure opposition was exploded. No one predicted that a humanitarian intervention in the affairs of a small island would lead to Australians and Britons being blown to pieces in a resort disco. There were all kinds of rational explanations for al-Qaeda. Purists bent over backwards to say it was the fault of the West because of Palestine or American bases in Saudi Arabia or Western support for the corrupt Egyptian oligarchy. There was a grain of truth in all of the above, but attempts to rationalise the irrational – whether it's Nazism or religious fundamentalism – always break down. Once a cult of death takes hold, it has a life and logic of its own. Al-Qaeda sent young men to kill and be killed for a dream as impossible as communism: the restoration of the Islamic Caliphate. In the new Muslim empire, which would stretch from Spain to Malaysia, laws would follow al-Qaeda's interpretation of the Koran and the victims would be Muslims who didn't comply (as they were in Taliban Afghanistan). What Islamic fundamentalism hated and feared was the best as well as the worst of the West – the separation of church and state, the substitution of man-made laws for the word of God and the emancipation of women. What was the guilty West meant to do? Take the vote from women?

The far-left couldn't handle fundamentalism and had to turn the war in Afghanistan into a war for oil. This time there were public plans to build pipelines. But America didn't behave as if it was on a land-grab for the oil companies. Before war started it told the Taliban it would be free to carry on persecuting women and hanging television sets from lamp-posts if it handed over al-Qaeda members suspected of involvement in the 11 September bombings. When the Taliban refused, it attacked. The overthrow of the Taliban had the beneficial side-effect of persuading two million refugees that it was safe to return home, but the United States didn't seem overly interested in securing territory for pipelines. The most frequent complaint after the war wasn't that America had been imperialist but that it hadn't been imperialist enough. It had left too much of Afghanistan in the hands of warlords and drug traffickers who were free to run vicious fiefdoms.

The confusions over Afghanistan, East Timor and Kosovo were trifling in comparison to the contortions over Iraq. Here was a country which had been supported in the 1980s by Europe and America (and, although everyone found it convenient to forget it, by the Soviet Union and the Arab world as well). In 1990 greed and militaristic aggrandisement drove Saddam to invade Kuwait and made him America's enemy. No argument convinced the opponents of the war that they were righteous more than the hypocrisy of their governments. A West which had armed Saddam Hussein and ignored his crimes was now saying it wanted to overthrow Saddam Hussein in the name of freedom.

For the life of me I couldn't see why people set so much store by consistency. Baathist tyranny was as bad in 2003 as 1983. The condition of the regime's victims hadn't changed. They needed help – and if the help was to come from the capricious countries which had once aided their oppressor, well, there was a restorative justice in that. However bad a regime sponsored by Bush would be, it would be better. But millions talked as if Western backing for Saddam in the 1980s gave him *carte blanche*, while airbrushing from history the memory that when America had been Saddam's ally, the left had been Saddam's enemy. The double standard was double-edged. It cut both ways. When America switched sides, the left switched sides.

Pure opposition led it into the trap of looking-glass politics. As universal principles were abandoned for opposition to the West whatever it did, the left matched the hypocrisies of power with equal hypocrisies in the opposite direction.

The East Timorese could write the book on Western perfidy and smelt the phoniness at once. José Ramos-Horta was one of the leaders of the struggle for independence and winner of the 1996 Nobel Peace Prize. He had begged Western governments to intervene against the Indonesian military. He watched the protests against intervention in Iraq in New York, Sydney, Cairo, London, Paris, Damascas, Madrid and Rome with growing bewilderment. 'Saddam Hussein has dragged his people into at least two wars,' he wrote in the *New York Times*.

> He has used chemical weapons on them. He has killed hundreds of thousands of people and tortured and oppressed countless others. So why, in all of these demonstrations, did I not see one single banner or hear one speech calling for the end of human rights abuses in Iraq, the removal of the dictator and freedom for the Iraqis and the Kurdish people?

The blunt answer to the Nobel Laureate was that the war's opponents weren't so different from the leaders they protested against. Because Blair's priority was to stick by America, he betrayed the deepest beliefs of many of his colleagues and supporters. Because the left's priority was opposing Blair and Bush, it broke the first commandment of the socialist religion and betrayed its comrades.

In the late 1980s you couldn't move in leftish London without seeing tears of pity for the victims of Saddam Hussein. Rivers were shed for Arab Iraqis; oceans for the Kurds. Christ but we cared. The Kurds were the largest people on earth without a state of their own. They were spread across Iran, Turkey, Syria and Iraq – and oppressed by all four countries. They had been promised a homeland after the First World War. In 1930 the Foreign Office explained to the League of Nations why the promise must be broken:

Although they admittedly possess many sterling qualities, the Kurds of Iraq are entirely lacking in those characteristics of political cohesion which are essential to self-government. Their organisation and outlook are essentially tribal. They are without traditions of self-government or self-governing institutions. Their mode of life is primitive, and for the most part they are illiterate and untutored, resentful of authority and lacking in any sense of discipline or responsibility. [In these circumstances] it would be unkind to the Kurds themselves to do anything which would lend encouragement to the sterile idea of Kurdish independence.[9]

Kindness for Kurds was to place them under the rule of quasi-fascist regimes which treated them as impure aliens. Turkish nationalists forbade the teaching of the Kurdish tongue. Iraqi Baathists persecuted them for the crime of not being Arab. Meanwhile the great powers played with them. In the early 1970s, Iraq was getting too close to the Soviet Union for America's liking, and annoying Washington's placeman, the Shah of Iran. Henry Kissinger and Richard Nixon encouraged the Iraqi Kurds to revolt. Saddam Hussein responded to the pressure and came to terms with the Shah. American, Israeli and Iranian military advisers did a midnight flit. Saddam sealed the borders and exacted his usual revenge. Even by the standards of the Cold War – even by the standards of Henry Kissinger – the betrayal of an ally stood out. The Congressional select committee on intelligence said that

> the president, Dr Kissinger and the Shah hoped that [the Kurds] would not prevail. They preferred instead that the insurgents simply continue a level of hostilities sufficient to sap the resources of [Iraq]. The policy was not imparted to our clients, who were encouraged to continue to fight. Even in the context of covert operations, ours was a cynical exercise.[10]

American backing for the Shah of Iran couldn't save him from the Islamic revolution of 1979. The world had little choice but to support Saddam's unprovoked war on Iran. A victory for the Ayatollahs would have left the Iraqi, Kuwaiti and Saudi oilfields at Iran's mercy. The left poured contempt on the West as

Saddam took the opportunity offered by international support to pour poison gas on soldiers and civilians alike. George Galloway and his left-wing colleague Jeremy Corbyn led the slating. Corbyn castigated the 'fascist' Saddam and the Western governments which supported him. There must be 'no trade, no aid, no deals while the present repression continues against people in Iraq', he declared.

In Harold Pinter, the Kurds had a playwright of genius on their side. *Mountain Language*, released in 1988, shows an anonymous people being forced into silence. A martinet guard bellowed at prisoners: 'Your language is forbidden. It is dead. No one is allowed to speak your language. Your language no longer exists. Any questions?' The mountain people Pinter had in mind were the Kurds, and a better dramatisation of how the world need never know of suffering because the sufferers cannot be heard has yet to be written.

On 20 January 2003, Dr Barham Salih, Prime Minister of the Kurdish government in Northern Iraq, went to a meeting of the Socialist International in Rome to renew his fraternal ties with all the nice white people. The Kurds had had one bit of luck since 1991, he said. They had taken George Bush Snr at his word and risen up after Saddam was defeated in Kuwait. When the world did nothing to help, the Baath Party regained control and Iraqi Kurds had to flee to escape Saddam's reprisals. Fortunately, television cameras were at the Turkish border to record the refugees freezing in the mountains. Fickle public opinion was mobilised on the Kurdish side. Britain and America agreed to enforce a no-fly zone in northern Iraq and a Kurdish statelet grew up in the safe haven. Villages which had been levelled by Saddam's ethnic cleansers were rebuilt. Although the same sanctions applied to the Kurdish enclave as the rest of Iraq, the infant mortality rate was half that in the Baathist-controlled areas because Saddam and his cronies weren't stealing bread from the mouths of children. There was a free media, women judges and all kinds of other attractions for Western liberals and socialists. These achievements, Salih said, could be a model for a free Iraq, but only if the Americans invaded.

He was explicit: there was no other way. Iraqis couldn't break the Baathist grip without outside help.

The Kurdish leadership was a touch confused by the arguments of its former friends. Among the demonstrators, Salih observed, were 'human rights activists who had noticed our plight long ago'. Now they were marching to keep in place the regime which caused that plight. Their chant was 'No War against Iraq, Justice for Palestine'. Did the converse apply? If international troops went into the West Bank to remove Israeli settlements, would millions take to the streets and demand: 'No War on Israel, Free Iraq'? Salih doubted it. 'Since when is justice for the Palestinians, and for the Israelis for that matter, to the exclusion of justice for Iraqis?' he asked. Other demonstrators said the war was all about oil. Salih didn't give a damn. 'Iraqis know that their human rights have too often been ignored because Iraqi oil was more important to the world than Iraqi lives. It would be a good irony if at long last oil becomes a cause of our liberation – if this is the case, then so be it. The oil will be a blessing and not the curse that it has been for so long.'

Above all, he tried to bang home the point that the choice wasn't between peace and war. The Baath Party war against Iraqis had been going on for decades. Hundreds of thousands had died in the struggle against tyranny. Salih asked his old friends to stick by their comrades and unite in an anti-fascist struggle:

> Today, I stand before you not only as a representative of the Kurdish people in Iraq, but also as a messenger for the oppressed peoples of Iraq. You have a role to play in that liberation, for your values, the values of the Socialist movement, are utterly opposed to the values of dictatorship and racism. Let us join together in the spirit of solidarity that has always animated Socialists, to make Iraq and the Middle East a place of freedom and peace.

Salih's was one of the most futile appeals for solidarity in the history of socialism.

Muslims were as deaf. The approved subjects for Muslim

protest were Kashmir, Palestine and Chechnya, where Muslims were persecuted by Hindus, Jews and Christians respectively. Iraq, where Muslims asked for help against persecution by other Muslims, could only be thought of as the fault of the West. Simple old Salih had failed to notice that the accident of history which had made Saddam an enemy of the United States had changed everything. The anti-war movement surfed a wave of bad faith.

Pinter spoke at the anti-war rally. He erupted with anger against 'a country run by a bunch of criminals'. He meant America. After Saddam invaded Kuwait in 1991, Jeremy Corbyn reassessed his position. He went from calling for sanctions on the 'fascist' regime of Iraq to be imposed to calling for sanctions on the fascist regime of Iraq to be lifted. There was an honest defence of the flip-flopping. You could be against sanctions and Saddam. George Galloway couldn't use it when he matched Corbyn's U-turn and went on to become Saddam's best British friend. In 1994 he greeted the brute with: 'Sir, I salute your courage, your strength, your indefatigability.' As the 1990s progressed, Galloway became a frequent flyer to Iraq. His private intimacies with the regime's leaders included an invitation to Tariq Aziz's Christmas party.

The Kurds were mountain people once again. When they asked their comrades to put aside their opposition to Bush and Blair until the greater good of destroying Saddam had been achieved, the 'illiterate and untutored' were told to head for the hills.

The principle of fraternity carries no obligation that you agree with your comrades. Fraternity, and common courtesy, requires only that you listen and argue with them as equals. But discussion of fraternal obligations would have meant considering the possibility that pure opposition and a consistent opposition to oppression were incompatible. It would have meant supporting Bush and Blair when they were against Saddam while continuing to oppose their policies when they conflicted with your other priorities (which is to say most of the rest of the time). Such a strategy was as inconceivable as a football fan supporting Manchester United for the first half of a match and Arsenal for the second. The Iraqi opposition wasn't beaten in argument. There was no argument. It was as if Saddam's opponents didn't exist

But because there was no fraternal debate, events cut the ground from under the anti-war movement. It had no explanation for the Kurdish freedom fighters placing themselves under American control, or the soldiers in the regular army and Republican Guard who refused to turn Baghdad into a second Stalingrad, or the crowds which tore down the statues of Saddam, or the Iraqis on the television who said that whatever fears they had about Western intervention they were glad Saddam was gone. All the the left could do was sit on the sidelines hoping for the worst. It couldn't make alliances with democratic forces in post-war Iraq because it had dropped them a decade before. A few played with idea that the remnants of the secret police, who shot at US troops, were a 'national liberation movement'.

The old word for the ability to switch the party line in an instant and indulge mass murderers is 'Stalinist'. The bulk of the marchers were anything but. Many were articulate and scrupulous people from the progressive middle-class who were proud of their 'communication skills' and 'networking abilities'. They would, I'm sure, have refused to be in the same organisation as anyone who showed the smallest tolerance of sexism or racism. But they allowed themselves to be organised by people who tolerated tyranny, who weren't over-disturbed by the murder of 20 million in Stalin's one-party state or hundreds of thousands in Saddam's one-party state. All the talk of the Seattle generation bringing a new politics to a new century ended with the same old scowling faces from the age of the European dictators back in charge. It was as if the supporters of fox-hunting and village post offices had allowed the British National Party to run the Countryside Alliance.

Political innocents recoiled. Ewa Robertson from Essex described the process:

I contacted Stop the War and threw myself into it; I canvassed, attended meetings, marched on 15 February, attended more meetings and a couple of local demonstrations. However, things did not feel right from the start and the more I probed, the less happy I became. Despite my ideological unsuitability, I was eventually selected for a 'people's assembly' at a meeting of hard-left individuals. I found the gathering at Central Hall, Westminster to be totally unrepresentative of British society and the conduct of the day-long meeting anything but democratic. Some reluctant supporters of Stop the War argue that it is the only umbrella organisation for opposition to the war, but this is an umbrella with holes.[11]

The Stop the War's coalition leadership included the cadres of the Communist Party of Britain, the Socialist Workers Party and the Muslim Association of Britain. The Coalition's chairman, Andrew Murray, wrote an article to celebrate the 120th anniversary of Stalin's birth. He acknowledged that Stalin had used 'harsh measures' but asked why 'hack propagandists abominate the name of Stalin beyond all others'. That there were 20 million reasons didn't seem to have occurred to him. Murray was on the politburo of the Communist Party of Britain (which must never be confused with the Communist Party of Great Britain). In a report to his comrades in March 2003 he said, 'We need urgently to raise the level of our Leninist education. Everything we are talking about, the imperialist crisis, inter-imperialist conflict, war, political strategy and tactics, are Leninist issues. We need to do far more to study Marxism-Leninism.' The anti-war protest had led to 'the rate of inquiries about party membership rising rapidly and that is welcome, but we need to ensure they are educated as communists and learn to work as communists'.

Opposition to a war against a dictator who modelled himself on Stalin was being led by men who could see the good in Stalin. When he was asked if he would describe himself as part of the 'Stalinist left', George Galloway equivocated. 'I wouldn't define it that way because of the pejoratives loaded around it; that would be making a rod for our own back. If you are asking did I support the Soviet Union, yes I did . . . The disappearance of the Soviet Union is the biggest catastrophe of my life.'

The Socialist Workers Party was a Trotskyist group which was formally opposed to Stalinism. It was a distinction without a difference. The SWP wanted to abolish democracy and replace it with a 'dictatorship of the proletariat'. If the history of revolutionary socialism was a guide then the proletariat would be shrunk to the bosses of the Socialist Workers Party come the glorious day.[12] The SWP called itself Marxist but cared little for the ideas of Karl Marx. Of all the Muslim groups it might have picked to co-host the anti-war demonstrations, it went for the supporters of Islam at its most bigoted. The Muslim Association of Britain had the usual difficulties of fundamentalists with the vexed questions of women's equality and gay rights. But it did have a clear line on what should happen to Muslims who decided they no longer believed in God: they should be executed. Marx abominated religion. For the crime of preferring feudal theocracy to bourgeois democracy he would have tied copies of *Das Kapital* round the necks of the SWP leaders and thrown them into the Thames. Pure opposition to western power reached its sinister terminus in the pact between the enemies of political freedom and the enemies of religious freedom.[13]

As the weeks passed, the foul smell, which was first caught with Tony Benn's refusal to confront Saddam, spread. The *Daily Telegraph* found documents in Baghdad which said that Iraq was sending Galloway hundreds of thousands of pounds a year from funds which were meant to be spent on feeding malnourished Iraqis. Galloway denied the charge that he was the hireling of tyranny and sued for libel. Who was right was a minor issue. What was worse: saluting Saddam's courage because you were bribed to salute him or saluting him unbribed and of your own free will? Tam Dalyell told a reporter from *Vanity Fair* he had an old explanation for Blair's policy. Dalyell 'thinks Blair is unduly influenced by a cabal of Jewish advisers. He mentions Mandelson, Lord Levy [Blair's chief fund-raiser] and Jack Straw.' Jack Straw isn't Jewish, although he did have a Jewish grandparent. Mandelson's father was Jewish, but Mandelson isn't. Only Levy was blatantly and shamelessly Jewish. That was enough. The Elders of Zion were running the twenty-first century as they had run so many centuries before.[14]

With leadership on the streets of this calibre, the left was bound to lose. It will always lose until it makes a clean break with totalitarianism old and new. If morality can't produce a rupture, the principle of self-preservation should be a sufficient motive. Perhaps it won't. Perhaps the vice is ineradicable. If it was a little late in the day to begin mourning the dead of the Nazi concentration camps in 2001, it was culpably negligent not to know by 2003 that the left had graveyards of its own. If it couldn't be done 70 years after Stalinism, it probably never could.

PART II

Bust

Peter Mandelson, the Trade and Industry Secretary, has
just returned from Silicon Valley apparently intoxicated by the
entrepreneurial air he was breathing there . . . He was told by
the Dean of Engineering at Stamford University, the
institutional godfather of Silicon Valley's recent success, that
'it was just plain OK to get filthy rich' in the United States.
Mr Mandelson replied that Labour was 'intensely relaxed'
about people getting filthy rich but added a crucial
qualifier – as long as they pay their taxes.

Guardian, 6 October 1998

SIX

The Big Tent

To their critics, Britain's millennium celebrations were a carnival of vacuity. The Great Exhibition of 1851 had told the world of the benevolent possibilities of science and manufacturing. The Festival of Britain had reflected the optimism and solidarity of the generation which survived the Second World War. The Dome had nothing to say. It couldn't celebrate the inventiveness of a native industry which had been battered for 30 years. It couldn't proclaim the united purpose of a nation which was divided by fantastic inequality and slowly fragmenting into its constituent parts. The absence of intelligent purpose did not, however, bother the Dome's supporters. Like official guides in the old Soviet empire, they held that spectacular scale could overwhelm questions of value. Moaners missed the point of a Dome which, whatever else you might say about it, was far, far bigger than domes in less fortunate countries. As the opening night approached, the PRs announced that the Dome would be capable of holding '18,000 double-decker buses', or '13 Albert Halls', or '3.8 billion pints of beer', or 'the Eiffel Tower on its side'. If you were minded to pick it up, carry it to the Canadian-American border and place it upside-down under Niagara Falls, you would gasp as you checked your watch and saw that it took '10 minutes to fill'.

The breath-catching design (by Mike Davies of the Richard Rogers Partnership) passed the sternest test for a new building: it was imprinted on the popular mind before construction had finished. David Hockney said Davies's creation would be 'most beautiful left empty'. His sensible suggestion was ignored. The Dome had to be furnished because it had an ambitious task to perform. 'The overall purpose of all millennium activity,' explained New Labour's special advisers shortly after they reached office,

> is to re-energise the Nation. The ultimate aim of the Company, therefore, is to change perceptions, more specifically:
> • to raise the self-esteem of the individual;
> • to engender a sense of pride in the wider community;
> • to enhance the world's view of the Nation.

Note the grandeur of the ambition: the Dome was to be a tonic for a grumpy public and an instrument of foreign policy. Note, too, the hubristic confidence which demanded the capital N in Nation at a moment when devolution and poverty weren't the only forces undermining national unity. Brussels ran much of domestic policy; Washington ran much of foreign policy; corporate interests dominated Whitehall; and the Blair clique dominated the Labour Party and, by extension, the national Parliament. When the government presiding over multiple fragmentation was too dim to realise what it was doing to the 'Nation', it was tempting to join those who dismissed the Dome as a void. 'What is the Dome for?' asked Jacques Chirac on a visit to Britain. Intellectuals and hacks alike couldn't help him out. The Dome, wrote the London litterateur Iain Sinclair, is a 'Disneyland on-message' that had 'nothing to do with bemused citizens'.

Yet if you could bring yourself to study it closely the Dome had plenty to say about the condition of the citizens of *fin-de-siècle* Britain. The first blaring message was that it made solid the continuity between Old Conservatives and New Labour. The Dome and the National Lottery which supported it were the creations of John Major. His peculiar brand of humbug was to invoke Orwell's decency and national unity while promoting the concentration of unelected power and a commercialisation of everyday life that undermined both. There was nothing New Labour liked less than being accused of being a continuation of the *ancien régime*. While Major babbled about warm maids and old beer, his successors professed to believe in modernity.

Simon Jenkins, a former editor of *The Times* and a quango-crat on the Millennium Commission, realised that it was essential to persuade Blair that the Dome wasn't another of John Major's clapped-out ideas. On 16 June 1997 he wrote to the new Prime Minister to warn him that young Euan Blair would be disappointed if his father disowned the Conservative legacy. 'Every child, including many from abroad, will want to see Greenwich in 2000 and tell it to their grandchildren [*sic*],' he said. Whether shrewdly or intuitively, Jenkins recognised the ruling class's change in style and played to the Prime Minister's desire to repackage Tory policies in modern wrappings. The world, as well as his son, was looking to Greenwich for a sign. 'German, French, Italian and American planners all concede Britain's leadership' in millennium celebrations, he wrote. The Dome would show that Great Britain was as great in 2000 as it was in 1851. 'Every Victorian machine said "Shown at the Great Exhibition". Every new one should say, "Shown at Greenwich" . . . I promise you, Greenwich is a future that will work. It will be Britain's proudest creation and proudest boast in the year 2000.'

Three days after what became known as the 'Euan letter', the Cabinet decided that the Dome must be built. I say 'decided', but in truth the discussion of 19 June 1997 showed that Cabinet government was as feeble as parliamentary democracy. Blair told his colleagues he wanted it to go ahead. 'If it's successful,' he said, 'it will recoup a significant part of the cost and could even make money . . . It can't just disappear. It must link in with other things we are trying to do: new technology, education, etc. We must make it clear it is for the whole nation, and is relevant for everyone.'[1] With that, Blair left the room, and his ministers discussed what should be done. Not one supported the PM unequivocally, while twelve were opposed. Gordon Brown was prescient. He said he had 'a series of worries'. The Dome was 'London-based, the objectives are not clear and it is not durable . . . It's public money and if anything goes wrong it will all come back to us.' Later he added, 'We are all agreed the present project isn't working and is a mess.' David Blunkett was 'deeply against it, frankly', because 'the design has no vision'. Ann Taylor, a Northern MP and the then leader of the Commons, said she would prefer the money to be spent 'on schools and hospitals instead'. Northern families wouldn't come because the costs of admission and a trip to London were too high. Clare Short said that other parts of the Nation had little time for the National celebration. 'I'm vehemently opposed. This will be a political disaster ... The whole of the West Midlands is very angry about the fiddled way it was decided not to go for the NEC.' (Birmingham had been persuaded to make an expensive pitch for the millennium celebrations to be held at the National Exhibition Centre instead of Greenwich. The contest was a fix from the start. London was always going to win.) Jack Cunningham thought that Blair's hopes that the Dome would make a profit were fatuous. 'It will cost three-quarters of a billion pounds,' he predicted. Margaret Beckett said five years ago she 'thought it would be brilliant to put it in Greenwich but now it has become bogged down in problems and controversy'.

And so it went on. The leaders of the once disputatious and democratic Labour movement predicted every aspect of the looming disaster. Blunkett identified the absence of an animating idea. Cunningham estimated the eventual losses with uncanny foresight. Taylor and Short were well aware of the resentment in the provinces. Brown had grasped all the reasons for the coming fiasco. If there had been a free vote, Blair would have been defeated.

There was no free vote. Labour's senior politicians had been reduced to nervous courtiers, more worried about offending the King than standing up for the wise use of public funds or, indeed, themselves. The monarchical nature of Blair's 'modern' regime is a theme which runs through this book. The leaked Dome minutes showed that monarchism was New Labour's style from the beginning, not a fault brought about by the slow corruption of power. No one was prepared to displease the sovereign. After voicing cogent objections Brown turned tail and fled with a politically prudent cry of, 'We need to support what the PM is suggesting.' His colleagues concurred. 'If Tony has made a decision, we have to support it,' said Robin Cook. Beckett let the cat out of the bag when she said that 'if the PM was here and said we should go ahead, we would all accept it'. Dissent could be muttered in private, but would never be spoken in the King's presence. The minutes of the next Cabinet meeting on 26 June don't include one minister repeating his or her doubts in front of Blair. The PM apologised for walking out of the last meeting and thanked his colleagues for having the sheer bloody guts to make a decision which had to be made. An unctuous Blunkett forgot his declaration that he was 'deeply against it, frankly' and told the PM that the Dome was 'an enormous challenge. We should be congratulated for moving on so quickly.' With this and many another congratulatory pat on their own backs, ministers fell in with their leader's vision of the future.

Blair told the public that 'this country is often good at knocking, good at running itself down'. He didn't mean it as a compliment. 'I believe it is time for ambition to drive out cynicism. It is about how we see ourselves as a nation. This exhibition will make a statement about Britain – about our creativity, our dynamism, our cutting-edge technology, our imagination.'

Dynamism was not going to be encouraged by extending democracy. After devolving power to the Celtic fringe, Blair fell for the fading charm of the unaccountable English state. Nor would he allow youthful energy to be directed towards redistributing wealth. Modernity lay in dispensing with such exhausted notions as constitutional reform and democratic socialism. Blair's future belonged to pragmatic and competent men and women: technocrats and meritocrats, uncontaminated by ideology, who knew what worked and were certain that they had the talent to deliver.

The kindest observers of the Dome were compelled to admit that competence was not the most striking virtue of its administrators. At around the time of the Cabinet meeting, John Prescott asked Gez Sagar, the Dome's head of press and parliamentary affairs, a good question. What was this Dome going to be? Was it to be Disney? Or Alton Towers? Was it an Expo? Was it a theme park or, well, what? None of those things, Sagar replied, but it was more difficult to say what it was going to be.[2]

Just so. Even those of us who have worked in the private sector all our adult lives, and learned as the years went by that its senior managers included an alarming number of crooks and halfwits, have retained enough faith to expect that any executive, however dunderheaded, would know it was time to abort when his underlings couldn't describe what a project was for. New Labour pressed on. It hired Stephen Bayley as consultant creative director and instructed him to give the exhibition coherence and purpose. He was unnerved by the mediocrity he encountered. Bayley suggested there should be a six-month break while everyone went away and asked themselves what they were trying to achieve.

In retrospect this, too, was a sensible suggestion. Bayley found that his suggestions weren't required and left. Michael Grade, one of several media grandees co-opted to advise on the Dome's contents, deployed the most shop-soiled of postmodern cop-outs when he was asked to answer Bayley's question. The Dome wasn't trying to achieve anything, he replied; there was no message delivered from above for the public to understand. Top-down élitist sermons from a patronising and paternalistic past had been discarded. The Dome was

> designed to reflect the current reality of our society at the start of the 21st century. The here and now, a time when individuals are taking more and more responsibility for their own lives . . . In 1851 and 1951 the great and the good created wonderful tableaux, then lifted the curtain and allowed the great unwashed to have a peep at how great their leaders were. This show is different. Here it is the people themselves who are the focus. It says: 'Think about your own life.' The people are in charge. They can make their own mistakes. They are not being told what to be or how to act. What the Dome is saying to them is: 'Here you are, folks. Here are the choices. You decide.'[3]

In other words, we're not being judgemental so don't you dare judge us, pal.

The 'folks' never had a choice. If the unwashed had been consulted, they would have chosen to spend their money on hospitals, or parks, or replacements for the flogged-off school playing-fields, or on anything which might have lasted. The élite's familiar covering of its back with the pseudo-democratic language of anti-élitism couldn't hide the nature of the Dome's management. It was just as hierarchical as the management of any project from the past that the cocksure Grade dismissed.

Squatting on the top of the pyramid was business. The Dome's failure was a corporate failure, a disaster which defined the intellectual and aesthetic limits of modern capitalism. The companies involved weren't as inept as that last, bald sentence makes them sound. Whatever you think of them, the commercial values of advertising saturate the culture, and most find them compelling. New Labour itself was an immensely successful advertising pitch which had turned the Conservatives from the natural rulers of the country to a fringe group of embittered pensioners. The Dome is remembered as a laughable flop. Only 6.5 million of the 12 to 15 million predicted visitors showed up, a third of the number who had visited the Festival of Britain. Given the scale of the failure, it is easy to forget that the Dome was still the most popular British attraction in 2000. The majority of sightseers said they had a good day out. What they couldn't say was that they had been inspired. Contrary to Jenkins's promise, they wouldn't remember the ideas the Dome raised for the rest of their lives and bore their grandchildren with tales of how it had opened their eyes to the possibilities of the new century. Funky politicians and sharp-eyed corporate sponsors were unable to extend their range. When they attempted to go beyond gesture politics and beguiling spectacle, they found engendering 'a sense of pride' was beyond them. Tony Blair had exclaimed in 1998 that: 'This is our Dome! Britain's Dome! And believe me, it will be the envy of the world!' The Nation was as unimpressed as the rest of the planet.

Visitors got a fuzzy notion of the Nation in 'Self-Portrait', a huge drum holding hundreds of pictures of aspects of British life. These, said the Dome guide book, were

> what the UK people feel are their best assets – qualities including the "British" sense of humour, creativity, inventiveness, culture and tradition. Within this, a series of larger-than-life sculptures offers a more critical view of the national persona and weaknesses of society.

I've always thought that any Briton who went on about the famous 'British sense of humour' didn't have one. The cultural historian Richard Weight said the guide writers' inverted commas around 'British' also said more than was intended. They suggested that at some level the new élite guessed that what it meant to be 'British' was a contested terrain.[4] But they couldn't bring themselves to celebrate or understand the Scots, Welsh, Northern Irish and, above all, the English. As Jack Straw explained in 2000, the English were a 'potentially very aggressive, very violent' people who had used a 'propensity to violence' to subjugate Ireland, Wales and Scotland. And used it again 'in Europe and with our Empire'. (Clearly there was nothing else to be done but cage as many of the beasts as possible, which Straw duly did when he was Home Secretary.)

Business leaders made much better company. The Dome was built by funds from the Lottery, a tax on the stupid and desperate. If it had been left to the private sector, there would have been no exhibition. First Michael Heseltine and then Peter Mandelson were determined to draw in business nonetheless. The lottery might have provided the necessary funds, but Tories and Blairites agreed that nothing worth having could be created without corporate sponsorship. Dome zones were designed expressly for the private sector. British Telecom said it would help only if its corporate image was enhanced. Exhibits on the theme of 'talking' were promised to please it. Adrian Horsford, the company's sponsorship director, explained his control of the national showcase thus: 'When the Talk Zone opened there were some things we were not happy with, but we put those right. We were quite closely involved with the development.'

The Corporation of London, a rotten borough which represents City bankers rather than Londoners, was given a space called the Transaction Zone. The name was later changed to the brutally simple Money, a title the crassest of agitprop revolutionaries couldn't have bettered. Other companies were more subtle. 'A highlight of the Dome,' explained the administrators in October 1999, 'will be the McDonald's Our Town Story where for 210 days people will perform and exhibit their town's past, present and future.' Our Town Theatre was the one national attraction at the exhibition. Every school was invited to produce a play. The best won the right to perform their work in Greenwich. Direction of what might have been a touching exploration of local histories was passed to a multi-national. It ran the competition as a thinly disguised advertising campaign. You can't blame McDonald's for seizing the opportunity. All companies in the youth market slobber at the thought of getting into classrooms. Schools are among the few areas of uncommercialised public space left, virgin territories where intrusion has a memorable impact on young minds. McDonald's helped drama teachers by supplying them with instructions and, when necessary, professional advisers. Teachers helped McDonald's by backing its promotions with the authority of the school. The teenagers McDonald's wanted as low-paid workers, as well as customers, learned that the corporation was the benign custodian of the histories and aspirations of their communities. The cost to McDonald's of sponsoring the McPlaylets would have been cheap at twice the price. No civil servant or minister worried that the company had spent the 1990s trying to silence the protests of two obscure green activists in the longest trial in British history. At the end of the libel action, Mr Justice Bell ruled that the evidence he had heard amply substantiated the defendants' claim that the company targeted 'susceptible young children to bring in custom, both their own and that of their parents'.

Rupert Murdoch's *Sun* attacked the Dome for wasting public money which might have been better spent on the National Health Service. The government was horrified. It had wooed Murdoch's NewsCorp with the eagerness of a fortune-hunting hussy chasing a filthy-rich old man. Blair thought the engagement had been announced and a *modus vivendi* established. New Labour would do what it could to facilitate the expansion of Murdoch's business interests. Murdoch would tell his Tory journalists to toe the New Labour line. Andrew Neil, a former editor of the *Sunday Times*, remembered the courtship beginning when Blair told him, 'How we treat Murdoch's media interests when we are in power depends on how his newspapers treat the Labour Party in the run up to the election and after we are in government.'[5] Murdoch noticed Blair's arousal. He responded in *Der Spiegel* with 'I could even imagine myself supporting the British Labour leader, Tony Blair.' Blair registered the come-hither look and began to exert himself. In July 1995 he made a 50-hour round trip so he could address Murdoch and his editors at a NewsCorp 'leadership conference' on the Australian resort of Hayman Island. The Murdoch press had smeared Michael Foot with the vile and ludicrous accusation that he was a KGB 'agent of influence'. Neil Kinnock, Foot's successor, was traduced daily. Foot and Kinnock were threats to media monopolists. Blair flew across the world to assure Murdoch that New Labour was submissive – it would be what NewsCorp wanted it to be. The party had embraced the market, Blair told Murdoch and his assembled execs, because 'the old solutions of rigid economic planning and state control won't work'.

In Utopian capitalist theory, markets are the enemies of rigidity because competition ensures that firms which don't bend to the desires of the consumer disappear. But in capitalist practice – and this really is basic stuff which even the leaders of New Labour ought to have got their heads round by the age of thirteen, or fifteen tops – competition also ensures that capitalism tends to monopoly. Successful companies wipe out existing rivals and have the resources to stifle fresh competitors at birth. (If you doubt me, count how many new supermarket chains have appeared in the past twenty years.) In its 1992 election manifesto, Labour (as it then was) recognised that media conglomerates poisoned free societies. A handful of companies must not be allowed to limit democratic debate by buying up and closing down the platforms for competing voices. Labour promised: 'We will safeguard press freedom [and] establish an urgent inquiry by the Monopolies and Mergers Commission into the concentration of media ownership.' Nowhere was ownership more concentrated than in the hands of Rupert Murdoch. He controlled the *Sun*, the *News of the World*, *The Times*, the *Sunday Times* and the BSkyB satellite network. The last had the greatest potential. Murdoch had the enticing possibility that he could own the satellite 'platforms' which delivered television to Britain and, by extension, decide which channels should be broadcast. He had proved already that he was happy to use the ownership of satellites to censor if the interests of profit demanded suppression. Murdoch stopped BBC World Service TV broadcasts to Asia from his Star satellite because the BBC's honest reporting had angered China's market-Leninist dictatorship, whose goodwill Murdoch needed to reach one billion Chinese consumers.

Blair dropped all the nonsense about freedom of the press and breaking up monopolies, and in 1995 took New Labour (as it had become) way to the right of the Tories. To the slight surprise of those who thought the Labour movement still had a purpose to it, Blair condemned the Conservative government for trying to tighten the regulations on limiting the ownership of TV stations by newspaper magnates. His complaint was that the Tories had gone too far and were daring to threaten the press barons. New Labour was now closer to Murdoch than the old man's old Tory friends. Blairism was 'sticky with Murdoch', as a Labour grandee, who became sick of the whoring of a party she had served all her life, told me. Murdoch was delighted. He and everyone else knew that Blair was going to win. Blair was now promising that regime change wouldn't mean a change in the regime's policies.

In the run-up to the 1997 election, the once-Tory *Sun* said the Tories were 'tired, divided and rudderless'. The British needed 'a leader with vision, purpose and courage who can inspire them and fire their imagination. The *Sun* believes that man is Tony Blair.'

The relationship was consummated with more love than is usual in these encounters. The Dome, however, wasn't a guest at the wedding. Its managers read the *Sun* and realised it hadn't been included in the pre-nuptial agreeement. Like the European Union, Murdoch had kept the Dome as a bit of skirt on the side. Conservative *Sun* journalists, who had submitted to the change in line without a resignation, were to be allowed to play with it.

As the barrage of insults grew, the millennium bureaucrats asked themselves how Murdoch could be persuaded to muzzle his yapping dogs. His family suggested an answer.

The fiercely meritocratic Murdoch, who had spent his life laying into the nepotism of the old British establishment, had recently made a brilliant business decision about the direction of BSkyB. The entrepreneur discovered that the most qualified person to fill the post of General Manager (Broadcasting) was none other than his very own daughter, Elisabeth. The Murdoch sprog was stepping out with Matthew Freud, a PR man on the Dome's executive committee. By mid-February 1998, the *Sun*'s criticisms had become savage, and much of the rest of the press was following its lead. Freud knew what he had to do. 'I talked to Liz about it,' he recalled, 'and then had a few minutes with Murdoch in LA.' Murdoch was won over by his daughter's intended. He promised Freud he would give the Dome £12 million in sponsorship on the serendipitous grounds that he and Her Majesty's Government were both in the entertainment business.

Freud then savoured 'the nicest call I've ever made'. He rang Rebekah Wade, the *Sun*'s deputy editor, to tell her the Dome was now the Murdoch family's pet. 'You may be interested to know . . . ,' he began. 'Oh fuck!' Wade cried, and produced an inspiring display of editorial independence. She executed a swift 'reverse ferret', as U-turns were known at the *Sun*. The editorial pages mapped the ferret's drunken progress.[7] On 12 January 1998, just before Freud lobbied Murdoch, the *Sun* thundered: 'This waste of public money should be axed, for that's what public opinion wants . . . that damned Dome has disaster written all over it.' Five days later, the *Sun* returned to its theme. 'The Dome has all the makings of the biggest white elephant of this or any other century. What a terrible monument to the human ego.' On 23 February, just after Freud charmed Murdoch, the *Sun*'s thunder disappeared as fast as a summer storm. It accepted that in the past the *Sun* had been the Dome's 'fiercest critic', but a reconsideration of the evidence had obliged it to think again. 'There is beginning to be an air of excitement about the Millennium Experience. Griping about it will achieve nothing. Instead we should all get behind it and ensure it is a success.'[8] Murdoch made Wade editor of the *News of the World* shortly afterwards, and editor of the *Sun* in 2003. Every good girl deserves a favour.

Murdoch was as jarring a choice as McDonald's as a sponsor for Britain's national celebration. He was an Australian who became an American for business reasons. His British media interests paid virtually no corporation tax, for all their tears for the under-funded NHS. The Murdoch press made profits of about £1.3 billion between 1987 and 1999. The *Economist* calculated that if corporation tax had been paid at prevailing rates the Inland Revenue would have collected enough for seven new hospitals or 200 new primary schools. As with McDonald's, no one in authority wanted to dwell on the unhelpful detail. Later, when the Dome's failures became too well-known for the *Sun* to cover up, it reversed the reversal of the ferret and went for the Dome for wasting the money of people who didn't dodge taxes, and proved once again that governments can't buy Murdoch: they can merely rent him.[9]

The creepy relationships between the Dome and business implied that it was little more than an easy vindication of the Marxist theory that the economic base determines the cultural superstructure. In truth, neither Marx's materialism nor any other philosophy which relied on intelligible links between cause and effect could account for all the Dome's contents. Many slipped their moorings to reason and floated away on a giddy swell. The exhibitions of 1851 and 1951 allowed industry to display inventions which would transform the spectators' lives. The Dome's attempt to revive the energy of the past in de-industrialised Britain descended into absurdity as raddled mutton was dressed as the millennium year's lamb. New Labour allowed the public a preview of the Dome's exhibits in 1998 when it unveiled powerhouse::uk (case and punctuation as in the original.) The powerhouse was four giant interlinked drums with inflatable walls, which were plonked in Horse Guards' Parade. Architects explained that the designers had chosen a 'pneumatic inflatable structure' because 'its transient and dynamic nature' contrasted with 'the formality of the traditional government buildings' in Whitehall. Among the exhibits shown to visiting heads of heads of state were 'an orthopaedic overshoe for cattle' and a 'device for trapping cockroaches in talcum powder'.

Maybe the organisers looked at the innovations and realised that Britain's 'cutting-edge technology' wasn't as inspiring as the PM and Simon Jenkins believed. For whatever reason, they filled the hole in the Dome with images of insipid concern and risk-free dissent rather than the triumphs of British manufacturing.

The Learning Zone presented a rotating video wall in which a huge library turned into a forest and back again. Whether visitors were meant to worry about the loss of woodland to the publishing industry, or celebrate the transformation of timber into knowledge, or nod and move on, or nod off for that matter, was as unclear to the viewer as it was, presumably, to the designers. A mock-up of a pier promised traditional fun for all the family. Its What-the-Butler-Saw machines presented images of environmental decay. No one could explain the connection. The Dome's official historian came closest when he revealed that the creators of the pier were drunk when the inspiration hit them.

The Mind Zone was meant to be filled with Britart from the Watersports School. But in one of their better decisions, the sponsors rejected 'Piss Flowers' by Helen Chadwick, a series of bronze moulds taken from cavities left after she had risked hypothermia for her art by peeing in the snow during a visit to Canada. Her holes were replaced by an enormous perspex case filled with thousands of leaf-cutter ants. The designers claimed that they symbolised 'communal, instinctive minds, working together, carrying bright flecks of leaf along paths designed to resemble the tracks of a silicon chip'. To the delight of the City and the political and media classes, the dotcom bubble was inflating with a speed which outpaced all previous speculative frenzies. What could be more fitting than a celebration in the Dome of the miraculous chips?

In their native South America, leaf-cutter ants are better known for their appetites than their symbolic representation of the Net. Each ant can carry 500 times its body weight in chopped leaves. About a million live in each colony. When they get hungry, the ant armies march in unstoppable columns. They strip trees in the rainforest and munch their way through the crops of destitute peasants.

Ruthless ants were an apt representation of the regimented style of the New Labour administration and the rapacious practice of business at the height of the bubble. But they couldn't begin to compete with the Dome's star turn, Faith Zone. The Dome was about to show that religion in the new century had retained all of its irrational power.

Britain is the most atheist country on earth, thank God. Observance is collapsing by every measure. In fairness, the Catholics and Protestants of Northern Ireland and the Jihadis of Finsbury

Park remain pious, but they aren't advertisements for faith which are likely to convert sceptics. Mandelson and Lord (Charlie) Falconer, his successor as Dome minister, couldn't, however, preside over a celebration which reflected the secular temper of the times. They had to find a space for God in the Dome, and not just because its ostensible purpose was to mark the 2000th anniversary – or thereabouts – of the birth of Jesus Christ.

Most twentieth-century British politicians were cheerfully irreligious in private. By the start of the twenty-first century, much of the electorate had followed them and abandoned God. A trifling 8 per cent padded out the pews, a third had no idea what Easter was meant to commemorate, Judaism had declined with each generation. Only Islam and the charismatic churches retained their grip on the minds of the credulous. The political class nevertheless chose the godless millennium as the moment to find faith. Among the leaders of New Labour in its first term, Tony Blair, Gordon Brown, Hilary Armstrong, Tessa Jowell, Lord Irvine, Chris Smith and Jack Straw were ostentatiously pious. Blair said he prayed every day, and may not have been lying. Before he dropped the idea of 'reforming' the House of Lords, he planned to give seats to sixteen unelected Anglican bishops and an unspecified number of equally unaccountable leaders from other faiths.

The Christian Socialist Movement was one of New Labour's most influential cliques. It was shadowed on the Tory side by the Conservative Christian Fellowship, a queer-hating sect which boasted of its friendship with the creationists in the American Christian Coalition. William Hague took their fellowship from the margins of his party to an office in Conservative Central Office. Iain Duncan Smith kept it there. At no time in the previous 100 years were British politicians as religious as they were in 2000 (and, I shouldn't have to add, at no time did the electorate regard its leaders with greater distaste).

Why religion appealed to the powerful was a hard question to answer. Traditionally, it was a means by which cynical rulers kept the dopey masses in order. But in twenty-first century Britain it was the cynical masses who were rejecting religion while the dopes at the top converted. In New Labour, finding God was an astute way to please Blair, a good career move. Atheist politicians said they also suspected religion provided a substitute for the Labour faith the party had abandoned. Piety also had an electoral advantage. In 2000 there was no longer a vigorous anti-clerical tradition in England because there weren't enough powerful clerics to generate opposition. A simple comparison made the point. In Ireland anti-clericals had to fight to free women from the Catholic church's bans on contraception and abortion. Women's emancipation depended on their victory. In Britain, anti-clericals who were determined to *écrasez l'infâme* were reduced to trying to rub out 'Thought for the Day' on the *Today* programme, which was an offence against all standards of intelligent discourse, to be sure, but perhaps not as infamous as Voltaire's Jesuit enemies. In a priest-lite land, Blair's image as a trendy vicar didn't hurt him. Vicars were generally seen as worthy men and women who may have been a bit wet but did good work for all that.

It wasn't until the Dome had closed that the nature of the Third Way spirit world became public. Cherie Blair's Catholicism and Tony Blair's Anglo-Catholicism and interest in Islam coexisted with paganism, Ouija board tapping, pseudo-science and New Age quackery. *The Times* was the first to shine a light on their mysteries when it broke the story of what the Blairs did during their stay at the Maroma Hotel, a pricey retreat on Mexico's Caribbean coast. Mrs Blair took her husband by the hand and led him along the beach to a 'Temazcal', a steam bath enclosed in a brick pyramid of an Aztec design. It was dusk and they had stripped down to their swimming costumes. Inside, they met Nancy Aguilar, a New Age therapist. She told them the pyramid was a womb in which they would be reborn. The Blairs became one with 'Mother Earth'. They saw the shapes of phantom animals in the steam and experienced 'inner-feelings and visions'. As they smeared each other with melon, papaya and mud from the jungle, they confronted their fears and emitted a primal scream. The joyous agonies of 'rebirth' were upon them. When the ceremony was over, the Prime Minister and his wife waded into the sea and cleaned themselves up as best they could.

Primal screaming was the invention of one Arthur Janov, who made the classic baby-boomer journey from politics to mysticism. Janov unveiled 'primal therapy' theory in 1970, when many baby-boomers were deciding that if enough people changed themselves, the world would change with them and there would be no need to fight the riot squad. You helped others by helping yourself. Janov told his patients to release their fears with primal screams 'so that you can be free in the present and free to build your future'. The cause of sexual liberation, to which the Blair wing of the British baby-boomers was true in its own way, depended in part on the personal becoming political, so I suppose the theory wasn't entirely egocentric. But Janov and thousands of other gurus led the way to a narrow individualism. As early as the 1970s, Christine McNulty of the Stanford Research Institute in the United States found a link between personal liberation and conservatism. She divided people by their attitudes and 'lifestyles' rather than their class. Regardless of their backgrounds, those who believed they had freed themselves from the chains of society to build their own futures were far more likely to vote for Thatcher and Reagan than any other group. Her colleagues thought she was mad. These were socially aware and socially concerned people who may well have marched against the Vietnam War. But the appeals of 'choice' and freedom from control were far greater than nostalgia for a vanishing youth. They had been taught that selfishness was the way to liberate the abused self. The surprise, in retrospect, was that anyone was surprised by their greed.[10]

The *Mail* took up the New Age theme in the autumn of 2002 and investigated the shamans who had attached themselves to the Blair court. Chief among them was Carole Caplin, Mrs Blair's confidante and personal trainer. The friendship led to a minor scandal because Caplin was carrying the child of Peter Foster, an Australian conman who had secured the Blairs two flats in Bristol at below the market rate. As telling as the free legal advice Mrs Blair gave to a crook who her husband's Home Office was seeking to deport was the religious world in which she and Caplin communed.

Caplin introduced her to Jack Temple, an 86-year-old homeopathic healer. Temple had built what he claimed was a 'Neolithic stone circle' in his back garden. He said the stones captured the healing energies of the stars, sun and moon and held them for the benefit of his paying customers. He gave me an exultant lecture on how he discovered the rocks in Pembrokeshire and transported them in two lorries to his home in Pyrford, near Woking, Surrey.

'I'm sorry,' I interrupted. 'The local authority and the National Trust allowed you to run off with an ancient monument?'

'The stones weren't in a circle,' he replied. 'They had been cleared so the field could be worked. They were dumped in a ditch and a farmer sold them to me.'

'I see. A farmer said a load of old rubble in a ditch was once a Stone Age religious site, and you paid ready money to get your hands on it. How did you know the stones were genuine stones, so to speak?'

An irritated note entered Temple's voice. 'I dowsed them with my magic pendulum, of course. I made the amazing discovery that each of the sixteen stones relieved stress in different parts of the body – the muscles, the brain and so on.'

I gave up, and Temple went on to explain that, after he moved the stones to Surrey, he went to the local garden centre and used his pendulum to divine the aura of the herb and alpine section. His trial of the plants was rigorous. He found only wild strawberries had the strength to 'contain nature's energy generated by the stone circle'. Temple planted his circle with strawberries and sold small packets of their dried leaves for £10 (plus £1 p&p) to Mrs Blair, the late Princess Di and Fergie. 'I believe I've helped the lame to walk, the barren to conceive, and the sad to smile,' Temple claimed in his autobiography. 'I've been able to reflate the lungs of children previously condemned to a life constricted by asthma. I've even seen the bald pates of middle-aged and elderly men begin to spring hair growth again.'

About the only miracle his pendulum and strawberry leaves couldn't guarantee was communication with the dead. Clairvoyance was left to Carol Caplin's possessed mother, Sylvia. She was a former ballet dancer turned spiritualist. According to a client, Caplin Snr said she could 'bring the light down' and open channels with the dead. Mrs Blair regularly visited the mystic's £500,000 house in Dorking, which was also filled with stones. 'There was a particularly active period in the summer when Sylvia was channelling for Cherie over two or three times a week, with almost daily contact between them. There were times when Cherie's faxes ran to ten pages.'[11]

Magic strawberries and conversations with corpses aside, Mrs Blair hired a feng shui expert to rearrange the furniture at Number 10 when she moved into Downing Street. She also took to wearing a 'magic pendant' known as the BioElectric Shield, which was filled with 'a matrix of specially cut quartz crystals' that surround the wearer with 'a cocoon of energy' to ward off evil forces – given to her by Hillary Clinton. Then there were inflatable flowtron trousers, auricular therapy and acupuncture pins in the ear.

The list is far from complete, but I hope you can see the awful dilemma Peter Mandelson and Lord Falconer faced. Hardly anyone wanted a celebration of religion. The few who did, however, were in power and willing to believe in anything and everything. When bishops complained that there was a God-shaped hole in the Dome which must be filled, Blair's underlings had to fill it, but with what?

The religious zone, 'Soul', was designed by Eva Jiricna in the spirit of New Age mysticism. Like Cherie Blair, Jiricna had a penchant for pyramids. Hers was to have a smoky-glass exterior which reflected all that was going on around it. Inside, the visitor was to be confronted with white walls and bright lights. The space under the floor's toughened-glass tiles would be flooded so the punters would feel they were walking on water. Simple benches were to line the walls. They would encourage visitors to 'hold hands and think about what they have in common rather than look at historic clues to what went wrong,' said Jiricna. The minimalist interior would be 'a contemplative space' which rejected established faiths because 'to me religion is dogma . . . Religion often cuts off other people's wings. And people, or at least their souls, want to fly. If you don't want war on your hands, you have to rise above religion.'

Poor soppy Eva didn't stand a chance. She had a war on her hands – a war she could only lose. New Age quackery may have been the sole popular superstition, but Jennie Page, the chief executive of the New Millennium Experience Company, was having none of it. She was a regular church-goer herself and, in any case, knew that Mr Blair, Prince Charles, the Archbishop of Canterbury, the Tory Party and the *Daily Telegraph* wanted traditional religion too. 'It was clear to me from Day One that we needed to accommodate dogma,' said Page. 'Soul' was renamed 'Spirit Level' and then 'The Faith Zone'. The top of Jiricna's pyramid was snipped off. Minimalism was forgotten as all kinds of knick-knacks were bunged into her pure space. Arguments about the contents were conducted by the Lambeth Group, a TUC of the faithful. The group comprised representatives of the different varieties of Christians, along with Jews, Hindus, Muslims, Buddhists, Jains, Bahais and Zoroastrians. Prince Charles was represented. His Royal Highness was determined that the Dome shouldn't be given over to the pursuit of pleasure. The clerics, whose faiths were incompatible and whose adherents had spent much of the previous two millennia murdering each other (and were soon at it again in September 2001), supported the Prince's notion that he could be Defender of all the Faiths when his mother got out of the way and allowed him to become 'our' unelected head of state. In a letter to the Lambeth Group, the Prince wrote: 'I was much heartened, and moved to read your affirmation of the essential unity of religion and the commonality of core values essential for sane, balanced and responsible living in any age.'

Page bent her knee before the twittering royal. She ordered that 'The Faith Zone' should be born once again and re-rechristened 'Faith Zone'. The definite article was purged because the 'the' was thought to imply that there was one faith, established Anglicanism, which was more important than the others, Judaism, Islam, Zoroastrianism and the like. The dogma the Dome had a place for was the ecumenical dogma that all established faiths were one-ish.

Twiddling with titles couldn't distract Mandelson for long from a financial embarrassment. Faith Zone, like all other zones, had to have a business sponsor because everyone agreed that the market was great and good. But no business could see the competitive advantage in consorting with religion in a godless land. One Dome manager confessed to praying before bedtime to the Good Lord for a capitalist to save him. Salvation came in the form of the Hinduja brothers. They were, obviously, Hindus. But Srichand Hinduja said he was with Charles Windsor and believed in the 'shared values of each faith'. He wanted the Dome to recognise that the human race must sow the seeds for 'peace, development and co-operation'.

As with so many other billionaires' piles, it was difficult to chart the growth of the Hindujas' wealth. The brothers – Srichand (SP) and Gopichand (GP) in London, Prakash in Geneva and Ashok in Bombay – were the sons of Paramand Hinduja. He was a Sindhi: a Hindu who fled Pakistan to escape the blood-lust in the faith zones of partition. He died in 1971, leaving his sons $1 million and some land in Iran. The boys turned their relatively modest inheritance into a fortune. They supplied pre-revolutionary Iran with Bollywood films and India with Iranian crude oil. They owned 40 per cent of Ashok Leyland, the Indian truckmaker, and had the rights to market the Gulf Oil brand outside Britain. The brothers were traders in India, Europe, the Gulf and the US. Weapons deals plumped

their portfolio. They represented Bofors, the Swedish armaments combine in Iran and India, and negotiated the sale of
German submarines to the Indian Navy.

Although the *Sunday Times* Rich List had SP and GP as the
joint eighth richest people in Britain in 1999, the title was misleading in several respects. London was SP's and GP's base.
They had a home in Carlton House Terrace, within a short car-
riage ride from Buckingham Palace, and an office round the
corner in Haymarket. But their wealth was based overseas, as
was the employment it sustained. They had no significant
investments in Britain.

If the above description makes GP and SP sound shady, they
didn't appear that way to the Westminster village. They were
ascetics as adept as any Blairite at delivering the tremulous platitudes of the pious. They held their fortunes in common; they
rejected alcohol, nicotine and caffeine (yes, yes, fine, I accept
this wasn't a strong point for the defence); and they gave generously to charities on three continents through the Hinduja
Foundation. I saw them at a diplomatic reception. They struck
me as polite and eager to meet new people, particularly if the
new person in the room was a politician. The brothers knew
George Bush Snr and Bill Clinton. The Queen condescended to
make their acquaintance. They graced Conservative fund-raising parties for Margaret Thatcher, John Major and Edward
Heath, before finding, along with many other rich men, that the
transition from Conservative to Labour was profitable and
painless. The Hindujas and the new government were all over
each other. Stephen Byers visited them to discuss joint ventures
between India and Powergen when he was Trade Secretary.
Patricia Hewitt popped into their mansion in Bombay when
she was on an official visit to India. Clare Short, Chris Smith
and Robin Cook took their advice. Mandelson needed them
most and knew them best. 'I asked: can we do something in the
Dome?' said SP in 1999, when he explained the Hindujas' offer
of £1 million to underwrite the costs of Faith Zone. 'Mandelson
started coming to our functions and receptions. He is sharp,

decisive and has a good grasp of the issues. Every businessman likes politicians like that.'

Much of the promised Hinduja money never reached the Dome. Once the free tickets for corporate entertaining and the tax advantages were deducted, the Hindujas' outlay was closer to £350,000 than £1 million. The same gap between the headline figure and small print could be seen elsewhere in the Dome's books. In the first of a series of increasingly incredulous reports, the National Audit Office found that one reason why Greenwich administrators made ever greater demands on Lottery funds was that a brag by Lord Falconer that he had raised £160 million in sponsorship was empty. The Dome was £45 million short of its sponsorship target, the auditors reported. The gap had to be plugged by yet more Lottery grants.[12]

Nevertheless, the Hindujas helped out, and the pulling power they received by bailing out an official embarrassment was palpable on the night of 3 November 1999. The Prime Minister and his wife joined Mandelson, Charles Kennedy, Jeffrey Archer and 3,000 other guests at a Hinduja Diwali party at Alexandra Palace. Mrs Blair was dressed to ingratiate. She wore an orange and white silk churidar kameez – a sari-style wrap covered by a puff-sleeved jacket – and a jewel on her forehead. SP's daughter picked the costume from the collection of Nita Lulla, one of the best British-Indian designers. Distinguished guests applauded the Hindujas for their broadmindedness and philanthropy. Lowlier souls moaned. 'Everyone around me thought it was a bit tacky,' Zia Sardar, a friend at the bash, told me later. 'The place was heaving and we were left parched and struggling to get a drink. David Frost came on and made a few bad jokes. Blair made a speech I've heard him give to ethnic minorities before. Cherie's dress was too flashily Bollywood.' The booze may have been pitiful and the company atrocious, but the grumpiest party-goers couldn't object when they were invited to sign the 'Hinduja Pledge'. The assembled revellers bound themselves to strive for tolerance and peace in the next century. Who could object to such well-meaning, if somewhat saccharine, sentiments? SP said he was happy to support the ecumenical mission statement of Faith Zone because 'I don't agree when we talk about Hindus or Christians, because we are all human beings. It's only which faith people follow that has created differences between us.'

His analysis was overly narrow. The struggles for temporal power – and for control of the weapons that secure it – also have their part in creating differences. As Peter Mandelson was about to find out.

SEVEN

The Cashondeliveri Brothers

In *The Moor's Last Sigh* Salman Rushdie presents us with the monstrous Abraham Zogoiby. The father of the hero is an ecumenical Indian tycoon who will deal with anyone regardless of colour, caste or creed. Zogoiby is hated by Bombay's Hindu fundamentalists who have a 'vision of theocracy in which one particular variant of Hinduism would rule, while all India's other peoples bowed their beaten heads'. Abraham built his fortune by associating with, and then supplanting, the Cashondeliveri brothers. He promotes shared values by encouraging corruption, 'an inter-community league of cynical self-interest' whose success may be 'a dark, ironic victory . . . [for the] godless crooked army that could take on and vanquish anything that the god-squad could send its way.' His son remembers Abraham telling him how the family business made its money:

> Armaments featured strongly, though the publicly listed activities of his great corporation included no such trade. A famous Nordic armaments house was negotiating to supply India with a range of essentially decent, elegantly designed and naturally lethal products. The sums of money involved were too large to have meaning, and as is the way with such Karakorams of capital, certain peripheral boulders of money came loose from the main bulk and began to roll down the mountain. What was needed was a discreet means of tidying away these tumbling boulders in a manner properly beneficial to those involved in the negotiations. The participants in the negotiations were of a great refinement, possessed of a delicacy that would have made it quite impossible for them to tidy away this rubble of lucre, even into their own back accounts. Not a whisper of impropriety could ever attach itself to their high names! 'So,' said Abraham with a happy shrug, 'we do the dirty work and plenty of pebbles end up in our pockets, too.'

Those ignorant of Indian politics would have read the passage and decided it owed more to magic than realism. (The Cashondeliveri brothers? Rubble of lucre? Where on earth do these bloody novelists get their ideas from?) *The Moor's Last Sigh* was published in 1996. On 22 October 1999, ten days before Blair and Frost raised half-empty glasses of insipid wine to global tolerance, Superintendent Keshav Mishra of the Indian Central Bureau of Investigation filed a 25-page affidavit at the court of special judge Ajit Bharihoke in New Delhi. The outline of his case was backed with 2,500 pages of witness statements and supporting documents. After years of obfuscation, the Bofors scandal, which had haunted the Hinduja and the Gandhi families, had jerked out of its shallow grave.

Rajiv Gandhi's Congress government had paid Bofors, the Swedish armaments manufacturer, $1.3 billion (£802 million) in 1986 for 400 Howitzers. Rajiv was then at the summit of his popularity. The airline pilot had never expected to be a politician. After his brother Sanjay died young and Indira Gandhi was murdered, he was pushed into taking charge of a Congress Party whose senior politicians had degenerated into a claque of monarchists. Rajiv's isolation from traditional politics allowed him to pull a trick which prefigured Blair's strategy a decade later. Rajiv posed as a bright technocrat who would stop the fixing of the old élite by opening up a secretive government. Indians were assured that his accession announced the birth of a modern India, a new India, an India impatient with ideology and ready to throw off the forces of conservatism. The appeal of the young leader was enhanced by his promise that middlemen would be cut out of Indian government contracts. In theory, the agents of western companies were supposed to provide local knowledge. In practice, as all half-way knowledgeable Indians knew, they bribed generals and politicians to secure orders.

The Bofors scandal rotted every principle Rajiv professed. Within months of the guns being delivered, Swedish radio reported that £30 million in kickbacks had been distributed to the Gandhi court. Rajiv denounced the allegations as a conspiracy against India, and then presided over the most perfunctory of inquiries. The Indian army's chief of staff said he had recommended pulling out of the contract but had been overruled by Rajiv's associates. The defence minister resigned rather than obey Rajiv's orders to stop his investigations into the contract.

With all the juicy allegations of larceny and intrigue to chomp on, it was easy to forget that the Bofors' Howitzers intensified the arms race between India and Pakistan, an arms race which left them in an unstable nuclear 'balance of terror'. The consequences for Indian democracy were as dire. The Gandhi family had glaring faults and committed many crimes, but at its best it upheld Nehru's ideal of a secular India. The scandal guaranteed Rajiv's defeat in the 1989 general election and gave the Hindu sectarians of the BJP their first taste of success. The BJP revived the Bofors affair in the 1999 general election in an attempt to undermine Rajiv's widow, Sonia, who had assumed the dynasty's hereditary title of Leader of Congress. It disinterred the corpse of her assassinated husband and threatened to charge it posthumously with criminal conspiracy. In a less decisive manner second time around, Bofors shot down Congress and maintained the power of the bigots.

The Hindujas appeared to have nothing to do with the affair until June 1988, when the Indian press published documents from the Swedish auditor-general identifying shell companies that had allegedly channelled Bofors' bribes. Detectives from the Central Bureau of Investigation followed the media accusations with their own inquiries in India and Sweden. The police alleged on 7 February 1990 that 'the Hinduja brothers are believed to be behind secret coded accounts in the names of Pitco/ Moreso/Moineao and AE Services of the UK' which were held in Swiss and Panamanian banks. Boulders of money had allegedly bounced to the Alps and the isthmus. GP and SP were incandescent: 'We completely deny that any such payments were ever received by our company or by any member of the family,' they said. They were so outraged by the slur they were willing to renounce Mother India in disgust. On 21 February 1990 they applied for British citizenship. Their change of allegiance wasn't just a gesture. As British citizens they would have the option of fighting and possibly blocking an extradition request from India at the High Court in London.

The then Conservative government turned them down. Doug McQueen, a Home Office civil servant, said the brothers hadn't spent enough time in Britain in the past five years to show that they had 'thrown in their lot' with this country. The Bofors allegations meant it was impossible for Whitehall to be sure that they were of 'good character'.

The character question should have been easy to resolve. Indian detectives persuaded the Swiss to freeze six bank accounts. Full discovery of the contents might have cleared the brothers' reputations. But each attempt to get at the evidence was blocked by the brothers' appeals to the Swiss courts, whose delicacy in investigating money tidied away in its banks was justly celebrated around the world. The case was mired in legal appeals until the autumn of 1999, when the Hindujas ran out of judges.

Their enemies in the BJP had an explanation for the Hindujas' love of lawyers. Arun Jaitley, the minister of information in the BJP-led coalition, told me in 1999 that only 'repeated appeals' to the Swiss had stopped formal charges being brought. 'If there is no evidence, why have the Hindujas been fighting the battle of their lives to stop us getting evidence from Switzerland?' The Hindujas justified the delaying tactics by saying that their legal transactions with Bofors would be twisted by their opponents if the records were released. As ecumenical opponents of Hindu fundamentalism, the brothers were the victims of a political vendetta, their spokesman said. The Hindujas went to India to face their accusers when charges were brought. The law's delays are the curse of Indian democracy and no verdict had been given by the court at the time this book went to press.

New Labour passed its verdict years before. The brothers

weren't just relieved of their money and thanked. Like so many of the party's business partners they were flattered and embraced, consulted on the great affairs of state and befriended. When the Bofors scandal hit the Dome, New Labour pundits yawned and asked if it really mattered in the greater scheme of things if businessmen got passports from a friendly government. Several replies were available. The promise of money had been followed by the granting of passports, and there was – to put it gently – a suggestion of favouritism. The Blair administration was also disgracing itself in 1999 by vilifying and persecuting asylum-seekers. Its appeal to the far-right was based on a claim that it wanted to stop economic migrants getting into Britain, and had nothing against genuine refugees. This was a foul lie which was made fouler by the spectacle of a government rushing to grant the protection of British citizenship to billionaire migrants implicated in the greatest financial scandal in independent India's history. More telling than both was, and is, New Labour's deference to the rich: a mental handicap which warps policies from the regulation of stock-market excess to the delivery of aid to the Third World.

No one was more eager to please the Hindujas than the Prime Minister. Dinners at Carlton House Terrace and the cheerless party at Ally Pally were accompanied by a warm correspondence. Blair treated the arms dealers as partners for peace. In July 1999 he told them, 'We will continue to encourage India and Pakistan to engage in the search for a just and lasting solution, which reflects the views of the people living in Kashmir. I hope that you will convey a similar message to your interlocutors in both countries.' (Why should you expect Blair to see the irony? The Hindujas' admitted and alleged weapons deals were small beer when compared against Blair's overriding of objections to selling arms to the murderous governments of Indonesia and Zimbabwe. If the Prime Minister didn't grasp that he couldn't be both an arms dealer and peacemaker, he couldn't be expected to laugh at the blackly comic spectacle of the Hindujas auditioning for the same parts.)

GP ended his letters to Blair with a chummy 'With kind regards and best wishes, GP Hinduja.' He was delighted by Blair's appointment of Keith Vaz, a family friend, as minister for Europe. GP wrote a note to praise Blair's vision of a more tolerant Britain. Blair replied: 'Let me once again express my gratitude to the Hinduja family for all that you are doing to make this vision a reality.' He signed off with a 'Yours ever, Tony.' Vaz later resigned in disgrace.[1]

A former adviser to the Hindujas recalled the feelings of his old masters for Blair and Mandelson when the romance was blossoming. 'Towards Tony Blair they [the Hindujas] were sycophantic, fawning, frankly arse-licking. To Peter Mandelson they were friendly – but it was a more equal relationship. They saw him as the gatekeeper to Blair – and that was the role he liked to play. Irrespective of whether he [Mandelson] was at Northern Ireland, Trade and Industry or a backbencher, the rich and famous were encouraged to queue up at his door to get to Blair.'[2] In July 2001, Downing Street admitted that the Hindujas had gone to Blair and his chief of staff Jonathan Powell with an offer to solve their crisis of faith at the Dome. Powell instructed Mandelson to close the deal. The PM encouraged his new friends to become the proprietors of the *Daily Express*, *Sunday Express* and *Daily Star* and keep them in the New Labour camp. Mandelson was a willing inermediary – and an unwilling fall guy.

The Home Office's objections to the brothers melted with Blair's victory in 1997. In July of that year, Andrew Walmsley, a civil servant in its Immigration and Nationality Depratment, recommended that GP Hinduja should become a naturalised British citizen. Mike O'Brien, New Labour's immigration minister, agreed. A year earlier, Walmsley had received a memo from Caroline Elmes of the Foreign Office's South Asian Department. She set out all the worries about the Hindujas. They 'are immensely wealthy, influential . . . and secretive,' she wrote.[3] Their business associates included a man under arrest on 'cheating charges . . . It is conceivable that the [Bofors] case could come alight.' Even if it didn't, she continued, 'at the very least they can be said to have sailed close to the wind in building their business empire'. Her warning was dismissed, as were similar alarms from MI6 going back to 1990. GP was still jetting all over the planet and failing to meet the residence requirement, but that didn't matter either. He got his passport. As the Hindujas had shown no interest in the Dome at that time, the best explanation for the indulgence GP received is the simplest: he was rich and New Labour liked the rich.

The demands for passports intensified a fortnight after the Hindujas met Blair and Powell. Either Mandelson or his private office contacted Mike O'Brien and asked if now was a good time for SP to become a British citizen. Mathew Laxton, O'Brien's private secretary, sent a message to Walmsley saying that their boss was 'keen to adopt a more positive approach to citizenship'. SP, too, didn't meet the residence requirement, but what the hell. On 5 October, O'Brien wrote to Mandelson saying that 'my officials advise me that his [SP's] current level of absences from the United Kingdom are not considered excessive and they are likely to look favourably upon any application'. SP was invited to contact Walmsley and informed that the civil servant would be 'happy to advise him'.4 On 14 October, the Hindujas agreed to underwrite 'Faith Zone'. Seven days later, SP made a succesful application for citizenship. In May 2000, yet another Hinduja – Prakash this time – popped up. GP wrote to Mandelson asking him if an application for British citizenship would be viewed 'in a positive way' by the Home Office. Mandelson gave the letter to Jack Straw. The then Home Secretary was more than eager to please the Prime Minister's favourite. But before Prakash could move to Britain, Mandelson was out and Straw was pretending that his department was a model of probity.

It's confusing being a leftish hack. You come across stories you believe cry to high heaven for attention, not just on ideological grounds but because they are 'good tales' in the jargon of the press pack. You bang on for years to no effect whatsoever.

Inevitably, you delude yourself on many occasions. But every now and then a subject you've raised explodes. I've given up trying to make predictions. There's no reason I can find why the Hindujas' patronising of New Labour became a sensation when the state-licensed extortion of the Private Finance Initiative didn't.

I banged on about the Hindujas and my articles[5] had their usual effect, which is to say none. About a year later my *Observer* colleague Antony Barnett persuaded Norman Baker, the Liberal Democrat MP for Lewes, to put down an astute question in the Commons. Baker asked the Home Office what representations Peter Mandelson and Keith Vaz had made about the Hinduja passport applications. The detail of what happened next has been printed many times and there's not much point in going through who said what to whom in anything other than outline.[6] The best way to understand why Mandelson has been the only Cabinet casualty of allegations of corruption is to look at the screaming jealousies at the top of New Labour. British civil society is weak, as I hope to show later. It has few independent means of subpoeanaing evidence. The guilty are dumped only when the members of the new élite stab each other in the back. There wasn't a square inch of unbroken flesh on Mandelson's by the time his friends had finished with him.

Mandelson told the *Observer*, 'To the limited extent that I was involved in this matter I was always very sensitive to the proprieties. The matter was dealt with by my private secretary. At no time did I support or endorse this application for citizenship.' The matter might have rested there. The *Observer* didn't lead the paper with the Mandelson piece. At the next Number 10 briefing, Alastair Campbell dismissed the story as the tittle-tattle of irresponsible journalists with a paranoid predilection to invent conspiracies where none existed. 'Mr Mandelson had not got involved in the matter – beyond being asked to be involved, which he had refused to do,' he said. There had been no lobbying of Home Office ministers on the Hindujas' behalf, Campbell assured the hacks. Chris Smith, the then Culture Secretary, told the Commons that Mandelson's 'sole involvement' had been to tell SP Hinduja that his application would be dealt with by civil servants 'in the normal way'. The story would have died if either of these statements had been true.

Neither was. The Home Office told Campbell that it would brief journalists that Mandelson had phoned O'Brien in 1998 to push along SP's passport application. Smith had inadvertently misled Parliament. The far grander figure of Alastair Campbell had inadvertently misled the press (not a hanging offence in itself, you understand, or even a petty crime, but Campbell would have lost face if journalists had been able to pin a liar label on him). Between them Campbell and Straw finished off their rival for the ear of the King.

The next day Campbell told the press that Mandelson's denials weren't convincing. There were 'difficulties and contradictions' in his account. He had had a 'very brief conversation with Mike O'Brien . . . Although Mr Mandelson had no recollection of the call, clearly it had taken place.' Mandelson told Channel 4 News that he hadn't forgotten a thing and implied that Campbell was lying. All Mandelson's friends deserted him as the third most powerful man in the Blair court tried to take on the second. Blair summoned Mandelson to Downing Street and searched for the courage to sack him. Doubting his resolve, Campbell went to a meeting of lobby correspondents and declined repeated opportunities to say that Mandelson had the Prime Minister's confidence. His silence was as good as a death sentence. The rolling-news bulletins reported that Mandelson had been sacked. Blair and Campbell ordered him to sign a resignation statement. He was gone – again.

Delight was unconfined. Campbell suggested to the press that a man Blair had trusted with handling the Northern Ireland conflict was on the edge of madness. He couldn't explain what had happened to anyone, 'including himself. I think he has been slightly detached.' Mandelson phoned Campbell and shouted, 'You swept me out in the gutter like a piece of old rubbish.' He then took up an old invitation to go to a Campbell

family party in Hampstead. He glowered mournfully at his exe-
cutioner across a crowded room, as if the heart-wrenching sight
would make the guilty Campbell realise what a swine he had
been, dive to his side, kiss the tears from the blotched cheeks
and coo that all was forgotten and they could carry on as if the
tiff had never happened. Split-ups at cider-fuelled school discos
have been managed with more grace.

Awkward questions about the Hindujas and the Dome
remained once the country had stopped its celebrations. Who
said what in disputed phone calls might have filled the news
pages for a few days, but wasn't the real point that the Hindujas
had offered £1 million and got their passports? If they were
unworthy of British citizenship, why was it acceptable to allow
them to sponsor Faith Zone? If no impropriety had occurred,
why had Blair fired Mandelson? If, conversely, Mandelson had
to resign for consorting with men accused of corrupting Indian
democracy, shouldn't Blair go too? What about Straw and
O'Brien? They, after all, awarded the passports. These matters
needed to be handled with the utmost tact and the greatest sub-
tlety. For the first time in his premiership Blair ordered an
inquiry into allegations of corruption. He had just the man for
the job.

Sir Anthony Hammond, QC, Knight Commander of the Order
of the Bath, Standing Counsel to the General Synod of the
Church of England and, in his time, Treasury Solicitor, Queen's
Proctor and legal adviser to the Home and Northern Ireland
Offices, crowned his career with a triumph. The Dome was his
opportunity. For the first time in the annals of the establishment, he whitewashed a whitewash. The tradition of the incurious public inquiry was already revered by the British
establishment. In 1983 the 77-year-old Lord Franks detailed the
blunders which led to the Falklands War. Two hundred and fifty
men died in the battle to retake the islands. Franks examined
the official papers which showed how their sacrifice might have
been avoided; how Margaret Thatcher's government had

missed the warning signals and practically invited Argentina to invade. But when it was time to condemn the someones who had blundered, a feeling of detachment descended on His Lordship. The sentiment was so powerful it detached him from the evidence and compelled him to conclude that 'We would not be justified in attaching any criticism or blame to the present government for the Argentine junta's decision to commit its act of unprovoked aggression.'

Sir Richard Scott's report on how Britain armed Saddam Hussein remains the epitaph of the long Tory government. His account of how ministers preferred suppressing evidence (which would save the innocent directors of Matrix Churchill from prison) to having their dealings with Saddam exposed left this reader never wanting to see another Conservative regime. But when he had to apportion blame, even Scott became an incurious inquirer. Although he had said that Parliament and public were 'designedly' misled, he concluded that ministers had 'not acted with any duplicitous intent'. Franks and Scott established the ritual of the incurious inquiry. The published evidence contains much that is fascinating, even sensational. But no attempt is made to connect it to the perpetrators.

Hammond bettered both Franks and Scott. His investigation was a masterpiece which the Rolls-Royce minds of the civil service will hold up as an example for future generations of mandarins. Everyone was cleared – twice. Like Lord Nelson at the Battle of Copenhagen, Sir Anthony had to refuse to see the facts he uncovered. The facts did not give up. They hollered and they bawled at Sir Anthony. But, like a quantum physicist, he found that they could be there and not there at the same time.

In his first report, he didn't address how the Hindujas had made their money. Nor did he ask why a Labour Prime Minister had turned to such people for companionship and counsel. He did look at the records from the Tory years when Foreign Office and MI6 warnings about Bofors and the Hindujas stopped GP and SP being welcomed as British citizens. Caroline Elmes of the FO had spoken plainly in 1996. But, said the lawyerly Sir Anthony, 'it should be noted that it [the FO] did not recommend that the Home Office should refuse naturalisation'.7 If Walmsley and O'Brien had gone back to the FO in 1997 when GP got his passport, they would have heard that the Indian government was collecting more evidence for the Bofors prosecution. Sir Anthony noted that the FO was not consulted, but was not concerned by the bureaucratic lapse. 'Whether the application should have been refused on the basis that the scandal cast doubt on whether Mr Hinduja satisfied the good character requirement is a matter of judgment.' 8 Sir Anthony, a QC who was acting as judge in this instance, was not going to be over-judgemental about the laxity of the Home Office. Walmsley and O'Brien had used their discretion with propriety, he concluded.

O'Brien, Campbell and Straw had made Mandelson resign because they said he had phoned the Home Office to press SP's case. Mandelson said he hadn't made the call. It was a trivial point. All agreed that Mandelson had been a promoter of the Hindujas' interest. Nevertheless, it was the point which had forced his second resignation. You might have thought that the claim and counter-claim couldn't both be right. Sir Anthony considered the unpleasant inference that one side must be lying and rejected it. True, there was no record of the phone conversation. Moreover Mandelson told Hammond 'that he did not have a ministerial telephone directory in his office, so would not have known how to contact Mr O'Brien'. Was this proof that a weak prime minister had been bullied into sacking an innocent man? Not at all, said Sir Anthony. The absence of the telephone directory was not conclusive proof. 'It is possible that Mr Mandelson could have used the No 10 Downing Street switchboard which would have connected him to Mr O'Brien's office.'9 Was, then, the architect of New Labour a liar? Not at all, said Sir Anthony. 'It is likely that Mr Mandelson spoke directly to Mr O'Brien. [But] Mr Mandelson's belief that he had not had a telephone conversation with Mr O'Brien was honestly held.'

Good chaps were everywhere. The Home Office was full of them. In 1998, when the Dome deal was on, Mandelson raised the matter of SP's status. Walmsley, a civil servant who has spent a fair proportion of his working life dealing with assorted Hindujas, neglected to write a formal report on his decision to speed up and then grant SP's application for citizenship. Suspicious minds wondered why. Sir Anthony said that although Walmsley's behaviour was contrary to 'good practice', managers in the directorate had assured him that 'Mr Walmsley was an expert on nationality policy and tended to keep a lot of the reasons for his decision-making in his head. The lack of minuting did not suggest that Mr Walmsley was being evasive or trying to hide the reasons for his decisions.'

Walmsley chose to deal with SP's 'high-profile' case himself rather than pass it to a junior official, as was customary. He told SP he didn't need to fill in a new application form. He could save himself from unnecessary paperwork by refiling the old one the Home Office had rejected. Walmsley then approved the application with a speed which would stun refugees who wait for years below the poverty line for a decision. Sir Anthony explained the silver service SP received thus: 'Mr Walmsley did not have the same volume of casework to deal with and Mr SP Hinduja's application did not need to join the queue of cases waiting to be processed . . . In line with his general philosophy, Mr Walmsley had wanted to be helpful.'[10]

More help was offered in May 2000 when Mandelson forwarded a letter to Straw from GP which asked if Prakash could join his brothers and become a British citizen. Straw wrote to his private secretary: 'Mara – Mr Mandelson raised this matter with me. Please have a word first then get some advice. ?Zola Budd.' The '?Zola Budd' was circled. Budd was a teenage South African athlete who was taken up by the *Daily Mail*. The paper hectored the Tories until they accepted her as a British citizen – thus allowing her to join the 1984 British squad at the Los Angles Olympics. In the final of the 3,000 metres Mary Decker, the pretty American favourite, fell over Budd's legs and Budd became the most hated athlete at the games. (No good deed may go unpunished, but the Budd story shows that a few craven deeds get their comeuppance too.)

Budd's application was processed in a record-breaking and rule-breaking ten days. Everyone over 35 knew that Budd's name and favouritism were synonymous; everyone, that is, except Sir Anthony. He reported that a scatterbrained Straw had told him 'there had been some attention focused on Ms Budd, an athlete, when she was granted British citizenship, but he could not recall why he had referred to her in this way at the top of Mr GP Hinduja's letter.' Hammond wasn't in the least suspicious. He did not 'regard this as significant'.[11]

Sir Anthony found that Straw had also sent a private letter to Mandelson about SP. The Home Secretary said he was 'following the matter up personally and will be back in touch as soon as I can'. Sir Anthony did not regard this as significant. Straw was doing no more than assuring his colleague 'that the matter was being dealt with efficiently and properly'.[12] Sir Anthony discovered that Straw's private secretary had then told the civil servant handling Prakash's application that the Home Secretary would like it dealt with 'helpfully' and 'quickly'. Sir Anthony did not regard this as significant. 'I am satisfied that the use of the word "helpfully" did not have any suspicious connotations,' he reported. 'Nor did it suggest that the Home Secretary wished to give Mr Prakash Hinduja any preferential treatment which he would not have offered in other cases of this kind.'[13] If the criminal courts had judges in Sir Anthony's mould, the prisons would be empty.

You won't be surprised to learn that he concluded that there was not a shred of evidence that the passports were a quid pro quo for bankrolling the Dome. His mandarin style would have carried greater authority if he had bothered to interview the Hindujas' aide, Darin Jewell, who was eager to give evidence. The Hindujas were furious that all reputations except theirs were being cleared. Jewell would have shown Sir Anthony draft agendas for meetings with Mandelson in August and October

1998 at which citizenship was top of the bill. In a statement to the *Observer*, Jewell said that the brothers met Lord Levy, Blair's fundraiser, in the autumn of 1998. Levy made it 'perfectly clear' that he was there at the specific request of the Prime Minister. Mandelson told Sir Anthony he had 'no knowledge' of the meetings. 'I have not,' concluded Hammond, 'considered it necessary to contact Mr Jewell. I accept Mr Mandelson's explanation.'

The admiring letters Blair exchanged with the brothers were leaked to Andrew Tyrie, a Conservative MP. Tyrie charged Blair with fostering the impression he was little more than a nodding acquaintance of the Hindujas when they were the PM's confidants. Sir Anthony would not examine documents which drew the Prime Minister into the affair. They were outside his terms of reference – terms of reference which had been drawn up by the Prime Minister. By not seeing what was in front of his nose, and by refusing to admit the evidence which others wished to place in this blind spot, Sir Anthony was able to conclude that neither the Hindujas nor ministers had sought to link discussions about financing the Dome with the receipt of British passports.[14]

It was a magnificent performance, a *tour de force*. But the gap between the excellent and the truly great is a chasm. Sir Anthony still lacked the final touch which would lift his work to the status of a bureaucratic genius. His chance to apply it came in 2002. Mandelson had regained the affection of the Prime Minister. He was convinced he could prove that he had never phoned O'Brien and therefore need never have resigned. If he could, there was a chance of returning to the Cabinet. The kindly monarch yielded before his old favourite's pleadings and ordered Sir Anthony to reopen the inquiry. This was Hammond's moment – the moment to apply the unprecedented second coat of whitewash. The hand of history was upon Sir Anthony's shoulders – and he grasped it. Public suspicions that there may have been the smallest connection between the Dome and the passports were again dismissed.

In his first report, Sir Anthony had printed a curious memo Mandelson had sent to Jennie Page on the subject of the Hindujas:

> I agree that they are an above average risk but without firm evidence of wrongdoing how could we bar them from involvement in sponsorship? We are right to reduce our exposure to them. I wonder how this involvement got publicity in the first place. Incidentally, if Mr S P Hinduja wishes to pursue his citizenship application he can do so without further involvement or commendation from me![15]

Sir Anthony saw nothing peculiar in Mandelson's linking of sponsorship and passports. Nor did he notice the minister's apprehension. Hammond's insouciance continued in his second report. He saw and passed over evidence that Mandelson's civil servants were as worried as their master. Mandelson's private secretary warned in a memo scorched with emphatically underlined words that it was 'perfectly legitimate for you to raise the case with Mike O'Brien. Agree that you cannot be seen to push this personally much further. No matter how justified SP's nationality claim is, the media and others will accuse you of improper influence. Advise we await the outcome of MO'B's own investigations – and avoid anything in writing for the time being.'

Put bluntly, there had to be be no paper trails if the appearance of neutrality was to be maintained. Mandelson himself was torn. On several occasions in 1998 he said he didn't want to use his influence to help the brothers, but he carried on helping them to the end. Everyone was worried except good old Sir Anthony. He didn't reverse his verdict about the phone call. Why should he, when propriety had been displayed by one and all?

> I have concluded that the new documents do not affect my original conclusion that both Mr Mandelson and Mr O'Brien behaved properly throughout . . . if anything they reinforce my judgement that Mr Mandelson was concerned both to act, and be seen to act, with propriety.

Mandelson was still out of power but his reputation was upheld. O'Brien, Blair, Straw and Campbell were in power and their reputations were also unblemished. The irreconcilable had been reconciled not once, but twice. The walls of Whitehall gleamed. Sir Anthony rose from a civil-service Salieri to a mandarin Mozart.

By the time Sir Anthony's report was published, the Dome had become a fitting symbol for the new century. Technocrats who prided themselves on their competence had lost a small fortune of Lottery money, a disproportionately large amount of which had come from the country's poorest people. According to the National Audit Office, the paperwork for 129 contracts had vanished. Sixty contracts had been awarded without competition, and the police were taking a keen interest in them.

An élite which built its power by denouncing élitism failed to please 'the people' whose humble servant it claimed to be. The political class and the CEOs it worshipped had found the task of inspiring the country they controlled beyond them. Those visitors who turned up could have toured a 'haven of tranquillity' and meditated on Faith Zone's associations with war in Kashmir and profiteering in New Delhi. They could then have moved to the Mind Zone, sponsored by British Aerospace, suppliers of Hawk aircraft to the slaughterers in General Suharto's Indonesian air force and contributors to New Labour funds. Nearby, they would have been able to gawp at giant screens sponsored by Rupert Murdoch, courtesy of his daughter's boyfriend, and make a detour to see how McDonald's had sequestered local history in the Our Town Theatre. A year or so later, they could have read Sir Anthony's report and marvelled at the sight of the old establishment riding to the rescue of the new. And a few months later, they would have heard that, after stunning losses, the Dome had been sold on very generous terms and that its management had been passed to Anschutz Entertainment Group.

Philip Anschutz, its head, had been the founder and chair-

man of Qwest Communications, an American telecom company which had been a wonder of the bubble market. In 1999,
Anschutz sold share options worth $1.5bn (£960 million). He
picked a good time to bail out of his company. By 2002, Qwest
had lost 90 per cent of its value after the American Securities
and Exchange Commission began an investigation into the
alleged inflation of profits. Its share price crashed from $65 to
$3.25. According to charges bought by the New York District
Attorney, Anschutz had other sources of income. He was
accused of awarding work to the investment bankers at Citigroup in return for 'hot' shares from the bank which were in
short supply. Anschutz allegedly netted a personal profit of $4.8
million from the sale of the sweeteners. He paid a fine of $4.4
million to settle the case, but neither admitted nor denied liability. Citigroup, the New York authorities continued, showed
its gratitude to Qwest by assuring its trusting clients that Qwest
shares were good buys.

The British government rejected as ridiculous calls from its
opponents to stop the sale of its symbol to an executive facing
serious charges. Qwest's accountants had done nothing to raise
the alarm about the state of the corporation's books. The auditors were from Arthur Andersen, a firm which also approved
the books of a company called Enron.

Nothing to say? Nothing to say! If they had stopped being so
doltishly high-minded, its dismissive critics would have heard
the Dome bellow as much about Britain as its predecessors in
1851 and 1951. In the words of the publicity for Faith Zone, the
Dome 'explored the values that underpin our society'.

EIGHT

'A Complication of Knavery and Cozenage'

History never repeats itself, but all bubble markets are the same. Bubbles begin when inventions become objects for speculation with an unknown potential to bring radical change and make serious money. Their real worth is unknowable, so extravagant predictions are plausible, or at least not provably false. The Dutch tulip-mania of the seventeenth century started with buyers bidding up the price of rare imported bulbs. Dutch gardeners loved their flowers, but the new bulbs weren't a great technological advance. The hope that new diving technology would allow wrecks laden with treasure to be salvaged created the mental climate for England's first great explosion of speculative fraud, the South Sea Bubble of 1720. The expansion of canals and the authentically revolutionary invention of the railways puffed Victorian bubbles. The Wall Street bull market of the 1920s, whose collapse threw the world into depression, fascism and war, was driven by shares in the new radio, aviation, cinema and automobile industries. That all four were important technologies in no way lessened the catastrophe of the Great Depression. In the 1990s, it was the Internet. The Soviet Union was dead. Capitalism had won and was delivering profitable inventions which had a limitless potential to tie the planet together. Like its predecessors, the dotcom bubble was pumped up by a geyser of techno-Utopianism. No one could stop it when, as Andy Grove of the chip-maker Intel intoned in 1998, like a Pope issuing a decree *ex cathedra*:

> Whatever can be done, will be done.
> If not by incumbents, it will be done by emerging players.
> If not in a regulated industry, it will be done in a new industry born without regulation.

Technological change and its effects are inevitable.
Stopping them is not an option.[1]

Resistance did indeed seem useless until the crash in 2000 wiped $215 billion off Intel's stock.

Market manias are an affliction of peace and plenty when lazy governments sit back and see no reason to check financiers. The South Sea Bubble followed the end of the long war against the French from 1688 to 1715. The Great Crash of 1929 followed the Great War of 1914 to 1918. The Internet began to rise after the end of the Cold War of 1947 to 1989.

Rising share prices entice new investors into the market. Envy plays its part: the sight of a daughter's layabout boyfriend getting rich quick is a spur like no other. The faster shares rise, the more money is poured into shares. Shares, naturally, rise all the faster, generating euphoria. New companies are launched to take advantage of the certainty that stocks must soar forever. As the market whirls faster, said Charles Kindleberger, an historian of crashes, 'speculation tends to detach itself from really valuable objects and turns to delusive ones. A larger and larger group of people seek to become rich without a real understanding of the processes involved. Not surprisingly, swindlers and catchpenny schemes flourish.'[2]

Politicians and regulators do nothing to curb the swindlers. With or without bribes, they are persuaded by the ideology of the roaring market that it is not only pointless but positively harmful to interfere. The perverse incentives of capitalism destroy the credibility of sceptics. Investors who pull out of the market early, because they realise the fantasy can't last, are punished when shares head onwards and upwards. The herd mentality of crowds protects conformists and damns nay-sayers until the inevitable crash.

The millennium crash wasn't as bad as 1929, but that wasn't for want of trying. Governments and businesses hailed a 'New Economy' in which none of the old rules applied. Enron, which sold itself as 'the world's coolest company', was adored by investors and politicians because it claimed to be using the twin blessings of the Net and privatisation to revolutionise the distribution of the essentials of life: water, light and heat. Enron was little more than a criminal conspiracy, but grew to become America's seventh largest corporation until its frauds found it out. Enron went bust in what was, in 2001, the greatest bankruptcy in the history of capitalism. It managed to hold the title for only a few months. WorldCom's losses soon bettered Enron's. WorldCom had ridden the telecom bubble, which was bigger than its dotcom twin. Neither WorldCom nor its rivals could say who would use the millions of miles of fibre-optic cable they laid, or what they would use them for. No matter.

The competition from this side of the Atlantic was fierce. Imbecile managers who were entranced by the telecom frenzy withered the value of Marconi, one of the most successful British manufacturing firms of the twentieth century, from £35 billion to £50 million. The implosion at Equitable Life began a collapse in saving schemes that forced the English middle classes to stop talking about house prices for a moment, and look to their pensions and endowments with nervous eyes. Even after the bubble had exploded, and shares had all but halved in value, a few in the City couldn't believe the miraculous 1990s had .gone. Like jilted brides clutching pictures of their lost lovers, Standard Life managers clung on to share certificates, hoping against all reason that the romance of the New Economy would return.

The world's financial 'community' threw money at dotcoms which had never made a penny profit – and in most instances never could. The mania wasn't confined to the Anglo-Saxon world. The country which suffered most from the dotcom and telecom boom was Germany – which was meant to have immunised itself against the ravaging effects of turbo-capitalism. At its peak in March 2000 high-tech companies on the Neuer Markt register had a combined market value of 234bn euros (£147bn). By October 2002, the index had lost 96 per cent of its value. German investors threw 3 per cent of the country's gross domestic product at US dotcoms just as they were about to fold. With splendid timing, Germany converted to Anglo-Saxon capitalism at the moment of its crisis.

Only tired stick-in-the muds carped. Only élitists wondered if millions of ordinary investors were out of their minds. For the rest, the excitement was too great to resist. The Net, privatisation, deregulation and the unleashing of entrepreneurial talent promised a life-enchancing cultural revolution.

In 2000 the *Financial Times* gave Enron its 'Energy Company of the Year' award – and the prize for the 'Boldest Successful Investment Decision' to boot. Every year from 1996 to 2001, a panel of corporate executives bestowed on Enron *Fortune* magazine's title of America's 'Most Innovative Company' – which, in a sense, it was. Staff writers on *Fortune*, the Almanach de Gotha of share-option guzzling CEOs, agreed. In April 2000 *Fortune* ran a piece by one Brian O'Reilly which summed up the Utopianism of a groovy market which promised to reshape the world:

> Imagine a country-club dinner dance, with a bunch of old fogies and their wives shuffling around halfheartedly to the not-so-stirring sounds of Guy Lombardo and his All-Tuxedo Orchestra. Suddenly young Elvis comes crashing through the skylight, complete with gold-lamé suit, shiny guitar, and gyrating hips. Half the waltzers faint; most of the others get angry or pouty. And a very few decide they like what they hear, tap their feet, start grabbing new partners, and suddenly are rocking to a very different tune. In the staid world of regulated utilities and energy companies, Enron Corp is that gate-crashing Elvis.

One Enron commercial identified the company's demands to deregulate power markets with the struggles of Martin Luther King, Mahatma Gandhi and Abraham Lincoln. The New Economy was freeing the oppressed from the regulation of industry by authorities which enslaved the free-born consumer. The global partnership of Arthur Andersen, Enron's bent accountants who were to go down with their client (after going down on their client), were the *consigliere* of the bubble world. Andersen audited the books of WorldCom, and, through its alliance with New Labour, helped push the British government to accept yet more privatisation and commercialisation. Its ads showed Andersen leading humanity to a radical future. One commercial opened with Andersen helping a Generation X-er get a net IPO up and running. Its eco-conscious hero rides a bike to work. He displays his feminine side by chatting with a pregnant co-worker. Kiddies on the school bus salute him. He doesn't wear a tie, and his staff don't give a fig for convention. They whizz across the office on skateboards or lounge at their desks munching pizza – chilling out until creativity moves them. In the background Iggy Pop's 'Lust for Life' hammers away.

In business schools, gurus and consultants said there was no need to regulate markets because revolutionary outsiders were breaking up the old corporate cartels. Gary Hamel, Professor of Strategic and International Management at the London Business School and Distinguished Research Fellow at Harvard Business School, fought off competition from dozens of equally frenzied boosters to earn the title 'guru of the dotcom decade' – an accolade which had executives clamouring to hear his descriptions of commercial apocalypse. In September 2000 he demonstrated to his own satisfaction that corporations were more likely to be the victims of globalisation than its masters:

> We now stand on the threshold of a new age – the age of revolution. It is going to be an age of upheaval, of tumult, of fortunes made and unmade at head-snapping speed. For change has changed. No longer does it move in a straight line. In the twenty-first century, change is discontinuous, abrupt, seditious . . . Global capital flows have become a raging torrent, eroding national economic sovereignty. The ubiquity of the Internet has rendered geography meaningless. Bare-knuckled capitalism has vanquished all competing ideologies and a tsunami of deregulation and privatisation has swept the globe. In the age of revolution, opportunities come and go at light speed – blink and you've missed a billion dollar bonanza. Never has incumbency been worth less. New winds are battering down the fortifications that once protected the status quo. Economic integration has blown open protected markets. Deregulation has destroyed comfortable monopolies. The Internet

has turned bricks and mortar into millstones. And venture capitalists pour millions of dollars into terrorist training camps for industry insurgents.'[3]

Corporations never looked less likely candidates for annihilation than in the 1990s. Just as revolutionary heroes and the once subversive dictates of cool were turned into the allies of business, so the cry 'The corporation is in danger!' was used to pretend that they struggled for life in a ferocious free market. They weren't components of quasi-monopolies or, in the case of Microsoft, an actual monopoly, but one bungled rebranding away from the gallows. Executives who saved them from the clear and present danger of the 'raging torrent' deserved every penny they earned. What would be the point of the US government taking anti-trust action against Microsoft or the British government breaking up the supermarket cartel (a more far-fetched thought, I readily concede) if terrorist insurgents were waiting to pounce on the smallest fault in the lumbering incumbents' business plans and do the breaking themselves? Shouldn't the public, too, turn away from safe securities or saving schemes and invest in the liberating companies of the future? What looks safe today may be valueless tomorrow. The insane valuations placed on Internet companies would be modest and becoming if investors could be persuaded that they were about to supplant the arthritic beasts of the old economy and sweep in profits from the four corners of the world.

Predictions that the Internet would unleash creative destruction of Hamel's kind were everywhere at the time. They are laughable now and should have been derided when they were made. The most successful Net companies sold either pornography or the opportunity to gamble. After them came the online retailers, which were usually established by existing supermarkets and department stores rather than 'insurgents'. The shops had found a new way to reach customers, but operated on low profit margins. Their Net arms were little more than the competitors of the catalogue companies which sent mail-order offers to farmers' wives in the sticks.

Take Amazon, one of the few Net companies to show a modest profit, eventually. It's handy to be able to order any book in print from its website, but any good bookshop should provide the same service. The possibilities for buying entertainment that Amazon and companies like it brought were a continuation of, rather than a decisive break with, the transformation brought by motion pictures, the telephone and phonograph in the late nineteenth and early twentieth centuries. Nothing the 'information revolution' delivered compared with earlier advances. Public sanitation in the 1880s did as much for public health as all the doctors in history. Electricity allowed clean manufacturing and an elimination of household drudgery via the washing machine and vacuum cleaner. The bicycle and car brought mobility. Only an idiot would say the Net changed nothing, but it couldn't compete with the light bulb or Model T. When the fit passed, the Internet was revealed as merely the next thing to do with a telephone line.[4]

Boring reflections on the real benefits of dotcom or telecom companies were as beside the point in the late 1990s as they were in the 1720s. As so often before, once the bubble fever caught, the damn thing took on a life of its own.

The bewilderment of the crash's victims lay in the cry I heard from many whose savings had shrunk, including Labour MPs who ought to have known better. They wanted to know how the brightest and best had presided over a disaster. It was unarguable that a large tranche of the cleverest graduates of the late 1990s went into finance or headed off to start up dotcom outfits. Wall Street and the City had their pick of MBAs, mathematicians and economists. Two economics dons – Andrew Oswald of the University of Warwick and Steve Machin of University College, London – found there were hardly any young British economists willing to teach the next generation. In 1998 only seventeen British students began studying for a PhD in economics, the essential qualification for an academic. The London School of Economics had no graduates beginning economics doctorates, an absence which raised severe Trade Descriptions Act problems. The government's economics service had to leave 30 per cent of its places unfilled. Able students were dismissing intellectual life and public service as beggarly occupations for no-hopers.[5]

A compensation for the entry of fine minds into stock picking ought to have been the presence of recruits with the intelligence to spot swindlers and catchpenny schemes. Surely they had the wit to know how to maintain the value of investors' savings? This touching belief showed how suspicion of speculation, part of the common sense of Western democracies after the Great Depression, was pushed to the margin in the 1990s. The financial press, the government, the Financial Services Authority and the Federal Reserve didn't know, or didn't say, that the last concern of a bubble market is the real value of investments.

They were proved to be wildly irresponsible, but at moments like the 1990s, being right is no defence, if the consensus is against you. Being right is the worst investment strategy you can follow. It is sane to be insane, profitable to be profligate. 'When the rest of the world is mad, we must imitate in some measure,' sighed the London banker John Martin at the height of the South Sea Bubble. (Martin's imitation of madness was too convincing. He didn't cash in his South Sea stock in time and lost everything.)[6]

Tony Dye was right from the start of the bubble. In 1995 he managed £50 billion for Phillips & Drew. The pension fund investments for ICI, Thames Water and many local authorities were in his hands, and he cut quite a figure in the City. His popularity evaporated because he had no faith in the dotcoms. An analyst from a City bank tried to get him to buy into a tech business. Dye looked at the bank's calculations and worked out it was claiming that the company would be accounting for 15 per cent of all the profits made in Britain in a few years. Dye phoned the bank and told it not to waste his time. He lowered his reputation further by saying 'pure greed or envy of new riches acquired by friends already playing the market suck

more and more people into the share-buying spree'. Such pro-
nouncements were bad for business. For presciently saying the
market was overvalued by trillions of dollars, Dye became a figure of fun. He was 'Dr Doom', said the *Guardian*; a 'laughing
stock', said *The Times*. His investments under-performed in the
market because he refused to touch bubble stocks whose values
were shooting up.

When the bubble burst, Phillips & Drew's funds outperformed
its rivals. Victory came too late for Dye. He resigned just before
his vindication. Although the mockers couldn't have been more
wrong in the long-term, in the short-term they won the prizes.
All that is necessary for shares to rise is for investors to pile in. If
a fund doesn't have Internet stocks, it can't sell on and make an
enormous profit. Traders don't have to believe that Net or telecom companies are truly valuable. They must just take the
money while the mania lasts. Of course, once the bubble bursts,
many investments are revealed to be valueless. But fund managers are judged in the short-term, and risk being fired it they
don't join the fun when prices are soaring and paper profits
being converted into hard currency. When the crash comes, all a
fund manager's colleagues are failures too, so no individual can
be blamed. As J. M. Keynes said, 'Worldly wisdom teaches that it
is better for reputation to fail conventionally than to succeed
unconventionally.' Stick with the crowd and you'll be OK.

The exploitation of the rationality of irrational herd
behaviour has been dignified with a financial theory: the
'Greater Fool Principle'. Success depends on an investor going
along with folly and buying hyped shares. The trick is to flog
them on to a greater fool just before the crash. The catch is that
no one knows when the crash will come. The potential calamity for society is that the longer a bubble is allowed to expand,
the worse the consequences will be when the crash does come,
as the world discovered after 1929 and Japan learned after its
roaring 1980s bull market fell apart and pushed the country
into apparently unending stagnation.

Keynes deployed an elegant image to illustrate how speculation had little to do with an informed understanding of a company's prospects:

> Professional investment may be likened to those newspaper competitions in which the competitors have to pick out the six prettiest faces from a hundred photographs, the prize being awarded to the competitor whose choice most nearly corresponds to the average preferences of the competitors as a whole; so that each competitor has to pick, not those faces which he himself finds prettiest, but those which he thinks likeliest to catch the fancy of the other competitors, all of whom are looking at the problem from the same point of view. It is not a case of choosing those which, to the best of one's judgment, are really the prettiest, nor even those which average opinion genuinely thinks the prettiest. We have reached the third degree where we devote our intelligences to anticipating what the average opinion expects the average opinion to be. And there are some, I believe, who practise the fourth, fifth and higher degrees.[7]

Or everyone does what they think everyone else will do. (After twenty years of watching journalism and the cultural industries, I should say in fairness that they outdo the City in their determination to follow this policy to the letter.)

Dye's Wall Street counterpart was Barton M. Biggs, the chairman of Morgan Stanley Asset Management. As the Dow and Nasdaq soared, he made heretical comparisons. The Internet was an interesting innovation, which might make money for a few, but clearly wasn't as important an invention as, for instance, air conditioning, which allowed people to work through the midday sun in the tropics and sub-tropics. The frenzy about the Net, which was sending the price of shares to 1929 levels and beyond, couldn't be justified. 'You've got stocks selling at absolutely unbelievable multiples of earnings and revenues,' he said in 1996.

> You've people setting up Internet pages to reinforce each other's convictions in these highly speculative stocks. Everybody's son wants to work for Morgan Stanley. Worthless brother-in-laws are starting hedge funds. In every market where it has happened – from the US to Japan to Malaysia to Hong Kong – it always ends in the same way.'[8]

The date of Biggs's warnings told against him. In 1996, the bubble had another four years of hot air in it. As greater and greater fools rushed in, the market ballooned. The longer the euphoria lasted (and the more damaging it became), the less attention was paid to sensible scepticism. Dye and Biggs were right. But, I repeat, it's no good being right unless you go public at one minute to midnight.

The Greater Fool Principle works in the most extreme cases. In 2002, the *Financial Times* and *Wall Street Journal* were shocked by the news that bankers could be swindlers. It wasn't brought by their reporters, but by the New York State's Attorney-General, Eliot Spitzer. He responded to the anguish of the greatest fools left with worthless Internet stock by investigating investment banks. They had an obvious conflict of interest. The banks' analysts were meant to give an independent view to investors of the merits of buying shares in this or that company. Their employers wanted to please the dotcom and telecom companies which paid them royally, and to attract new business by flattering potential customers. Henry Blodget of Merrill Lynch was an analyst who was treated as a cross between a film star and philosopher by the financial press. Nothing dampened his enthusiasm for Internet companies. Their shares must be bought, he said, because they were '(1) growing amazingly rapidly, and (2) threatening the status quo in multiple sectors of the economy'.[9] You were a fool not to pay any price because the prospect for profit stretched to the far horizon. Blodget was more circumspect in private. Spitzer examined Blodget's emails. Why, asked a friend of the analyst, was Merrill telling its clients to buy the stock of an Internet company called GoTo.com?

'What's so interesting about GoTo except banking fees?' he wrote under what he thought were the lobby terms of Wall Street insiders.

'Nothing,' replied Blodget.

Merrill wanted GoTo's business and if it told its duped investors to 'buy' GoTo shares, the grateful company would be encouraged to take its business to the bank. 'GoTo was a paradigm of what was wrong at Merrill Lynch,' Spitzer's spokesman Darren Dopp explained as the bank was forced to pay a $100 million fine. 'Not only did they use [positive] ratings to solicit investment banking business, they used negative ratings to punish those who took their business elsewhere.' The analysts, who were supposedly separated from Merrill's banking business by an iron curtain, knew perfectly well what was expected of them. One, Kirsten Campbell, complained to Blodget in 2000 about the pressure from management to make GoTo look like a share with 'amazingly rapid' growth potential. 'I don't want to be a whore for fucking management . . . We are losing people money and I don't like it. John and Mary Smith are losing their retirement because we don't want Todd [GoTo's chief financial officer] to be mad at us . . . The whole idea that we are independent from banking is a big lie.'

The job of the well-named Jack Grubman at Citigroup's investment arm, Salomon Smith Barney, was to fuel the excitement for telecom shares. Grubman had been freed to pump up the telecom market by Bill Clinton, who had deregulated it in 1996. In one private email, he admitted his bank supported 'pigs' in its superficially objective research briefings for customers because it wanted the pigs to bring their custom to Salomon's investment bankers. In another, Spitzer found Grubman complaining to a colleague that 'most of our banking clients [whose shares Citigroup was commending] are going to zero and you know I wanted to downgrade them months ago but got a huge push from banking. I wonder what use bankers are if all they can depend on to get business is analysts who recommend their business clients.'[10]

Citigroup stuck with the telecom company WorldCom to the end – $140 million in banking fees encouraged it to stay loyal. Although most of the attention was on the dotcoms, the telecom bubble was ten times greater, and when it burst the losses totalled around $1 trillion. The manias were connected. What powered the telecom bubble was the belief that there would be an insatiable demand for Net access from the billions aching to give money to dotcom entrepreneurs. Thirty-nine million miles of fibre-optic lines were laid in the US during the bubble – enough to circle the globe 1,566 times. Bernie Ebbers, World-Com's boss, bought up rivals to ensure that he would lead the 'bandwidth revolution'. Investors threw money at the company because the US Department of Commerce and every – and I mean every – Net pundit said it was an indisputable fact that 'Internet traffic was doubling every 100 days'. After the crash, it became embarrassingly clear that Internet traffic was toddling along at about one tenth of the rate the 'doubling every 100 days' figure implied. Shamed analysts tried to find the provenance of their favourite statistic. It had come from WorldCom.

By that time WorldCom was bust, and Ebbers had gone off with a $408m loan from the company. The dead telecom companies did leave a marvellous fibre-optic network behind, while the dotcoms left nothing. But as of September 2002, only 2.7 per cent of the fibre was being used. The rest was 'dark fibre', so called because it wasn't connected to homes or offices. Perhaps archaeologists will dig it up in a thousand years and try to work out what it was all for.

Grubman cheered on WorldCom, telling investors that Ebbers was a leader of 'vision and boldness'. He dismissed questions about his pumping of a stock in which Citigroup had an interest with one of the best quotes of the millennium: 'What used to be a conflict of interest is now a synergy.'

Exactly. The synergy broke down in April 2002, when Grubman was compelled to mention that he had a few reservations about WorldCom. A week later he resigned. WorldCom disappeared in June.

Cynics might think pure greed made the banks lie about the dotcoms and telecoms to the dupes who listened to their investment advice. But Spitzer discovered glorious emails which showed that Grubman didn't just lie to protect his $20 million salary: he did it for the kids. Like many an arriviste before him, Grubman found that wealth couldn't satisfy if it didn't bring status. The surest way to announce his elevation to the New York aristocracy was for his twins to be accepted by the 92nd Street Y kindergarten. Few social climbers could scale this summit. The nursery admitted the offspring of Woody Allen, Michael J. Fox and Sting, but had the social confidence to turn away Madonna's child. In the better districts of Manhattan, rejection was held to blight the prospects of two-year-olds for the rest of their days. To save the young from ruin, parents press-ganged family and friends to speed-dial the school when applications for places opened in September. It was usually impossible to get through. The lucky few who did hired consultants to coach children who were scarcely out of nappies for the entrance tests. The authors of *The Manhattan Family Guide to Private Schools* recognised that desperate measures were necessary. 'Do use pull if you have it,' they advised, before counselling against trying to bribe the admissions office.

Citigroup may not have taken their warning to heart. Sandy Weill, Citigroup's CEO, was a close friend of Mike Armstrong, the CEO of the AT&T telecom company. Weill sat on AT&T's board. Armstrong sat on Citigroup's board. In 1999 Grubman sent investors a rare cautionary briefing about AT&T shares and then hastily withdrew it. Weill later admitted that he had asked Grubman to take a fresh look at his rating, but denied he had pressured his employee to be nice about his friend. Spitzer found that Grubman had replied to the request from the boss by asking Weill to help him give the twins the start they needed at 92nd Street. Weill was engaged in a fight for control of Citigroup with his then co-chairman John Reed. He needed Armstrong's support in the boardroom if his office politicking was to succeed.

The following events occurred in quick succession. Grubman upgraded AT&T shares from a 'hold' to a 'strong buy'. AT&T gave Citigroup $45 million of underwriting business. Citigroup gave the nursery $1 million. The nursery admitted the Grubman twins. Reed was forced out of Citigroup. Grubman downgraded AT&T stock. And Spitzer found an email from Grubman to a friend in which he said: 'I used Sandy to get my kids into the 92nd Street Y pre-school (which is harder than Harvard) and Sandy needed Armstrong's vote on the board to nuke Reed in showdown. Once the coast was clear for both of us (i.e. Sandy clear victor and my kids confirmed) I went back to my normal self.'

Merrill and Citigroup were following standard banking practice. Bear Stearns, Goldman Sachs, Morgan Stanley, JP Morgan Chase, Lehman Brothers, UBS Warburg, Credit Suisse First Boston and Deutsche Bank were all fined for misleading investors .

Now suppose you had the services of a computer hacker in the late 1990s. Suppose you knew that in the private opinion of the most powerful banks on Wall Street and in the City dotcom and telecom shares were 'pieces of shit' and 'pigs'. Would you have used your inside knowledge and steered clear of the shares? Not necessarily if the markets for both were rising. The Greater Fool Principle would still have applied. If you bought and sold quickly, you would have had a large unearned profit.

Most who poured into the market weren't wised-up sceptics who capitalised on the idiocy of others, however, or the knowing players of Keynes's beauty contest. They were true believers in the grip of exultation and denial. What motivated them was the desire to get rich quick. Their desire was heightened and reinforced by the madness of crowds. Among the throngs were people who had got rich quick by believing in technological revolution. Their stories inspired and emboldened the rest. The 1990s were filled with suckers who didn't want an even break. They were ready to be defrauded; in a sense, they defrauded themselves.

The most cynical minds can degenerate in the bubble world. In 1710 Jonathan Swift looked on the new breed of dealers who gathered at Exchange Alley in the City.

> Through the contrivance and cunning of stock jobbers there hath been brought in such a complication of knavery and cozenage,

such a mystery of iniquity, and such an unintelligible jargon of terms to involve it in, as were never known in any other age or country in the world.

The collapse of the South Sea Company in 1720 made his outburst seem an understatement. The company had taken over Britain's national debt. It had no income apart from interest payments on the debt it received from the government it had bribed. As it never sent one ship to trade in the south seas, it could only have been a small success at best. Modesty did not become John Blunt, the company's avaricious director. Lush riches could be secured by inflating the share price. ''Twas his avowed maxim, a thousand times repeated, that the advancing by all means of the price of the stock, was the only way to promote the good of the company,' wrote the anonymous author of *The Secret History of the South Sea Company*, a contemporary account of the scandal. An explanation of the shares' intrinsic values must be avoided, continued Blunt, because 'people must not know what they do, which will make them all the more eager to come into our measures'.[11]

The people didn't disappoint Blunt. A frantic population tripped over its heels in the race for stock. Swift looked on with a jaundiced eye. He wrote to a friend: 'I have enquired of some that have come from London, what is the religion there? they tell me it is South Sea stock; what is the policy of England? the answer is the same; what is the trade? South Sea still; and what is the business? nothing but South Sea.' Swift nevertheless invested in South Sea stock. Shares rose from £100 to a peak of £1100 before they crashed – taking with them nearly every bank and a fair number of aristocrats and country gentlemen.

Isaac Newton got out early with a healthy profit, and declared that he could predict the motions of the heavens but not the madness of people. You can almost see him looking round the room to check there was a scribe with a quill to record his remark for future dictionaries of quotations. But the madness was too infectious for the great scientist to resist. The lure of profit within weeks – days! – pushed him to jump back in. He lost £20,000 and refused to allow the words 'South Sea' to be uttered in his presence for the rest of his life. As for the capital's ravaged economy and the humbler citizens who depended on it, a newspaper poet wrote:

> All things are hushed, as law itself were dead;
> Poor pensive Fleet Street droops its mournful head;
> The Strand's a desert grown; the town's undone;
> Some hang, some drown and some distracted run.[12]

The 1990s differed in one respect from the 1720s. The discipline of economics was invented in the interim, and its disciples were on hand to proide justifications for the millennial mania. The 'efficient market hypothesis' had dominated conventional economic thought since the 1970s. It asserted that bubbles weren't possible because investors were engaged in the scientific study of corporate earnings. This was an optimistic point of view. When the human race is engaged in the search for power or status, it variously exhibits unnecessary cruelty, fantastic expectations, inexplicable folly, heroism, altruism, camaraderie, bravado, surges of hope, panic attacks, pigheadedness, superstition, covetousness and spite. The search for love isn't always as different as it should be. When, however, we come to the search to find wealth, the most important task of many lives, humanity is meant to be rational. To simplify, the 'semi-strong' form of the efficient-markets hypothesis maintained that whatever stock markets decide was indisputably right. It was an updating of Adam Smith's belief that an 'invisible hand' guides apparently selfish transactions to promote common prosperity. However, it differed from Smith in an important particular: the prominent and beneficial role the hypothesis assigned to speculators. Markets were efficient because share prices reflected fundamental values, the theory ran. They incorporated all relevant information. Ignorant investors could briefly inflate the price of a stock. But then informed speculators intervened and pulled a share price back to its true level.

Supporters of market efficiency had to believe that the bubble wasn't a bubble and that scientific speculators had spotted that the fantastic prices for dotcom shares were reasonable.

Speculators were heroes. They increased the wealth of nations by identifying new ventures which needed funds and dug up the information which made markets efficient. They scrutinised the policies of politicians as well as companies and punished those who did not act efficiently in the market's interests – interests which turned out to be identical to the interests of everyone else. Hadn't George Soros saved Britain by pushing sterling out of the Exchange Rate Mechanism? Weren't the markets ensuring that the Third World found contentment by punishing governments which deviated from the enlightened guidance of the International Monetary Fund on the ludicrous grounds that their peoples were suffering?

The myth of the 'New Economy' had to be invented. It was needed to span the chasm between the scientific markets of efficient theory and the riotous markets of speculative practice. Looking at the previous profit performance of dotcom and telecom companies wasn't 'helpful', because most of the dotcoms hadn't made a profit. New Economy theorists therefore argued that profits were a liability – they showed that a company wasn't investing enough. The essential task was to spend money to grab market share. In the end, the winners would take all, and those who had backed the winners would make a killing.

Without profit figures to guide them, New Economists looked at the size of dotcom turnovers, which were meant to indicate their potential to become global giants. That didn't work either. In the end everyone gave up trying to find evidence. They relied on the assertion that the efficient market was always right. The Internet was heralding an astonishing future of new marketing opportunities and spectacular increases in productivity. George Gilder, a former speech writer to Ronald Reagan and a noisy booster of Net shares, wrote in 2001 that the New Economy, 'far from being over-hyped, is still pitifully under-appreciated.' (Anyone who took him at his word and bought the stocks he recommended would have lost a fortune.) On CNBC, a gormless business channel, and in the *Wall Street Journal*, a gormless newspaper, pundits insisted that the Dow share index would rise from 10,000 to 36,000 or 50,000.

Their cries might have been ignored. Alan Greenspan, however, was unignorable. After initially warning of 'irrational exuberance' in the markets – but doing nothing to restrain it – the Chairman of the Federal Reserve recanted and told Congress that the new computing power had created 'exceptional' times – a once- or twice-in-a-century phenomenon that will 'carry productivity trends nationally and globally to a new higher track'. He refused to raise interest rates and stood back as foreign money poured into the American markets. Greenspan was the object of devotion by sycophants who resembled cultists. His word was enough. Virtually all Tony Blair's and Gordon Brown's policies came from America. Only Bill Clinton meant more to them than Greenspan. In 2002 – that is, after the explosion of the bubble – New Labour awarded Greenspan a knighthood. The citation read that the gong was for his 'contribution to global economic stability'.

Greenspan's endorsement meant that all the ingredients for capitalist catastrophe were boiling and blending nicely. Markets were cool and liberatory. Their critics were élitists who presumed to know better than the millions of ordinary people who bought shares online or founded Net businesses. There had been genuine growth and genuine prosperity after the fall of the Berlin Wall, although admittedly most of the benefits had been enjoyed by the rich. There was also real technological innovation, and its silicon chips doubled well as gambling chips. The perverse incentives and herd passions of the market ensured that shares would rise to death-inviting heights. The banks had every interest in keeping them up there. The theorists of efficient markets and the New Economy were on hand to justify the unjustifiable. There was no need to look back to 1929 or 1720. History was at an end, as Francis Fukuyama said.

Capitalism and democracy had triumphed and the world would turn no more.

Professor Fukuyama's reports of history's death were premature. The old girl wasn't in her grave just yet. She was preparing to reassert herself with a vengeance.

All that was needed to make the necessary conditions for a smash-up sufficient was a final touch. In *Devil Take The Hindmost*, his history of crashes from the Dutch tulip-mania on, Edward Chancellor writes that if a crisis is to develop 'it is essential that speculation should be unchecked by political interference'. A 'common feature' of all manias from the seventeenth century to the twentieth is 'a combination of laissez-faire and political corruption'.[13]

Squaring politicians is essential because politicians have the power. The anti-capitalist movement is at its most blinkered when it claims that corporations are now stronger than governments. However novel the ability of companies to shift money and jobs around the world is, and however restrictive the limits on the autonomy of national governments have become, corporations remain weak. When all is said and done, they are hierarchical associations for the production of profit. They can't raise armies or levy taxes or enact legislation. Governments can do all three, and can turn nasty if they have the inclination. They can increase interest rates, tax share dealings, restrict the buying of shares with borrowed money, bring to justice the crooks who infest all bull markets, send the Fraud Squad into investment banks, ban companies from going public on stock markets until they have a proven record of making profits, insist that auditors owe a duty of care to workers and suppliers and – although this would take a revolution – require companies to have on their boards elected workers' representatives who have a greater concern for the long-term health of a business than execs protected by seven-figure severance packages.

Above all, politicians can warn. In his study of how the Great Crash of 1929 was preceded by the delusion that a 'new era' of invention and productivity guaranteed perpetual prosperity, J. K. Galbraith wrote:

> Actually, not even new legislation, or the threat of it, was needed. In 1929, a robust denunciation of speculators and speculation by someone in high authority and a warning that the market was too high would almost certainly have broken the spell. It would have brought some people back from the world of make-believe. Those who were planning to stay in the market as long as possible but still get out (or go short) in time would have got out or gone short. Their occupational nervousness could readily have been translated into an acute desire to sell. Once the selling started, some more vigorously voiced pessimism could easily have kept it going.

Contrary to both the opponents and supporters of globalisation, business needs governments. Politicians must be persuaded to privatise and abandon restrictive regulations; to keep their noses out of the private affairs of conglomerates. They must be made to believe that the market is the answer.

Enron wasn't unique in suborning politicians. It was simply the best. With bipartisan permissiveness it seduced Republicans and Democrats in Washington, Tories and Blairites in London and secularists and sectarians in New Delhi. After its collapse, most of the ventures for which *Fortune* and the *Financial Times* heaped prizes on its executives were revealed to be whited sepulchres. But in the political influence-peddling market Enron's status as a world-leader has remained unchallenged. Its reputation grows with each revelation. Nobody did it better.

NINE

Bribed and Unbribed

To Kenneth Lay, controls on business were worse than burdens: they were blasphemies. 'I believe in God and I believe in the free market,' the Enron chairman told the San Diego *Union-Tribune* in 2001, the year his company broke all fraud records. When he died God would 'look at the way I treated people, the opportunities I've created for people [and the] standards of living that have been impacted for the better', and admit him to heaven. Jesus had promised as much. He had walked among men because 'he wanted people to have the freedom to make choices'.[1]

Lay's expectation of an eternal share option for CEOs may yet prove bogus. But no one could doubt the strength of his zeal for capitalism. A reporter from the *Economist* noticed it at a meeting of energy executives in London in 1999. Enron's market capitalisation had increased nine-fold in a decade, observed a member of the audience – 'How will you top that?' 'We'll do it again,' was the defiant reply. As Lay received the applause of true believers, he turned to an aide and said, 'Some of these guys finally seem to get it.' Long before Enron imploded, the *Economist*'s journalist wrote: 'Spend long enough around top Enron people and you feel you are in the midst of some sort of evangelical cult. Mr Lay with his "passion for markets" is the cult's guru. His disciples are Enron's managers, an intelligent, aggressive group of young professionals all of whom "get it". The "it" is the rise of market forces.'

There are many ways of telling the Enron story, and I'm sure all of them will be tried as books on the corporation flood out. For me the best way to understand the bankrupting of Enron and the messianic capitalism of the 1990s is to chart how the corporate corruption of public life accompanied the religious devotion to markets. 'Corruption' usually means the granting of a favour in return for a cash bribe. With parties spending more and more money on persuading fewer and fewer people to vote, instances of such straight bribery are bound to increase. But corruption isn't always as simple as the saloon-bar maxim 'politicians are all in it for themselves' insists. The instruction to 'follow the money' is often the Watergate scandal's silliest piece of cod-wisdom; the corruption of the mind can be more important than the corruption of the pocket. Many of the most dangerous policies and disastrous initiatives are completely lawful, but their legality doesn't make them less disastrous. Bribed politicians and officials must live with the slight risk of being caught and punished. Most of the millennial disasters were organised by men and women who weren't punished because they weren't breaking the law. The American saying 'the scandal isn't what's illegal: the scandal's what's legal' – an updating of Bertolt Brecht's 'better to be a bank owner than a bank robber' – recognises that the biggest crooks aren't crooks in the eyes of the law.

With the exception of the brief and quickly reversed stock-market panic of 1987, Wall Street rose continuously from 1982 to 2000. The long bull market impressed all contenders for power. No serious political force in Britain or America was opposed to the surge in privatisation or deregulation. What was new about New Labour and New Democrat politicians was their embrace of the distant past. The alleged progressives took politics back to the pre-social democratic or, in America's case, pre-Roosevelt era as they abandoned their residual suspicion of the destructive power of capitalism. Not all of them believed in God, but every last one of them believed in the market. Changing this deep ideology is a far more formidable task than persuading the cops to get out of the canteen and investigate bribery and corruption, although that would be a start. It will require an intellectual revolution.

Left to its own devices, the political class will privatise and deregulate without a cheque being sent to a Swiss bank account. Most politicians and bureaucrats would have bent over backwards for Enron without asking for a penny. Enron took no chances. Just to be on the safe side, it sprayed money to the world's élite like a sprinkler feeding a lush lawn.

Most histories of the corporation begin by saying how Enron started as a boring company, formed by a merger of two energy businesses in 1985. It got on with running 40,000 miles of pipeline from its headquarters in Houston, Texas, until hubris infected its managers. They embraced the tenets of the New Economy and brought the most arcane Wall Street dealing practices to the energy market. 'We are participating in the New Economy and the rules have changed dramatically,' Enron said in its 2000 annual report. 'What you own is not as important as what you know. Hard-wired businesses, such as energy and communications, have turned into knowledge-based industries that place a premium on creativity.' Nemesis followed this witless futurism with classical inevitability. Not owning enough to cover the debts assumed an old-fashioned importance when the world at last realised that the only creativity was in the accounts department.

The moral that virtue lay in the dull but honest work of generating and supplying power is satisfying. Unfortunately, it can't be drawn. For the past 25 years, Anglo-Saxon business has held that the first duty of a company is to provide 'share-holder value'. Enron showed that shareholder value led to valueless shares. The corporation was a machine for inflating its share price and its executives' share options by whatever legal or illegal means were necessary. It was as willing to milk the old economy as the new. Investors who punished the smallest failure to meet profit expectations demanded no less. The money and lobbyists Enron threw at the Blair government were essential elements in its campaign to receive permission to build gas-fired power stations. Neither business was at the cutting-edge of technological change. Enron spent millions on 'educating' Indian politicians on the virtues of the free market. India then signed the largest, and worst, deal in its independent history to build a boring old power station. From California to Mozambique, Enron fought to win any contract it could report as a profit in its next quarterly financial statement, however disastrous the investments looked in the long run. The logic of shareholder capitalism is that short-term returns must be maximised at all times and regardless of the consequences. No investor worries about how and in which sector of the economy profits are made or cares about the long-term prospects of a deal.

Lay was the son of a Baptist preacher. He was Enron's public face, the schmoozer who charmed the politicians and analysts. While Lay was all smiles, Jeff Skilling, his deputy, was a hard-faced bully. John LeBoutillier, one of his teachers at the Harvard Business School, remembered that when he asked the young Skilling what he would do if a product he was selling was killing the customers, Skilling replied: 'I'd keep making and selling the product. My job as a businessman is to be a profit centre and to maximise return to shareholders. It's the government's job to step in if a product is dangerous.'[2] His attitude towards his subordinates was encapsulated in advice he gave fellow executives at an energy industry strategy conference in 1997. 'You must cut costs ruthlessly by 50 to 60 per cent,' he roared. 'Depopulate. Get rid of people. They gum up the works.'

Brutal words, but honest in their way. The contemporary business talks of its staff being its 'greatest asset', but employees are its greatest liability. Their wage bill is often the corporation's greatest cost. Although it is near to impossible for workers to strike in Britain and America, they can imitate the subjects of the former Soviet Union and go on internal strike. They can refuse to be motivated. They can be surly when they are passed over for promotion. They can presume to know better than managers whose promotions they regard as rewards for sycophancy. They can gossip, mock and email friends and lovers on company time. They can arrive late with hangovers and leave early to acquire hangovers. It is a regrettable fact that a large proportion of humanity is unfit 'to meet the challenge' of contemporary business. If contemporary business could do without them, it would.

Skilling's way round the people problem was the Peer Review Committee, a quasi-Maoist institution which fermented poisonous office politics at Enron's Houston headquarters. What employees called 'rank and yank' or 'bag 'em and tag 'em' was a personnel tool wielded by one-fifth of US companies.[3] At Enron, 5 per cent of employees were identified as 'superior' and placed in Level One. Thirty per cent were 'excellent', 30 per cent were 'strong' and 20 per cent were 'satisfactory'. The last 15 per cent were in the 'needs improvement' category and placed in the lowest level: Level Five. The rejects were given a desk and a phone and told to find a new job in the corporation. Climbing back up the ladder was all but impossible, and most of the yanked accepted a pay-off.

The rankings bred cronyism and vendettas. An employee selected five people to provide 'feedback' on his or her performance. If they were sensible, they also found a sugar daddy in the senior management who would watch their backs. Deals were struck and mutually advantageous promises given and received. Unfortunately for the complacent, the employee couldn't stop crueller colleagues giving their two-penny worth. If others loathed him, they were encouraged to denigrate. If they had nothing against him, they still had an incentive to go for him on the precautionary principle that there would be one less space in the corporate dustbin if their colleague was pushed down into Level Five.

The result was war to the knife. 'It was a pit of vipers,' said one employee. 'You can't believe how brutal that process could be. You had people attacking other people's integrity, morality and values.' A second said that his colleagues would find the files detailing rivals' deals and play about with the numbers until profits became losses. 'Because of the complexity of the math, it could take you weeks to figure out what had been changed, and by that time your deal was shot down or you were fired.'[4]

The prizes for clambering over the bodies of the slain were extravagant. Graduates fresh out of business school were promised bonuses of $1 million if they did what they were told. 'I remember one trader going crazy because his bonus was only $500,000,' a former Enron employee told the Houston *Chronicle*. 'He was cursing and screaming and throwing things at his desk. He thought because he was so brilliant, they should be paying him a lot more.' The rewards and the punishments encouraged fraud. If you went along with the fiddles of the management and their 'independent' auditors from Arthur Andersen, bonuses flowed. If you spoke out, you risked being yanked.

The internal politics of corporations may seem a minor matter, of concern only to a few thousand rather greedy employees. But frauds at Enron, WorldCom and companies like it redirected and deepened the crisis caused by the bursting of the dot-com and telecom bubbles. The fall of a ramped-up market had already been accelerated by the attacks of 11 September. The discovery of lavish white-collar crime kicked it down further. 'Enronitis' intensified the pounding of pensions and endowments. The disease was the fear that other corporations were as crooked. In many cases the allegation was scurrilous. The libelled firms were profligate, incompetent, over-valued and over-exposed. To call them criminal was outrageous. But the truth matters no more in a bust than in a boom. If the herd assumes the worst, the worst is what it gets. (Or, to restage Keynes's beauty contest, if the herd assumes that the herd assumes the worst, then the worst is what it gets and so on to the third, fourth and fifth degrees.) The apparently parochial policies of Enron aided and abetted the robbery of the wider world.

Enron was fêted because it brought the techniques Wall Street and the City financiers had developed for share trading to hundreds of commodities. Its gas bank offered stability to gas producers and suppliers in a deregulated market. Call and put options, swaps and other derivatives allowed gas producers and suppliers to pay for an option to sell or buy gas at a fixed point in the future. It was a useful service because it allowed business to plan ahead, but it was also a risky undertaking. If Enron didn't cover its commitment to, for instance, sell to a hospital a fixed amount of gas at a fixed price in six months then it would be in the red on the deal.

Enron marched out of energy and into new markets. Gas consumption is dependent on the weather. For a premium, Enron sold weather derivatives which protected against a wet summer hitting tourism or farming, or a warm winter reducing demand for power. As with gas and the weather, so with electricity, pulp, paper, oil, coal, paper and metals. In all, Enron offered deals in 1800 products and thirteen currencies. 'We made the gas market in the United States what it is today,' said Robert Hermann, an Enron lawyer. 'We decided we could do the same thing with electricity, and we were well on our way to doing it. Then we thought we could do it with anything. We had people who thought they could sell hairballs if they could find the buyers.'[5] To make Enron spankingly modern, deals were online. Buyer and seller could log on and trade. 'The net changes everything,' Skilling enthused. It was pushing the traditional corporation into an era of 'disintegration'. Deregulation and market forces would force companies to break up into hundreds of niche players. Enron would 'wire those firms back together cheaply and temporarily' through its online markets.

Perhaps you can begin to see why Enron caused such a fluttering in the hearts of the financial 'community'. The derivatives it offered were the inventions of banks and brokers. But instead of selling options on shares, it created markets where none had existed before. As it produced standardised contracts which could themselves be traded on by their owners, you might say that it extended the realm of money by creating new currencies. Lay and Skilling were noisy members of the free-market consensus which saw a world where stock-market solutions could hedge against every risk to business and, indeed, the planet. Among the hundreds of markets Enron entered was the market for trading permits in the production of greenhouse gases.

The potential for growth was beyond the imagination of the plodding mind. Of the $65.5 billion in assets Enron claimed in 2000, nearly $21 billion were financial derivatives. In the 2000 annual report Lay and Skilling said that when they put together the developed world's wholesale gas, power, energy services and broadband markets they provisionally estimated a '$3.9 trillion opportunity for Enron', and that estimate 'just scratched the surface'.

Enron was to control the world's energy not just by owning power stations but by controlling the markets in which power was traded. It sold the same services as a Wall Street investment house, but Enron always took care to avoid regulation. It wouldn't go near the share and banking markets which were regulated by the American Securities and Exchange Commission. It ensured 'big government' didn't apply the same standards to derivatives contracts in the energy market it hoped to dominate by buying big government with small change.

Enron's oldest friends in politics were a charming couple: Senator Phil Gramm, a Texan Republican, and his wife Wendy, who served as chairwoman of the Commodity Futures Trading Commission from 1988 to 1993. When Bill Clinton won the US Presidency in November 1992, Mrs Gramm was a lame duck. She and everyone else knew she was a political appointee whose job would go to one of Clinton's friends when he divided the spoils of his victory in January 1993. On 16 November 1992 Enron asked her to remove energy derivative contracts and swaps from government oversight. Although Enron was only a medium-sized company at the time, the name might have rung a bell in Mrs Gramm's head. Enron had given $34,100 to Mr Gramm's campaigns. She had a conflict of interest. To make matters worse for Enron, the commission normally spent a year examining technical and legal complexities before deciding whether changes to the rules were in the public interest. The claims of propriety and good government required her to pass the decision to her successor. Mrs Gramm ignored both. She rammed through Enron's waiver in less than two months. Two of the five seats on the commission were vacant at the time. The three sitting members were all Republicans. One, Sheila Bair, argued against Enron, saying that a 'dangerous precedent' was being set. Her protests did no good. Wendy Gramm insisted that Enron and other suppliers of energy derivatives must be removed from US government oversight in all circumstances. She ruled that even contracts 'designed to defraud and mislead' should be spared from regulation. Glen English, a US Congressman who kept an eye on the markets, said in May 1993 that she 'had opened the door to serious fraud. In the eighteen years I've been in Congress, this is the most irresponsible decision I've come across.'[6]

Six days after giving Enron *carte blanche* Mrs Gramm left public service. Five weeks later, she joined the Enron board. Lay described attempts by his critics to find connections between her private affluence and public squalor as 'convoluted'. Mrs Gramm said her decision to deregulate futures contracts had nothing to do with Enron's contributions to her husband's campaign. Enron's revenues from futures contracts went from $4.7 billion to $6.1 billion in 1993. Mrs Gramm received about $1 million from Enron between 1993 and 2001, a poor payment in the circumstances.[7] Senator Gramm's remuneration was as paltry. His campaigns received $97,350 between 1989 and 2001. Again it is the stinginess of the tip which shocks.

Enron took on risk as it offered options to protect others from risk. On every deal it needed to offset the risk that, say, it hadn't miscalculated the future price of gas. It was also borrowing heavily to fund its very Old Economy power stations. If the costs of a new station overran, its profit would be hit and share price (and bonuses for executives) would take a pounding. Enron's business was horribly dangerous, but for almost a decade no one noticed because the magic of accountancy made the risk vanish into thin air.

Traditional accounting procedures didn't allow profits to be booked until profits had been banked. If a company owned an office block, its cost as an asset on the books was the price the company paid for it. The property market might have gone through the roof, but the company either wouldn't be able to recognise the increase in value until the asset was sold, or would be compelled to log the paper profit in a special account plastered with health warnings.

Conservative accounting procedures are disheartening in a bubble. The paper value of companies' and individuals' assets is soaring, but the bean-counters refuse to acknowledge the fabulous growth. A new way of counting was needed in the New Economy, and 'mark-to-market' accounting was invented to turn paper fortunes into gold. Accountants reassessed the value of assets regularly by marking them against a rising market. Changes in the market value were reported to profit-hungry shareholders in balance sheets and income statements.

Mark-to-market accounting isn't villainous in itself. An investment fund will measure the value of the shares it owns at the end of a day's trading, not the price it paid for them weeks or months before. It's a reasonable exercise as long as no one takes the results too seriously and thinks that the profits are in the bank. As with shares, so with housing. In Britain and America the stock-market bubble was followed by a consumer boom fuelled by a property bubble. As British house prices rose by between 25 and 30 per cent in 2002, despite a stagnant economy, owners borrowed against the market 'value' of their homes. Both countries held off a slump with a wild spending splurge based on mark-to-market accounting. If borrowers had been told that the value of their homes wasn't the price of comparable properties they saw in estate agents' windows, but what they paid for them five, ten or twenty years ago, no one in my part of London would know what to talk about at dinner parties. Mark-to-market accounting can seem innocuous. But even with simple assets, there are dangers. Anyone who believed that the mark-to-market market value of endowments or pensions was fixed in 2000 should have learned better by now. The same lesson may be learned by those who have borrowed against the mark-to-market value of their property because they thought 'my house is earning more than I am'.

Traditionalists aren't always wrong, in short. Accountants who wouldn't let profits be booked until they had been received were following two sensible maxims: no one can see the future; and unrealised value is no value at all.

Shares and houses are easy to mark against the market. They can be checked against the FTSE 100 and estate agents' prices. Assigning a market value to long-term corporate contracts is wide open to fraud because there is often no market to judge the contract against. If you dispense with the conservative insistence on counting money only when it is received, you allow bent companies and fee-hungry auditors to make it up as they go along. The American authorities knew that mark-to-market accounting allowed virtual profits, but did nothing about it. In 2001 the US Financial Accounting Standards Board organised a conference at which the audience was shown how the value of a power contract could bounce from anywhere between $40 million and $153 million depending on what accounting assumptions were used. The obvious step would have been for the government to intervene to protect the public. But the success of free-market ideology had been total. Governments couldn't intervene and shouldn't intervene, and all Tim Lucas, a regulator from the accounting board, could manage was to throw up his hands and cry: 'There's no way to do it!'[8]

Many who worked at Enron remembered the day when they found out that Arthur Andersen, Enron's auditors, was allowing a racket to proceed unchecked. Brian Cruver, a bright young recruit, was told of the rottenness in the state of Enron by a colleague who, if not the ghost of Hamlet's father, was white-faced and red-eyed and wholly without illusion. He explained that all deals had to be submitted to Enron's Risk Assessment Department. The office belied its prudent title by hiking up the projected profits. The value of deals for accounting purposes was nearly always higher than the estimates from the staff who had done the trades believed possible.

> 'Where does the gap between the two figures come from?' [asked the unworldly Cruver.]
>
> 'From anywhere and everywhere they can get it . . . economic assumptions, price curves, or just out of thin air. They usually aren't trying to come up with the real value of the deal; they are trying to make their individual bonus targets . . . No one is going to resist these guys when their bonuses – and the Enron stock price – are riding on it. They justify it as working for the shareholder; you know, increasing shareholder wealth.' He paused to catch his breath. 'If I had a dime for each time someone chewed my ass to push an overvalued deal through . . . I mean, I've gotten phone calls like bleep bleep bleep Skilling bleep bleep bleep Skilling. Everything that happens in Enron is driven by two things: the PRC process [the rankers and yankers in the Peer Review Committees] and earnings per share.'

Cruver paused himself and mulled over what he had heard. 'What Middleton dumped on me that day,' he recalled,

> was the systemic reality of the magnificent Enron – that if people wanted to survive the PRC process and meet their personal bonus targets, then they often needed to inflate the deal value . . . With inflated deal value, they could deliver bigger earnings to senior management who in turn would deliver them to Wall Street and investors.[9]

Enron was a Ponzi scheme: a pyramid-selling swindle which required it to pay old investors with the money from new investors and run faster and faster just to keep still. As long as it could announce new business and book untested promises of profit, its shares would carry on rising and the losses on inflated deals could be hidden away in offshore accounts. But should the flow of deals slow, the losses would bring the pyramid down.

Cynthia Harkness, an Enron lawyer, had the facts of life explained to her in her first week. She was introduced to mark-to-market accounting by the company's Chief Financial Officer, Andrew Fastow. He told her that when Enron made a deal it declared all the profits years before it received them because that made the company look good and sent the share price sky-high. Harkness heard him out and then checked she had understood him correctly:

> 'Andy, it seems to me that if you do a ten-year deal and suck all the earnings out in one year, you will then have to keep the profit coming in through years four, five, six and all the way to ten by doing more of these deals. How are you going to do that if the market changes? Book more deals?'
>
> 'Yes, you have to keep doing more of these deals each year,' said Fastow.[10]

Booking more deals became progressively more difficult for Enron, and its executives persuaded Arthur Andersen to allow them to use ever more inventive accounting tricks to make the real state of the company vanish. 'Special-purpose vehicles' (SPVs) were designed to sweep loss-making contracts from Ernon's published accounts and create profits out of thin air.

Enron was borrowing heavily but didn't want the debt to depress its share price and credit ratings by appearing in the books. It parked the debt and risky investments in the special vehicles, whose liabilities weren't included in the Enron accounts. In theory, the vehicles weren't formally owned or controlled by Enron – they would be illegal if they were. But no one was checking, and Fastow was allowed to put his own money into partnerships which he effectively controlled. He was responsible for Enron's finances while at the same time negotiating with Enron on behalf of the special purpose vehicles. The negotiation was with himself and he was taking a cut from both sides. As well as being paid by Enron, Fastow and several colleagues were making money from the partnerships.

Lord Wakeham, the former Conservative energy minister,

was a member of the Enron board who sat on the company's audit committee. Neither he nor his colleagues saw anything wrong with the vehicles. Nor did the banks. Merrill Lynch, Credit Suisse First Boston and others which were hyping dot-com companies they knew to be 'pigs' went along with Fastow and Lay because they wanted Enron's business and weren't prepared to upset a customer by asking too many questions. The partnerships allowed Enron and Andersen to pull all kinds of stunts. Enron shares were issued to the SPVs and their value increased as the share price rose. This seemed a good scam when Enron's share price was shooting up. The trouble came when the share price started to fall and took the partnerships down with it. Bank loans to the special vehicles, meanwhile, were passed on to Enron and presented to the public as income rather than debt.

Hundreds of American politicians had an incentive to let Enron have its way. Enron's campaign contributions went from a trickle to a torrent in the 1990s. When the cash supplied from energy companies to candidates running in 1990 campaigns for Congress and the governorships of US states was added up, Enron was nowhere – it couldn't make the Top 20 of corporate donors. By the 1992 elections, Enron had broken into the charts at Number 18. It gave $300,000 or so to members of Congress. As the company's revenue increased from $13 billion in 1996 to $100 billion in 2000, so did Enron's welfare payments to the political class. All in all, Enron gave $6 million to national politicians in the 1990s, $2 million of which was spent on the 2000 presidential and congressional elections. Seventy-one US Senators and 187 members of the House of Representatives received Enron money.[11]

The Bush family must have regarded Lay as a kind of friendly uncle so generously did he shower the parents, children and all their friends with presents. When George Bush Snr ran unsuccessfully for a second term against Bill Clinton in 1992, he asked Lay to head the Host Committee for the Republican National Convention in Houston. Lay agreed, because, 'as an industry, we've pretty much gotten what we felt we wanted ten or fifteen years ago' from Bush.[12]

Lay found work for former members of Bush Snr's court. James Baker, Bush's Secretary of State during the Gulf War of 1991, was taken on by Enron to lobby the Kuwaiti government Bush's administration had saved from Saddam Hussein. Just after he joined the corporation, Baker flew to Kuwait with the recently deposed Bush to renew old friendships. Seymour Hersch of *The New Yorker* interviewed General Norman Schwartzkopf, who had commanded the American advance. The general responded with honourable contempt to the idea that he might imitate Baker. 'In the Arab world, your position in government may get you through the door, but it's the personal relationship that gets you the contract. American men and women were willing to die in Kuwait. Why should I profit from their sacrifice?'

When George Bush Jnr ran for governor of Texas, Lay and other Enron executives worked for his campaign and gave it $146,500. After Bush won, Lay lobbied the governor to restrict Americans' rights to sue corporations. Governor Bush agreed to 'reforms' which capped punitive damages for companies causing reckless injury or death, diluted the Texan Deceptive Trade Practices Act and prohibited Texan cities from suing gun makers and sellers. Strangely, the 'reforms' applied only to consumers. They did not limit the rights of corporations to sue business competitors for commercial losses. Stranger still was Enron's effort to outlaw actions against accountants who swore blind that fraudulent accounts were honest.[13]

When Bush Jnr stood for president in 2000, Lay was one of the first members of Bush's 'Pioneers', a select group whose volunteers pledged $100,000 a head to the cause. Enron put its private planes at the Bush campaign's disposal, and gave it $1.1 million. In the interval between Bush's victory and his inauguration, Lay was among three dozen corporate backers Bush invited to an opulent Houston hotel as he waited to be sworn in. The President-elect and the most overpaid executives in

America agreed that their country faced disaster unless the taxes on rich men such as themselves were cut yet further. Lay must have felt an avuncular pride as he saw Bush give White House jobs to former Enron alumni.

At about the time Bush was starting work in the White House, the lights were going out in California. The state, whose $1.4 trillion economy is the tenth largest in the world, the state which claims to show the way to the future with its film and high-technology industries, the state which, really quite famously, relies on electricity, was hit by Third-World power cuts.

In the 1990s the state government of California did what all governments were meant to do and deregulated power. The old utility monopolies, which had generated their own electricity and sold it at regulated prices, were broken up. They were instructed to sell their power plants and buy electricity on the open market. Enron and its competitors realised they could hold the free market captive. They let their power plants stand idle and withheld electricity until the price peaked. In the summer of 2000 prices were five times higher than in the summer of 1999. The utilities were heading for bankruptcy. They had to buy, but weren't allowed to pass the ramped cost to consumers. In 1999 California's wholesale power bill was $7 billion. In just one month in 2000 – June – it was $3.6 billion. As the bill became unpayable, the blackouts increased. Enron, which made $1.8 billion from the crisis, developed strategies with schoolboy nicknames such as 'Death Star', 'Fat Boy' and 'Red Congo' to milk the state. Enron would overload transmission lines and get paid for relieving the congestion it had caused. Tim Belden, the head of Enron's West Coast trading arm, pleaded guilty to fraud charges in 2002, and told how Enron had developed a dodge called 'the ricochet'. It would generate power in California where prices were capped, move it out of the state, and then send it back with a huge mark-up.

'I probably shouldn't say this,' a grinning Skilling told a conference of energy executives in Las Vegas. 'But what's the difference between California and the *Titanic*? At least the lights were on when the *Titanic* went down.'[14]

California was following the privatising example which had been pioneered in the Britain of the 1980s. Enron was there at the high-noon of Thatcherism. In 1989 it broke out of America by lobbying the Conservative energy secretary, John Wakeham, to allow it to build what was then the world's largest combined heat and power station at Grangetown, near Middlesbrough. Enron seemed to be pushing at an open door. The Tories were determined to finish off the industrial power of the miners, which had already been crippled by Arthur Scargill's disastrous strike. The 'dash for gas' would deliver the fatal blow. The miners, whose labour had sustained Britain for centuries, were to be thrown on the slag heap. Wakeham eased the passage of the deal and brushed aside objections. As we saw, when he left government he belatedly metamorphosed into a British Wendy Gramm. He received a place on the Enron board which, just before Enron fell, entitled him to £80,000 a year plus £4,000 a month in consultancy fees.

Enron's British division remained, however, in a dangerously exposed position. It appeared to have made an enemy of the Labour opposition which had sprung to the defence of the mining communities which had stuck with the party in good times and bad. Labour promised to revive coal by imposing a moratorium on gas-fired power stations. As the 1990s wore on and a Conservative defeat became a certainty, Arthur Andersen and Enron found it made good commercial sense to get to know an opposition which had gone from Labour to New Labour.

Enron moved on from Britain to establish plants on every continent. The mother of all deals was the Dabhol power plant on the coast of the Arabian sea near Bombay. A series of superlatives were attached to the venture. Dabhol was the largest electricity generating plant in the world and the biggest foreign investment in Indian history. Enron achieved another first. It compelled Human Rights Watch and Amnesty International to issue reports about human rights abuses by a corporation rather than a government for the first time in their histories.

In 1992 India announced that it was liberalising its economy. The state government of Maharashtra took New Delhi at its word, and began negotiations with Enron. It took Enron only three weeks between May and June 1992 to agree a 'memorandum of understanding' with the liberalising Indian authorities on how to bring privatised power to Bombay and its hinterland. Everything about the deal stank. The World Bank said the Indians hadn't provided 'an overall economic justification of this project'. It refused to supply loans because 'the conduct of the negotiations show the sole objective was to see that Enron was not displeased – it is as if Enron was doing a favour . . . The entire negotiation with Enron is an example of how not to negotiate.'

Indians were required to pay a fixed charge for electricity, even if they didn't need it. The Indian Central Electricity Generating Board was staggered by the financial implications. Enron, which was to own 80 per cent of Dabhol, and its partners were to invest $3 billion. The Maharashtra state government agreed to pay them in return $1.3 billion a year for twenty years, or $26 billion. The price was provisional. The cost could go up if fuel prices increased. To make the deal sweeter, Enron was to receive its billions in US dollars, not rupees. Enron would be protected if the Indian currency fell against the dollar – which it usually did.[15]

The Hinduja brothers' enemies in the sectarian BJP were dead against Enron. As were Shiv Sena, the BJP's partners in the Bombay government and a more dangerous and thuggish group. Both parties condemned the agreement between the Congress leaders of Maharashtra and Enron as a 'scandalous' and 'corrupt' selling of Mother India to grasping Westerners. During election rallies, Gopinath Munde, who became the state's deputy chief minister, said that Dabhol could easily be built by Indian companies. Instead of relying on cheaper native talent, Congress was allowing Enron to make huge profits off 'the backs of India's poor'. The Hindu nationalists promised to stand up for India against the thieving foreigners and 'bundle Enron into the sea'.[16]

The BJP/Shiv Sena coalition won the 1995 state elections. For a few months it looked as if it would stick to its pledge. The new government brought proceedings in the High Court in Bombay. Its lawyers alleged that Enron had won the contract with bribery. The BJP and Shiv Sena had a political interest in smearing their opponents, but, given that Enron had thrown money at politicians in America, the accusation wasn't beyond belief. Linda Power, the Vice-President, Global Finance, for the Enron Development Corporation, appeared to give it credence when she told a sub-committee of the US House of Representatives:

> Our company spent an enormous amount of its own money – approximately $20 million – on this education and project development process alone, not including any project costs. Why do we, and other developers, include such things in our project? To win local support and the support of the authorities, and contribute to the general improvement of conditions in the area.

Enron said there was nothing sinister in her reference to 'educating' the authorities, but after they had looked at how the deal had been done, Indians weren't reassured. There had been no competitive tendering. An inquiry by the new BJP government could find 'no reason cited in any file note or correspondence as to why another bidding party could not have been involved . . . It is this one-to-one dealing with Enron and absence of competition that led to secrecy and lack of transparency in the negotiation.'[17] If Enron got its way, 'high-cost power will be given precedence over low-cost power', the inquiry concluded, 'and that is clearly not in the best interests of the State'. The contract was to be torn up and Enron 'thrown into the sea'.

The BJP appeared to be implacable opponents. But as 1995 turned into 1996, their determination to stand up to the Houston corporation mellowed. The BJP's claim in the Bombay courts that the deal 'was conceived in fraud' was withdrawn. It agreed to renegotiate the contract and signed a new deal – which differed from its predecessor in that it was worse for Maharashtra. Congress had agreed for the first stage of the power station to be built. The BJP-Shiv Sena alliance gave Enron permission for Stage I and Stage II. The approval of New Delhi was still required. Fortunately, a minority BJP government was in power in May 1996. It lasted for thirteen days. On its last day, as a no-confidence motion was going through Parliament, the cabinet met for an emergency working lunch, and could think of no more pressing task before it returned to opposition than to approve and guarantee Enron's contract.

The people of Maharashtra found themselves in a position the Americans and the British would recognise: however they voted, Enron won.

The plant was to be built on hills by the Arabian Sea whose red, volcanic soil was covered with scrub and small farms. Enron wanted agricultural land, which was to be obtained by compulsory purchase. Peasants were to be chucked out of their homes. Dabhol's discharges looked as if they would imperil the local fisheries, while the 8,338 litres of fresh water per minute Enron would need to keep the plant generating would empty rivers. What really infuriated everyone was that, after enduring all of this, they wouldn't be able to afford the power.

With no democratic option left, mass protests began. Except in one case of stone-throwing and another where a water pipeline was cut, the patient opposition didn't resort to violence. The same could not be said for the authorities. The BJP mobilised all the resources of the state to suppress protesters on Enron's behalf. The Bombay Police Act had a catch-all clause. It forbade 'the public utterance of cries, singing of songs, playing of music, the delivery of harangues, the use of gesture or mimetic representations and the preparation, exhibition or dissemination of pictures, symbols, placards or any other object or thing which may in the opinion of such authority offend against decency or morality'. Which seemed to cover every-thing.

Hundreds of protesters were arrested each day. Habeas corpus was forgotten and 'externment orders' were used to prevent protesters going near Dabhol. Police beatings went on for months. The account of one demonstration by Ataman More, a fisherman, is typical of hundreds in Human Rights Watch's files. 'We were stopped at the site. We told the police that we were peaceful demonstrators and would go to hold our rally. The police fired tear gas and lathi-charged us.' Women in their eighties were beaten and dozens were held in the Enron compound which at this – and at 30 other demonstrations in 1997 – doubled as a private prison. Amnesty International reported that in June 1997, courageous officers armed with batons arrived at a fishing village when the men were at sea and beat and imprisoned women and children.

The police were keen to take out educated leaders. Sadanand Pawar, an economics professor, told Human Rights Watch that 'they wanted to see how strong I was mentally, since I had never been in jail. I told them I would continue agitating, it is my birthright. I was put in a terrible cell with bad smells and filth. [The police said] "You are a professor, you earn well, why do you want these headaches".' Enron's opponents claimed it had bought the law. In a sense, they were right. The costs of stationing officers at Dabhol was met by Enron.

The Third Wayers in the White House looked on with an approval which should make some of their former supporters think again about their heroes. In my extensive experience of liberals, self-doubt is a rarity. They are masters at condemning corrupt Conservatives or Republicans. They argue that it was a global tragedy that Al Gore was beaten by George W, as Bush was just a puppet of his corporate paymasters. And so he was, but so was the Clinton-Gore administration.

Lay may have subbed two generations of the Bush family, but his affection didn't limit his circle of friends. Between 1993 and 2002 Enron gave $2 million to the Democrats. The Clinton administration gave Enron $2.2 billion in loans and insurance. When it looked as if the Dabhol plant would be stopped in 1995, Clintonites fought to save it. Clinton's ambassador to India, Frank G. Wisner, and the rest of the administration hammered home to India that it would suffer. 'Failure to honour the agreements between the project partners and the various Indian governments will jeopardise not only the Dabhol project but also most, if not all, of the other private power projects being proposed for international financing,' said the Department of Energy. Britain and France were as appalled by the insubordinate natives. Kenneth Clarke, the Chancellor of the Exchequer in 1995, warned India that pulling out of the Enron deal could have repercussions for British investment. An official in the Indian Power Ministry told the *Far Eastern Economic Review* that 'the Indian government was clearly intimidated by Enron's clout'. America and Europe were sending the same message: pay Enron or your economy gets it.[18]

No one fought harder for Enron than Wisner. His mission accomplished, he left the diplomatic corps of the United States in the summer of 1997. Like Wendy Gramm and Lord Wakeham before him, he found a new career. Lay appointed him to the board of directors of Enron Oil & Gas on 28 October 1997.

The bullying was for nothing. The Dabhol deal proved too burdensome for Maharashtra to bear. By 2000 the cost of Enron power was twice that of other suppliers. The obligation on Indians to buy it for 21 hours day and night whether they needed it or not (which most days they didn't) threatened to burn the state's resources. Civil servants worked out that by 2003 Maharashtra would be giving as much to Enron as it was giving to all its schools and colleges.[19]

Maharashtra pulled out in May 2001. Lay warned again that India would be hit with economic sanctions if it didn't pay Enron off. 'There are US laws which could prevent the US government from providing any aid or assistance to India going forward if, in fact, they expropriate the property of US citizens,' he said. India risked 'sending an incredibly damaging signal to the international capital markets and investment community'. The Bush administration took up his cause. Colin Powell, Dick Cheney and an army of minor officials shrieked and bellowed. In *Anatomy of Greed*, Brian Cruver describes how the executives spoke in private. As the Dhabol deal was falling apart, he bumped into a manager who was knocking back glasses of Johnnie Walker Blue Label at $50 a shot in a Houston bar. Enron was heading for bankruptcy, and the executive warned Cruver that the world was about to learn that

> we got huge cans, huge buckets of worms. Warehouses full of crates, full of buckets of worms ... That Dabhol plant in India. The local protests and police raids aren't because Indians don't want power; the police didn't drag a pregnant woman naked into the street and beat the shit out of her for business reasons. It's an issue of human rights and human disrespect. The Indians on Enron's side get bribes, while opponents get arrested. Land gets stolen, water resources are destroyed. It may not be Enron in the streets wielding the baton, but it is Enron arrogance and Enron greed that pushes a project to that dilapidated state.[20]

A few days after the whisky tears flowed, Enron was bust. The special-purpose vehicles could not longer carry the weight of its frauds. As I mentioned, the debts which were taken off the books and hidden in the partnerships were backed with Enron shares. When the value of Enron shares began to fall, the value of the assets in the special vehicles began to fall. Enron had to sell more stock to meet its debts, which in turn reduced the value of its shares, which in turn reduced the value of the collateral backing, the special-purpose vehicles.

Not everyone had turned their eyes from the danger. Carl Bass, an Andersen partner, emailed head office to confess to 'a jaded view of these transactions'. Enron complained to Andersen that Bass had a 'caustic and cynical attitude'. Andersen took Bass off the Enron account. By 2001, no amount of wire pulling could hide the fact that the special-purpose vehicles were being used to hide losses. In 2001 Enron announced that it had lost $618 million in partnership deals. Three weeks later it said $586 million of the income it had reported to investors had vanished. A fortnight after that it blushingly admitted that it had to repay another $690 million in partnership debt. Its share price went from $90 in 2000 to a few cents in December 2001. Andersen staff were caught tearing up documents in the Enron offices. Shredding machines couldn't save either company. They were heading for the knacker's yard as the bubble built on the promise of a Net-powered, privatised Utopia imploded.

The financial and political worlds were stunned when Enron went under with losses of $100 billion; shocked beyond measure that a reputable company whose executives were the confidants of senators, presidents and ministers could have been nothing more than a swindle. Their surprise was a fitting epitaph to the millennial bubble. The holders of respectable opinion couldn't make the connection between Enron's corrupt behaviour in California and India, and the corruption of its finances. The links between morality and business had been severed.

Given Enron's record, what did they expect? Honest accounting? Let me try a homely comparison. Suppose you hired a builder who had permission from the Inland Revenue to file tax returns without a shred of supporting evidence. Suppose it was common knowledge that he financed the governing and opposition parties on the local council, gave jobs to planning officers who found in his favour, threw up rickety buildings which collapsed on their inhabitants, bullied his employees, beat his wife and set club-wielding private security guards on anyone who complained. Would you feel you had the right to be surprised when he ran off with your money?

TEN

Because I'm Worth It

In the mid-1990s, as the bubble was preparing to rise, I was working for the *Independent* at Canary Wharf. The tower stood incongruously in the old dockyards of London's East End. It was if a giant bird had flown off with a Manhattan skyscraper and dumped it on a whim between the Thames and the slums. Fear of the thieving habits of the poor neighbours and of an IRA which kept bombing the place meant that it was ringed with security guards. There were CCTV cameras on walls and above desks. The windows wouldn't open and you needed a swipe card to get through every door. There was then no tube connection to central London. Once office workers had schlepped in, they were stuck. It was impossible to nip out to visit anyone. Naturally, the owners of the *Independent*, *Mirror* and *Telegraph* groups decided that an isolated lock-up was just the place to put journalists working on seven national newspapers. That would teach them to waste company money by running off and talking to people.

The move to Canary Wharf hadn't suited the *Independent*. The paper was in an apparently unstoppable decline. Its owners attempted to prevent closure with a bold stroke. For the first time in British journalism a national newspaper was to sell itself as a think-tank pamphlet. Senior editorial positions were filled with middle-aged but svelte men who had found the elixir of permanent freshness in the ideology of modernity. Two were ex-communists: Charles Leadbeater and Martin Jacques. They had wound up their party and formed Demos, a think-tank aligned to Tony Blair's New Labour project. Geoff Mulgan, a former Trotskyist and the director of Demos, became a contributor to the opinion pages.

Reporters have a fierce craft consciousness. By definition, editors who have not proved they are hard enough to cover a multiple murder by a three-in-a-bed, two-timing love rat are effete time-wasters who will bring certain ruin to a paper. To make matters worse for the largely leftish hacks, the ideas which were driving the *Independent* appeared to be conservative. Yet however much reporters wanted to resist, they found it hard to get a grip on their adversaries. The Demos crowd didn't talk like Tories. They appeared to care about inequality and insecurity, and rejected the accusation of conservatism with irritated impatience. The very notions of 'left' and 'right' were dead, we were told. In their place was the new paradigm which was to be found in the tiger economies of the East – until they had the bad manners to collapse – and then in Silicon Valley. The new century was bringing an interconnected world which would make a nonsense of all that had gone before.

In the end we were unnerved as much by the jarring tone of voice as by what was said. Leadbeater and the rest had lost their faith in socialism, but in their conversation you could still hear the sharp accent of Marxist teleology. The gap between 'is' and 'ought' was hardly worth arguing about. History was steaming down the tracks. Questioning its inevitable destination was as pointless as arguing for the restoration of the Stuarts. After receiving a long lecture on the futility of doubt, Peter Wilby, the editor of the *Independent on Sunday*, staggered out of an editorial conference. 'These people used to go to Moscow and say, "I've seen the future – and it works!"' he bellowed. 'Now they go to Singapore and cry, "I've seen the future – and gosh!"'

Our colleagues were presenting us with a preview of the Blairism of the bubble years. Mulgan left Demos to become special adviser to Tony Blair in Number 10. Leadbeater left the *Independent* to become a management consultant, an adviser to Peter Mandelson and an author. His 1999 book, *Living on Thin Air*, will be essential reading for historians struggling to understand how it was that a Labour prime minister embraced the market at the moment it went mad.

The highest in the land welcomed *Living on Thin Air*. Blair said Leadbeater was an 'extraordinarily interesting thinker' who 'raises critical questions for Britain's future'. Mandelson added that Leadbeater had 'set the agenda for the next Blair revolution', and commended him as 'the sort of intellectual that is useful to government because his head is firmly in the real world' – an unintentionally appealing image of Leadbeater as a bottom-waggling ostrich. From the modernising wing of the Tory Party, Chris Patten said the author was 'intellectually fascinating' and the provider of 'a fund of insights'. Leadbeater himself was no less grandiose. He dedicated his book to the Prime Minister and told him that *Living on Thin Air* was 'a blueprint for what a radical modernising project will entail in years to come'.

Coming to terms with the project isn't easy. From the first page, the startled reader learns that for this member of New Labour the personal isn't political but world historical. Leadbeater begins with a statement of 'where I am coming from'.[1] When people ask him what he does, he 'finds it hard to come up with a clear, concise answer'. The best he can do is tell them that he is a 'knowledge worker', one of 'the people who live on their wits'. He is not yet 40, but has already had several 'mini-careers'. He 'sometimes marvels' at the risks he is taking until he realises that surviving on contacts and creating and selling knowledge is all he, and we, can do. Secure careers making solid goods are vanishing. Soon the world will be filled with programmers 'providing service, judgement, and analysis', manipulating information – and each other. Soon 'we will all be in the thin air business'.

Modernity has its discontents. 'The kids are perplexed by my lifestyle. They like me being around, but part of them would quite like it if I had a proper job to go to in an office like other people's dads.' But kids can be a commodity as well as a nuisance and providers of the defining Third Way manifesto. I refer, as many of you will have guessed, to *We're Going on a Bear Hunt* by Michael Rosen and Helen Oxenbury, the winner of the 1989 Smarties Prize for children's fiction. Leadbeater tells us

that the picture book – one of the young Leadbeaters' favourites
– is the 'unlikely starting point' for an answer to the question:
'How to find greater security in an environment as hostile as
the modern world?' His précis of the plot provides guidance. 'A
family sets out to find a bear, only to meet a series of daunting
obstacles: deep mud, a cold river, a dark forest, a violent storm.
At each of these the family chants: "We can't go under it. We
can't go over. We'll have to go through it."' Leadbeater is so
impressed by this advice he repeats it in the concluding sentence of his book. If we are to flourish in the modern world we
must learn that 'we'll have to go through it'.

His mother, too, can be pressed into service. She toiled in
kitchens 'as a daughter and a wife when she could have been
studying for a degree or starting a business. The lengthy learning
process that lies behind my mother's roast beef with crispy Yorkshire pudding was made possible only by a social division of
labour in which men went out to work and women stayed at
home.' His mother's craft is anachronistic. But hold on there,
more women may work now, but we have fast-food restaurants
and ready-to-eat cook-chill meals from Marks & Spencer and
Tesco. Most wonderfully, we also have Delia Smith, 'who
explains much of what the modern economy is about'. Leadbeater is too busy to sit in her kitchen and learn 'at first hand
what makes her chicken in sherry wine vinegar quite so tasty'.
But he can still 'follow her recipes', and through them learn that
'globalisation is good for our palates'. All over the world, profits
are going to the writers of recipes that can be reproduced – think
of Bill Gates's software! – while their customers are acquiring
knowledge not just of how to make the best marinade for a
corn-fed, free-range quail but of hundreds of other skills. Globalisation isn't just scrumptious, he says: 'Globalisation is good.'

The ideologue of Blairism tells us he likes Thai noodles and
foreign holidays. He commends his travel agent, one Philip
Davies of Real Holidays in Islington, north London. Presumably Davies sent him East. If he did we must thank him for providing Leadbeater with a stimulating break. For it was on the

shores of an Oriental sea that Leadbeater had an Archimedean flash and realised that humans could organise the leisure sector, because they weren't crabs.

> Each evening hundreds of crabs scurry across the idyllic beach at Krabi in Thailand. They form a fractious, self-governing community which in many respects mirrors our own. They fight over territory, squabble over food and get along with just enough cooperation to survive. What distinguishes humans from crabs, apart from their lack of claws, is the degree of cooperation we are capable of. Crabs and sunbathers may share the same beach but crabs have not built beachfront hotels, with swimming pools and restaurants, served by nearby roads and airports, to which planes are guided by sophisticated computers.

Pedants might have objected that the lack of claws is not the only difference between humans and crabs. We don't wear shells on our backs, to name one, and are rarely served as *hors d'oeuvres* in the better restaurants. Leadbeater was arbitrarily demonising one crustacean for its failure to attract inward investment while ignoring the market failures of others. How many oysters, for example, have been change agents in the tourism industry? And who but a fool demands room service from a lobster?

General readers were faced with a more troubling question. Why did Blair, Mandelson and Patten believe Leadbeater was a genius? It wasn't just the crabs. Unforgivably, he couldn't get *We're Going on a Bear Hunt* right. The family does 'go through' all obstacles in its search for a bear crying: 'We're going to catch a big one. What a beautiful day! We're not scared.' When they confront their quarry in its cave, however, the bear turns nasty. The family runs screaming all the way home, barricades the door, dives under the bed and cries 'We're not going on a bear hunt again!'[2]

Yet beneath the confusion there was a clear purpose. Like many of the former Marxists in New Labour, Leadbeater had gone from global revolution to global capitalism but retained a consistent contempt for the boring Labour movement which tried in its muddled way to make people's lives better. The

Blairite ideologists had no time for muddle. They were certain that there was a New Economy and Britain was in it. Trying to regulate the future by breaking up cartels was a hubristic defiance of the gods of the market. 'The best competition policy,' said Leadbeater, 'is not to restrict monopoly but to promote innovation.' In any case, public officials were unfit to regulate. 'The pace of change is moving so fast in these industries that law-makers, judges and regulators are too slow and their tolls too cumbersome to keep pace.' And as for Old Labour's love for manufacturing and redistributing wealth, they were as dated as the horse-drawn plough. 'The real wealth-creating economy is dematerialising' into cyberspace and into brands. 'The new economy will make it far more difficult to raise money for public spending through the old tax system.'

Instead of whining, we should worship the entrepreneurs who were riding the wave of the future. Leadbeater's hero was Paul Drayson, a venture capitalist who developed a gas-propelled gun which allowed patients to have a vaccine injected without the torture of a needle pricking the skin. Drayson's was a heart-warming story. Leadbeater tells us that he found love as well as a business opportunity when he went to the home of Brian Bellhouse, the inventor of the prickless needle. His eye was caught by Bellhouse's daughter Elspeth. After winning the rights to market the invention, he won the hand of the girl too. Drayson's and Bellhouse's gun scarcely deals with the most pressing medical problems facing humanity. Slothful regulators might wonder why health-service resources should be wasted on a luxury treatment for patients who go queasy at the sight of a syringe. But Leadbeater prohibits us from asking questions of worth and utility. Drayson has invented 'a brand, not just a device,' he rules, and deserves to enjoy his rewards. 'Drayson was motivated by the prospect of making money. It is only by treating people like Drayson and Bellhouse as heroes for creating wealth from knowledge that Britain will develop a fully-fledged entrepreneurial culture.'

*

'Chronocentrism' is the technical name for the malady – the egotistical belief that your age is poised on the cusp of history, that the world has never before seen what you are seeing. New Labour was chronically chronocentric. It needed the bubble, and the bubble needed New Labour's thin air to inflate it. Blair and his allies believed their party had lost four elections on the trot because it was associated with militant trade unions and declining manufacturing industries. It was a dated 'tax and spend' movement dedicated to squeezing money out of the aspirational and throwing it at lumbering bureaucrats. Whatever the truth of the argument – and there was truth in it – the problem Labour faced was that there was no point in having a Labour Party if it didn't stand up for the interests of labour. The bubble offered an escape. There was no need to worry about the old ways of politics and society when history was destroying them. Organised labour was being replaced by self-assured freelancers who were setting their own terms and running their own lives as they strode from job to job. They would laugh in your face if you told them they would be better off being a salaried drone in a creaking bureaucracy. The old distinctions between managers and workers were breaking down. Hierarchies were being smashed and old élites overthrown in a revolutionary change which a party of the left could and should support. Best of all, the bubble was resolving a hitherto insoluble dilemma. Inequality need no longer trouble New Labour. The gap between rich and poor may have been widening by the day, but if the rich were meritocratic 'heroes' in the Drayson mould, why should the poor be anything other than grateful to them for providing the jobs which lifted them out of penury and idleness?

For the first two years of New Labour's rule Gordon Brown imposed a freeze on public expenditure as severe as anything the Tories had managed. But as revenues from workers in the City and financial services ballooned, he could increase spending without significant rises in taxes. Money poured into the Treasury and poured out into education, health and the relief of poor mothers and pensioners. The assumption behind Brown's policy of spending without tears was that the casino wheels would turn for ever.

Of course New Labour loved the bubble – the bubble freed it from the vice of its history. Its leaders spoke in the bubble dialect. In 1999 Brown said he wanted to move Britain 'beyond the old and self-defeating choice between Old Left over-regulation ... and the New Right belief in unfettered markets.' Liberation would come by equipping 'people to master ever faster waves of technological, financial and global change in a way that is sensitive to the needs of all'. Tony Blair promised in 2000 that he would 'achieve leadership for the UK in the global digital economy' which was about to transform the world. His apparently bizarre condemnation of 'the forces of conservatism, the cynics, the élites, the establishment' at the 1999 Labour Party conference made sense to those initiated into the reasoning of the bubble world. Conservatives weren't only actual Conservatives who held back, for instance, women. Union leaders and Old Labour MPs could be small-c conservatives if they tried to trap people into jobs for life instead of sending them off to surf the wired world. Cynics could be those who laughed at the brave hopes of the Net entrepreneurs and paid more attention to the share options the entrepreneurs were pocketing than the visions they were promoting. Élitists could be old-fashioned businessmen who thought the world owed them a living, or academics and environmentalists who got in the way of change. The government's job wasn't to intervene but to 'facilitate' the creation of 'human capital' with 'education, education, education'.

Jon Cruddas, who was Blair's adviser on trade unions after the 1997 election, said he kept running into the dogmas of Leadbeater and the other chronocentrics in Downing Street. The New Economy reinforced 'an in-built hostility to organised labour and labour-market regulation from some of those within the Labour government,' he said as he looked back. It explained 'the failure adequately to address the legacy of a deregulated employment law inherited from the Conservative governments.'

Cruddas and Ian McCartney, the industry minister, fought an exhausting battle to get Blair to accept a small rollback of the Conservative anti-union laws. A minimum wage was introduced at a miserly level and workers were given the right to vote for trade union representation. The scraps thrown to appease Old Labour were all that was going to fall from the top table. Cruddas knew there was no reason to hang around and left Downing Street in 2001 to become the MP for the Old Labour seat of Dagenham.[3]

For the majority of the British the world of *Wired* magazine was incomprehensible. True, the decline in manufacturing from the 1960s had been precipitous – although ten million still earned a living with their hands. But the typical British worker didn't dump his laptop in the back of a people-carrier, wave goodbye to his confused children and speed off for a morning brainstorming with Channel 4 and an afternoon redesigning the Department of Trade and Industry's website. The growth in employment in software engineering and computer programming in the 1990s was modest in comparison to the increase in the number of sales assistants, data input clerks, receptionists, care assistants and nursery nurses. The fastest growing occupation of the decade, the career which led the drive towards full employment, was hairdressing. The new workforce wasn't composed of self-confident freelancers who could name their price.[4] Britain's reliance on a low-wage, low-productivity economy was as dispiriting as ever. The struggle to cope with toiling through the longest working days in Europe was particularly draining for women. At least 25 million manual and menial service workers in the working and middle classes needed a Labour government to strengthen their employment rights. What they got was Tony Blair's boast to the *Sun* in 1997 that his government would ensure that Britain 'will still have the most restrictive union laws in the Western world'. On this pledge, it is fair to say, Blair was as good as his word.

Their employers didn't need trade unions. Whatever doubts might be expressed about their managerial abilities, they were world-beaters at closing deals for themselves. From 1996 to 2002, the highest-paid directors of stock-market listed companies had double-figure percentage pay rises each and every year. In 2001 *Management Today* found that the average salary of the chief executives of British companies was £509,000 – up by one third on 1999. They were the best-paid bosses in Europe. The only executives to earn more were American executives. British salaries were 33 per cent above French chief executives, who were the next highest paid on £382,128. Swedish executives had to get by on £311,400, while the Germans, at the bottom of the pay pile, were close to beggary with £298,223. The Germans received eleven times more than their average shopfloor worker in manufacturing. The average French boss was worth the same as fifteen workers. British executives were 'worth' 25 times as much, and British workers in manufacturing were the lowest paid in the developed world, with salaries of £20,000. They were also the easiest in the developed world to fire. In one sense Leadbeater was right. Many people involuntarily enjoyed portfolio careers because it was so easy for their employers to throw them out of one career and force them to look for another.[5]

Averages conceal as much as they reveal. In 2000 when Vodafone took over Mannesmann, a rival German mobile phone company, Chris Gent, its chief executive, was awarded a £10 million bonus to supplement his £6.9 million salary and share options. How much the options were worth to him was was not disclosed, but in 2001 Vodafone announced that all its executives could make £28 million from share options over the next three years. Few institutional investors complained at the time. Vodafone was in the telecom business. No rewards were too great for the revolutionaries of Anglo-Saxon capitalism who were hacking out the the path to the future. The perverse incentives of a bubble market applied. Every pension fund manager bought Vodafone shares because every other pension fund manager was buying Vodafone shares. The herd pushed the price to a peak in January 2000 when Vodafone represented 12 per cent of the FTSE 100 index, and its shares were worth 400 pence. They fell to 80p by 2002, when Vodafone recorded a loss of £13 billion, the largest in British corporate history.

When the drug companies Glaxo and SmithKline merged in a deal which promised huge cost savings and a flood of new drugs, the share options of Jan Leschly, the SmithKline chief executive, were valued at $100 million (about £60 million at the time). Jean-Pierre Garnier, the chief executive of the merged company, began on a starting salary of £7 million. The merger produced a lacklustre company. Profits and the share price fell by 2002. Garnier still got his £7 million. If Glaxo's performance got worse and he was sacked, he would have been entitled to a pay-off of £22 million. The promised reward for failure was too much even for the tolerant City and provoked a revolt by the pension funds.[6] Garnier's income was dwarfed by that of Philip Green. According to the *Sunday Times* Pay List, the tycoon behind the BHS chain took £157.7 million in dividends on the shares he owned in the store in 2002.

Numbers of this size boggle the mind. They were put into a kind of context on 14 March 2003 when the BBC ran its annual fun-fest, Red Nose Day. Over eighteen years it had become Britain's greatest exercise in communal giving. The relentless cheeriness ground down all but the meanest. In 2003 comedians and singers once again donated their services gratis to raise money to relieve poverty at home and in Africa. There were messages of support from Bill Clinton and Julia Roberts. Tens of thousands pestered their friends to sponsor them to dress up as chickens or sit in baths filled with cold baked beans. Most got promises of money, if only to make them go away. Twelve thousand telecom workers gave up their spare time to man credit-card lines. About one million school children wore red noses, and 20,000 schools ran fund-raising events. The organisers estimated that all in all five million people bought noses and contributed to a record-breaking total of charitable donations from the public and business of £35,174,798 – or a shade under one quarter of what Green had pocketed the previous year. Comic Relief wouldn't have made the Top 10 of the *Sunday Times* Pay List. It would have languished in the charts at number 16, just behind Madonna, who made £36 million.

A look at executives doesn't begin to cover the redistribution of wealth from from the bottom and middle of British society to the top. In December 1999, the bubble peaked when the FTSE-100 hit 6930. By January 2003 it had fallen to 3460. While the markets climbed, lawyers, accountants and investment bankers could reach out their hands and snatch away the money which might comfort them in the hard times.

In 2000, 61 City lawyers who advised on corporate tax (the avoidance thereof), mergers and acquisitions made more than £1 million a year.[7] In the law, as elsewhere, class divisions within professions and trades were as great as class divisions between professions and trades. Lord Irvine, Tony and Cherie Blair's former pupil master, was a member of the legal 'million-pound club'. A Hong Kong businessman reputedly gave him the first seven-figure brief in English legal history. Blair appointed his old friend to the constitutionally monstrous role of Lord Chancellor, a post which made a nonsense of the separation of powers by combining the offices of Speaker of the House of Lords (the legislature), member of the Cabinet (executive) and appointer of the judges (judiciary). The post was abolished after Irvine retired. Blair also elevated Peter Goldsmith to the peerage, and appointed him Attorney General. Goldsmith defended the interning of Arabs after 11 September without charge or trial before judge and jury. He had been one of the highest paid commercial QCs, making more than £1 million a year.

Lord Grabiner was without doubt the most expensive lawyer in London in the 1990s. He rarely touched a case worth less than £100 million and charged £800 an hour (or 216 times the then minimum wage) for his services. After being ennobled by Blair he applied his forensic mind to the scandalous greed of the undeserving poor. In 1999 the Tories demanded that claimants of unemployment benefit who were suspected of working in the black economy must be forced to sign on every day to keep them out of mischief. New Labour responded with a rare display of radical anger. Jeff Rooker, a junior minister, said the Conservatives had descended into 'right-wing madness'. David Blunkett cried that the cost of this lunacy would be £540 million a year, as thousands of staff would have to be recruited to monitor the workless. Unemployed people who lived miles from a benefit office would see a slice of their tiny incomes frittered away on bus fares. All would waste time when they might be looking for a job. The critics were silenced by Gordon Brown, who transformed insanity into prudence within seconds and conceded that the Tories had an arguable case. He asked Lord Grabiner to investigate. Grabiner responded by recommending that claimants suspected of – but not convicted of – working illegally should be presumed guilty and forced to report daily.[8]

The prominence given to millionaire briefs helped explain why an administration dominated by lawyers assaulted the presumption of innocence, trial by jury and double jeopardy. Their insensitivity to liberty appeared inexplicable: it was as if a government of doctors had poisoned the wells. But men like Irvine and Grabiner hadn't spent their days in front of juries. They hadn't learned from seeing the police lie through their teeth why people had fought for liberties for centuries. They had gone to where the wealth and the status was – the commercial bar. They were as likely to argue in boardrooms as courtrooms. A solicitor in an East End firm might deal with the criminal justice system, but if she relied on legal aid for an income she would be lucky to make £40,000 a year, and would never meet Irvine professionally or socially. The distance between them was unbridgeable. They might both have been born into similar families and gone to the same university, but in the pleasures they enjoyed and their experience of the law they had as much in common as players for Manchester United and Doncaster

Rovers. They played different games in different worlds. The Blair government reacted to fetters on their power with booming, 'Do you know who I am?'

By 2000 no other country in Europe had as many accountants as Britain – at 250,000 they outnumbered all their rivals in the European Union put together. Companies preferred accountants on their boards to engineers because short-term management of the share price was more important than producing goods – especially when share options made the level of the stock a matter of intense personal interest. Accountants had a state-guaranteed monopoly of auditing, which in no way inhibited them from prostituting their independence by trying to flatter the corporate clients they were meant to be policing into buying additional services from their firms. Selling tax advice and management consultancy was where the money was. They had every incentive to keep their paymasters sweet by turning a Nelsonian eye to dodgy figures.

The tax advice they produced was on how corporations and the super-rich could find ways not to pay it. No one could be sure how much money they helped divert from the exchequer, but Prem Sikka, Professor of Accounting at Essex University, and Austin Mitchell, a Labour MP so far beyond the pale he was out of sight, estimated that £85 billion a year escaped the Inland Revenue by being channelled to offshore havens, the successors of the pirate statelets of the Spanish Main. If the wealthy had paid their share, the tax burden on the working and middle classes might have been reduced or something more might have been done about the gridlocked roads or the joke of the railway system or the 20,000 old people who died each year from cold-related diseases or the cumulative 25-year under-investment of £275 billion in the NHS or the useless police force which could clear up only 18 per cent of crimes or the unemployment benefits which were the lowest in Western Europe or the state pensions which were as miserable. In short, the majority of the population might have had better lives.[9]

Finding ruses to avert this catastrophe was a skilled job which required the services of men and women who had the right to expect to be well rewarded for their services. British accountants were the best paid in the world by a mile. Their average salary, including bonuses, stood at £82,000 in 2001. Foreigners looked on with envious appreciation. The next best paid were the Swiss, whose average income was £46,000. Rewards were at their highest in the 'big five' accountancy firms. Most kept their secrets, but Ernst & Young revealed in 2001 that 411 partners had each received a £449,000 bonus on top of their salaries.[10]

The rest of the City fared as well. In 2000 mergers, acquisitions and the dotcom and telecom bubbles created an estimated 2,000 bonus millionaires in the City. They weren't entrepreneurs or risk takers, but employees who were also drawing their regular salaries. Mergers were their cash cow. They did little to improve companies' performance, but they excited speculative interest. Vodafone's investment banks charged Gent £400m for advice on buying Mannesmann and other services. So impressed were UBS Warburg and Goldman Sachs with the size of their fees they filled the 60-acre grounds of Hampton Court with marquees and threw what became known in the City as the 'King of Parties'. The host for the all-night banquet under the hammer-beam roof of the Great Hall was Robert Gillespie, global head of corporate finance at UBS Warburg. His work for Vodafone had helped him find the money to begin building a 39-bedroom home in the Chilterns. The recently knighted Sir Chris Gent was the guest of honour. The market was about to crash. A few executives at Enron and WorldCom were wondering if their lies were about to catch them out. Millions of trusting people who had invested with funds as apparently reputable as Standard Life were about to learn that unregulated capitalism is a giddy thing. As the night wore on and successive toasts were proposed, the guests would have been base ingrates if they had not raised a glass to New Labour.

The worst fate for a satirist is to be taken at face value. In 1958, Michael Young, one of the authors of the 1945 Labour manifesto, invented the concept of 'the meritocracy' after he looked at the country he had helped create and decided he wasn't sure he liked the way it was going. *The Rise of the Meritocracy* is set in 2034. Jobs are given on the basis of merit, which comes down to the ability to pass exams. The meritocratic élite is insufferable. An aristocracy which knows it is where it is because of an accident of birth may on occasion show humility. Getting rid of it was an advance, but Young said he wanted to use mockery to show how 'if the rich and powerful were encouraged by the general culture to believe that they fully deserved all they had, how arrogant they could become, and, if they were convinced it was all for the common good, how ruthless in pursuing their own advantage'. Those excluded by the meritocracy's rise revolt in 2034 and demand to know who set the criteria. The rebel manifesto states: 'Were we to evaluate people, not only according to their intelligence and their education, their occupation and their power, but according to their kindliness and their courage, their imagination and sensitivity, their sympathy and generosity, there would be no classes.'

When *The Rise of the Meritocracy* was published, Young said he was warned by a classical scholar that he had committed a gross solecism. It wasn't done to invent a word by mixing Latin and Greek. 'I would, she said, be laughed to scorn.'[11] It didn't work out like that. Instead of attacking his linguistic inconsistency, the targets of the satire were delighted. To be a meritocrat was to hold power on the basis of merit, and who could propose a preferable system? The co-author of the 1945 Labour Manifesto found to his 'disappointment' that New Labour had decided that promoting a meritocracy was its *raison d'être*. In opposition, Tony Blair feared that the meritocratic Utopia might never be reached. 'We are light years from being a true meritocracy,' he sighed in 1995. But he was not downhearted. 'I want a society based on meritocracy,' he proclaimed in April 1997. After winning power, he made his revolutionary programme clear. 'The Britain of the élite is over. The new Britain is a meritocracy.' The New Britain was coming and nothing could stop it because 'the old establishment is being replaced by a new, larger, more meritocratic middle class.' Meritocracy would be democratic because 'the meritocracy is built on the potential of the many, not the few'. It would be profitable because 'the meritocratic society is the only one that can exploit its economic potential to the full for all its people'.[12]

The question raised by Young's rebels remained as valid as ever: who evaluates? Educational achievement was the generally accepted measure. The late 1990s produced a craze for exams, and, although there were complaints about the pressure on children and the quality of the marking, parents continued to judge schools on their performance in exam league tables, while New Labour aimed to get 50 per cent of the young to pass the exams necessary for a university education. The private schools were as keen on tests. They had abandoned their preference for good chaps over swots years before and become centres of academic excellence. These developments appeared benign, but they couldn't conceal the stresses of a meritocracy. Intellectually successful private schools allowed the coached children of the rich to secure the best grades. Self-made men or women who 'deserved' their wealth could buy advantage for their children. Their families would move from a meritocracy to an aristocracy of wealth in a generation. Given the unprecedented sums being made in the City and business as a matter of course, the new aristocratic dynasties could survive for decades on the fruits of a few years work by their founders.

Their rise was accompanied by a popular line of mockery against the apparently ridiculous BA (Hons) courses in golf management, media studies and hotel catering which were offered in the old polytechnics to the children of the less fortunate. The laughter missed a huge social change. Trades which used to be open to eighteen- or sixteen-year-olds required job applicants to have a university education. With the abolition of grants and the introduction of tuition fees, the cost of training was passed from employers to potential employees and the taxpayers who picked up the remaining bills. Children without degrees, usually working-class children, were disqualified by the absence of qualifications from careers which were open to their predecessors.

Young and others worried what would happen to the working class when it was told that its failure wasn't the fault of the class system but its own innate stupidity. There were signs of working-class demoralisation, particularly among boys and young men. Turnout in elections was at its most miserable in working-class constituencies whose natural leaders had taken advantage of higher education and joined the bourgeoisie. By the turn of the new century, working-class Members of Parliament were going the way of country squires. Trade-union leaders had degrees. John Prescott was the only working-class member of the first Blair cabinet and was derided daily.

There might still have been resistance. A normal response to a country where one man could make four times as much as the Comic Relief appeal would be to change it. But – and here is why the Hampton Court revellers should have toasted New Labour – how were the proles meant to bring about change? By voting New Labour? The U-turn by the natural party of egalitarianism had made change impossible, however the electorate voted. In opposition, Labour had fulminated against the 'fat-cat bosses' of the privatised utilities who earned what was by the standards of the bubble a pathetic £400,000. In government, it was confronted with wage inequality at its greatest since records began in the 1880s. It decided that once the examination process stopped, merit was to be judged by one criterion: money. The more a man had, the better, wiser and more inspiring he was.

In 1998 Peter Mandelson told one of the leaders of the dotcom 'revolution' in Silicon Valley that no millionaire or billionaire need fear his government because 'New Labour is intensely relaxed about people getting filthy rich'. Mandelson's gushings pointed to the failure of the Blair government to curb calamitous speculation in the markets. The adoration of wealth and love of the bubble world prevented it from performing its duty and warning the public of a potential disaster. Like the Clinton administration, the Blair regime made the crisis worse. In the autumn of 1999, journalists asked Eddie George, the Governor of the Bank of England, whether he thought all the dotcom and telecom stocks were running out of control. George, who had been given the ridiculously inapt nickname of 'Steady Eddie' by the financial press, said that hi-tech stocks 'provide a better underpinning of equity values than perhaps has been appreciated'. Bubble shares were solid investments that were, if anything, undervalued. George, like the ministers he served, reserved his anger for the real enemies of economic stability. When working-class fire officers demanded a salary of £30,000 in 2002 – or about 1/7500th of what the head of BHS took home – the Governor of the Bank of England cried that economic disaster would follow. Accepting the fire officers' claim would detonate a pay 'explosion' which would cause 'a generalised push on inflation'.[13]

Business became the model for government. If public services could not be privatised, then they should be run as if they were private companies. Every new public work had to be built under the terms of the Private Finance Initiative. It had been introduced by Kenneth Clarke when he was Chancellor in the Major government. He cheerily admitted afterwards that the PFI was a dreadful idea. He had only accepted it as a temporary expedient because the Major government had enormous debts and he couldn't raise money any other way. The most numerically challenged child could understand Clarke's criticism in an instant. The government allowed private consortiums to borrow money to build everything from new hospitals to the modernised London Underground. They borrowed at a far higher rate than the government could obtain, and then they took their profits. The firms managed the public works for 30 to 60 years and received mortgage payments from the taxpayer for their buildings and services. New Labour saw the magic word 'private' in the Private Finance Initiative and fell in love. It turned Clarke's stopgap into a foundation of public finance. The excuse for the imprudence was that the risk of costs over-running was passed to the private sector. But the buck always seemed to stop with the public. An early PFI scandal was provided by – who else? – Andersen Consulting, sister company of Arthur Andersen, which won the contract to supply a new National Insurance computer. It was 'rubbish', said the then social security minister, Jeff Rooker. Pensioners, widowers and benefit claimants suffered. When asked why Andersen had been forced to pay only 10 per cent of the cost of the shambles, Dawn Primarolo, the Treasury's Paymaster General, said she wouldn't make the management consultants pay more 'for fear of jeopardising future relationships'.

Because of the sweetness of the relationship between state and commerce, hospital beds and community health services were cut, as trusts struggled to meet the extortionate bills for the private buildings. What should have been a cause for celebration – the opening of a modern hospital – provoked citizens' revolts. In Kidderminster, the people of Middle England were so infuriated by the downgrading of their excellent local hospital to meet the expense of building a PFI hospital in Worcester, they rejected all the major parties and elected an independent anti-PFI MP in the only shock result of the 2001 election. New Labour pressed on. It handed control of the refurbishing of the London Underground to a gaggle of private companies, none of which would be clearly responsible when trouble came, and a few of which were on the edge of bankruptcy. For all their faults, they were private, and therefore superior to the elected representatives of Londoners.

A meritocracy implies the punishment of failure alongside the rewarding of success. The rewards for the fortunate were enormous. New Labour gave Britain the lowest rate of corporation tax in the developed world. The upper rate of income tax bit into the wealth of the middle class but didn't hurt the super-rich. Modest proposals to bring in a new rate at 50 per cent for income above £100,000 were dismissed by the government as a dangerous tax on success. At local level, the Council Tax wasn't a great deal fairer than the poll tax. The top band was capped on properties worth more than £320,000. Money went out of the City and into London property after the death of the dotcom bubble. In boroughs such as Camden, the most expensive properties on Hampstead Hill were worth 30 times more than the former council flats of the working-class. The top rate was only three times higher than the bottom rate.[14] Property taxes were the hardest taxes for Arthur Andersen's finest to find a way round – you can't put your home in a Jersey shell company. New Labour ensured that their burden fell on the working and middle classes.

Mandelson was right. New Labour was truly relaxed about the filthy rich. And the filthy rich were equally untroubled, and became the funders of last resort for the political class. To speak of parties becoming increasingly dependent on corporations, as I foolishly did in the 1990s, understated the case. Parties didn't need corporations when there were such extremes of wealth. Lord Sainsbury gave £8.5 million from his personal fortune to New Labour between 1997 and 2003. The Tories received a £5 million cheque from Stuart Wheeler, a spread betting tycoon. One man could do more for a party than the raffles and fundraising drives of tens of thousands of party members.

The justification for the inequality which allowed cheques of this size to be dashed off lay in the 'winner takes all' theory of globalisation. If David Beckham scored an astonishing goal in 1950, only the 70,000 or so spectators at Old Trafford would see it. In the new century a billion people could watch. In 1950, Beckham could play only in the old English First Division. Today he would be welcomed, and is welcomed, at any club in the world. In 1960, the only channels were BBC and ITV. They controlled the market, and performers in sport and elsewhere had to accept their rates if they wanted to work. In a media-saturated age, celebs who could hold the attention of the fickle channel-hopping audience were in control.

Business was no different from entertainment, the theory held. Executives who could build a global brand in the ferocious free market were worth almost any price. The moment early in the life of the New Labour government when the committed feminist Harriet Harman ordered Labour MPs to cut the benefits of the poorest women and children, while Tony Blair hosted a party for the disc jockey Zoë Ball, the loud-mouthed talkshow host Chris Evans and other celebs in 10 Downing Street, wasn't as sickening as it appeared. To true meritocrats, it wasn't sickening at all. Evans and Ball were rich because they deserved to be rich. If single mothers had talent or initiative, they wouldn't need benefits. They would be running BHS or hosting the breakfast show on Radio 1. Any yobbo could risk his life to save the lives of others in the fire service, any slapper could struggle to bring up a child on a dismal estate, but only Paul Drayson could be Paul Drayson and only Chris Evans could be Chris Evans. Their uniqueness meant that different standards applied.

After the bubble burst, meritocrats continued to be rewarded while their companies went to the dogs. In a crowded field, Lord Simpson stood out as the silliest man ever to head a major British company. He took over GEC, a successful manufacturing firm which built everything from washing machines to radar for fighter planes. The speculators weren't keen on Lord Weinstock, Simpson's predecessor. GEC had £2.6 billion in the bank when Weinstock retired, and, although later events were to prove that Weinstock's cautious approach to business was amply justified, the City wanted a 'sexy' company. Simpson delivered. He changed the company's name from GEC to Marconi in 1999 and threw Weinstock's reserves into the bubble mania. New Labour gave him a peerage. The City gave him a standing ovation. Marconi built up £4 billion of debt as it bought telecom and dotcom companies. In 2000 Marconi was worth £34.5 billion and its shares traded at £12. By August 2002, it was worth £50 million and the shares traded at 3.6p. Ten thousand workers lost their jobs. Simpson got a £1 million pay-off.

Nor was Leadbeater's hero Paul Drayson always the risk-taking, caution-defying buccaneer of chronocentric theory. After the 11 September attacks, the government worried that al-Qaeda might release smallpox in Britain. The £32 million contract to provide a vaccine went to Drayson's firm. His rivals pointed out that Drayson had contributed to New Labour funds. They didn't allege corruption but were surprised that the contract wasn't put out to competitive bidding. Drayson explained there had been no competition 'for reasons of national security'. Pressing though those were, the United States, which had more to fear from al-Qaeda, invited bids for a smallpox vaccine from ten companies. A businessman who gets a fat contract in these circumstances can be described as lucky, but not, I think, a 'hero' who creates 'wealth from knowledge' and brings to Britain 'a fully-fledged entrepreneurial culture'.

In 2001, the last year of his life, Michael Young watched the ghastly masquerade pass by and reflected on how his prophecies in the *Rise of the Meritocracy* had been all too accurate:

> So assured have the élite become that there is almost no block on the rewards they arrogate to themselves ... The old restraints of the business world have been lifted and, as the book also predicted, all manner of new ways for people to feather their own nests have been invented and exploited. Salaries and fees have shot up. Generous share option schemes have proliferated. Top bonuses and golden handshakes have multiplied. As a result, general inequality has been becoming more grievous with every year that passes, and without a bleat from the leaders of the party who once spoke up so trenchantly and characteristically for greater equality.[15]

ELEVEN

Thank You for Not Smoking

There's always a danger in polemical writing of inventing a golden age which never existed. I'm sure this book has implied subconsciously that public debate was once rational, public life was once pristine and the public once enjoyed eighteen pints of bitter and a fish supper and still had change from half-a-crown. I therefore hope I'm not suffering from false memory syndrome when I think back to when politicians took it for granted that capitalism could be crooked. Even the Thatcher administration had its exclusion zones. In 1982 it stopped Arthur Andersen receiving government contracts because the accountancy firm had failed to spot that taxpayers' money was vanishing when it audited the books of the DeLorean car maker. For a company to be blacklisted by the Tories was the corporate equivalent of being thrown out of the Gestapo for the use of excessive force, but Andersen's provocation was spectacular. It didn't warn ministers that John Zachary DeLorean might as well have had 'spiv' branded on his forehead.

By the time the DeLorean affair was over, the best that could be said of him was that he had had a hand in the production of one of the cultural hits of the 1980s: the DMC-12, which played the role of Michael J. Fox's time machine in the *Back to the Future* films. The stainless-steel sports car with gull-wing doors carried a 130 h.p. Renault engine which could thrust it from nought to 60 m.p.h. in eight seconds. It looked marvellous at the car shows. The trouble came when DeLorean tried to sell it.

DeLorean was sure his baby would succeed and show the world that he couldn't be ignored. The son of a Ford factory worker, he had grown up on Detroit's east side during the Depression. He climbed the ladder of the US motor industry until, in the early 1960s, he became the manager at General Motors who created the Pontiac GTO. The 'hot rod' was a smash – 250,000 were sold in its first five years. DeLorean's salary went to $650,000 (a lot of money in those days, and these days, now I come to think of it). Success turned him into a swinging industrialist. DeLorean could be seen at Hollywood parties with his steel-grey hair coiffured into a helmet, his shirt unbuttoned to his waist and Raquel Welch or Ursula Andress on his arm.

In 1972 he married Christina Ferrare, a model who was half his age. He didn't like the boring old corporation men who ran the car industry, and the suits didn't like him. In 1973 he 'fired GM' and set off on his own as a maverick risk-taker with a vision to build the DMC-12. The car was going to prove that he could take on Ford, Chrysler and GM, and revolutionise the American motor industry. *People Weekly* had described him as the 'Detroit dream merchant', and DeLorean looked around to find investors who could make his dream come true. He needed $175 million. Sammy Davis Jnr and other celebrity friends helped out, but the bulk of the investment – $156 million – was put up by Her Majesty's Government on condition that the DeLorean Motor Company factory was built in Northern Ireland. The Conservatives' motives were admirable. Unemployment in Northern Ireland stood at 20 per cent and ministers hoped, perhaps naively, that the 2000 new jobs at the DMC factory would diminish support for Catholic and Protestant terror groups.

DeLorean risked a little of his own money – $700,000 according to reports at the time – and lived well. He had a twenty-room apartment in New York, an estate in New Jersey and a ranch in California. He made damn sure DMC's New York offices were in a skyscraper as high as the GM building round the corner. His salary was $500,000 in 1982. His fortune was put at $28 million. If the business had succeeded, then British tax-payers wouldn't have minded subsidising his princely lifestyle. What the auditors from Arthur Andersen failed to notice was that the business was a disaster. Walter Strycker, the company's chief accountant, warned Andersen that money was heading off in all directions. 'We thought John had abused the position of CEO at the DeLorean Motor Co., and that he had taken money that did not belong to him,' Strycker explained. Andersen accepted DeLorean's assurances that everything was on the level and dismissed Stryker's concerns. The factory began producing in 1981. The DMC-12 was good to look at but it cost half as much again as its competitors in the sporty car market. Only 8,500 were sold before the factory went into receivership.

The events of the next few years suggested that Andersen might not have been the most alert of watchdogs. An American federal grand jury indicted DeLorean for income tax evasion and mail and wire fraud after hearing evidence that he had diverted the funds of investors in DMC into his private bank account. He was acquitted of fraud but ordered to pay $9 million to creditors. Another jury told him to pay his lawyers $10.3 million in outstanding legal fees.[1]

Fraud wasn't the only charge thrown at him. While the British government was trying to extricate itself from the disaster, DeLorean looked around for a new source of funds. In October 1982, he was arrested during an FBI sting and charged with trying to import cocaine with a street value of $24 million. He claimed he had been set up and variously said he was the victim of a plot by American car-makers or Margaret Thatcher or the IRA. For good measure, he added that his children's lives were in danger. He was acquitted of all charges after a judge ruled that the FBI operation had been a clear case of entrapment. His wife left him. DeLorean became a born-again Christian.

The British government sued Andersen for negligence, fraud and breach of duty. Andersen's good name and its endoresement of DeLorean had persuaded Britain to invest in the doomed car. The auditors should have blown the whistle when suspicions about his financial dealings were raised by his colleagues, the Tories argued. They accused the accountants of concealing and delaying the discovery of its own 'breaches of duty' as well as of the allegedly 'fraudulent scheme of DeLorean'. The case was to drag on until Blair came to power more than a decade later. In the interim, juicy British contracts for advice on the privatisation of just about everything that wasn't nailed down went to Andersen's rivals.

The original Arthur Andersen was the son of Norwegian immigrants to Chicago who set up shop just before the First World War. He was scrupulous to the point of self-righteousness. When a railroad tycoon demanded that he approve accounts that had been inflated Enron-style, Andersen replied that there wasn't enough money in the city of Chicago to persaude him to pass cooked books. The tycoon took his business elsewhere. When his company went bust, Andersen's reputation for probity was made. But that was in 1914.

Arthur Andersen knew that business depends on honest numbers. Workers, investors and suppliers need to know they're not giving their labour, money and goods to a firm which is likely to disappear. For the numbers to be honest, the auditors have to be independent. But by the 1990s the governments of Britain and America, and the commercial lobbyists they listened to, were willing to destroy one of the bedrocks of capitalism in an effort to keep the accounting industry sweet. In New Labour London and Bill Clinton's and George Bush's Washington the Big Five firms of the accountancy cartel were forces regulators learned not to mess with.

The US Securities and Exchange Commission watched the bubble grow with prudent concern. 'The stock market had reached dizzying heights, and the corporate numbers game had grown more and more brazen,' recalled Arthur Levitt, its chairman in the 1990s. 'It began to appear as if the towering market rested on fictitious numbers.'[2] Independent auditors were needed to test the claims of share boosters, but independent men and women were thin on the ground. Independence would entail that auditors didn't own shares in the firms they were auditing. They weren't likely to rush to expose their clients if their investments would fall. Three-quarters of PricewaterhouseCoopers partners who were randomly sampled in the US by Levitt's staff were breaching the rules on the need for auditors to declare an interest in shares in companies they inspected. A revolving door between the Big Five and their corporate clients further dampened what independent spirit remained. Enron was stuffed with former Andersen employees. At Waste Management, a garbage company, also audited by Andersen, executives and auditors were accused by the Securities and Exchange Commission of manipulating financial statements to hide costs of $1.7 billion. From 1991 until 1997 every chief financial officer and chief accounting officer at Waste Management had previously worked as an auditor at Andersen. Fourteen ex-Andersen employees were still handling its finances when it went under. At Enron and Waste Management auditors hadn't exposed companies which might offer them a new career.

The greatest curb on independence was, however, the conflict of interest at the heart of the policing of business. In 1981 the average accounting company derived 15 per cent of its income from consulting services. By 1999, consulting delivered half of annual revenues.[3] An auditor wasn't going to make a fuss about bent executives if half his firm's turnover depended on persuading those same executives to buy advice on installing computers and dodging taxes. Andersen was making $25 million a year from its audit work for Enron and $27m from its consultancy services. It expected its Enron business to grow to $100 million. It was as if the police were allowed to sell services to criminal suspects.

Levitt could see that corporate standards were collapsing. Companies were restating their profits with alarming regularity. Between 1991 and 2000 the number of complaints from American investors to the SEC doubled. Reform was in the public interest, and Levitt decided to take on the Big Five. It was a battle he could only lose:

> Soon I was spending all my time deflecting a barrage of phone calls, visits, and letters from House and Senate members. Within a

month of issuing the proposed rule, I received negative letters from 46 members of Congress and two-thirds of the Senate Banking Committee's Securities Sub-Committee.

The Big Five had become Big Players in the money race which determined who had the funds to win American elections. In the 2000 Congressional and Presidential contests they doled out $14.5 million to candidates for Congress and the President. 'And boy did those donations get results,' said Levitt as he watched his reforms being gelded.

Levitt's defeat was a triumph for Harvey Pitt, a former SEC lawyer who was hired by the Big Five to lead the assault on his former employer. In November 2000 he secured a second victory when George W. Bush won the presidential election and decided that Pitt was just the man to head the SEC. Phil Gramm, Enron's senator from Texas, was at the scene of the mugging. He warned Levitt that the Senate would consider cutting the SEC's funds if it insisted on auditor independence.[4]

A few minor restrictions came in, but the world's stock markets were left free to float up to the stars on the back of the American boom. Andersen was left free to carry on helping Enron as only it knew how.

Enron's collapse lay in the future. While they were lords of all they surveyed, Enron and Andersen were free to tackle their local difficulty in Britain. Andersen was eager to get its name struck off the Tory blacklist. Enron feared that a Labour government would keep its promise to end the dash for gas-powered electricity and destroy the corporation's hopes of expanding from beyond its base at the gas-fired reactor in Teeside.

Both responded to the advent of New Labour with tried and tested strategies.

In the summer of 1996, Blair invited Roy Hattersley to address a seminar for 90 promising New Labour MPs at Templeton College, Oxford. Hattersley's Jurassic views weren't in favour, but the leadership was aware of how little experience of government Labour politicians had after almost two decades out of power. Hattersley and a few other old-timers were instructed to tell the next generation what they should expect if they became ministers. He lectured the MPs on how they must master their briefs and win the respect of civil servants. He warned them that in government they must be prepared for any crisis the media seized on, real or imagined, to be their responsibility.

As he warmed to his theme, the blood went to his head and he went too far. Mere managerial ability was all very well, he continued, but it wasn't enough. As Labour politicians they needed to remember that their democractic socialist principles would be their true and constant guides. There was no point in having politicians if all that was required was good managers. There were technocrats outside Parliament who could manage departments better than any MP. Politicians were elected because they had a clear view of how the world should go which they applied to whatever opportunites or misfortunes befell them in office. Without ideology, they would preside over an aimless mush of an administration. In years to come, people would look back and ask what the point of them had been.

His audience was disgusted. It hadn't heard anything as crude in years. Young politicians, led by Geoff Hoon, heckled the eminent Hattersley with bellows of 'What's wrong with being a good manager?', 'What's wrong with managerialism?'

Hattersley was too taken aback to notice that the seminar was sponsored by the experts in modern management from Arthur Andersen. New Labour was following Andersen. Or perhaps Andersen was following New Labour. By the end, it was difficult to tell the difference between the two.

Andersen had despaired of the hard-hearted Tories ever forgiving the small matter of the missing $156 million, and had been sinking its claws into Labour for years. Its best hope of winning back government business was to see the government change. The idea that the Labour Party would be amenable to the wooing of John DeLorean's accountants would once have been ridiculous. Before 1997, the party was committed to banning auditors from selling extras to their clients.

But Andersen had a better reading of politics than most commentators and nearly all Labour Party members. A beautiful friendship began. In 1994 Patricia Hewitt became head of reasearch at Andersen Consulting. A team of Andersen accountants advised New Labour on how to impose a windfall tax on the privatised utilities when it came to power. Geoffrey Robinson MP, Gordon Brown's ally, enthused about the quality of the work in his autobiography:

> It was a research exercise that would have been inconceivable in the cramped conditions and with the limited resources already stretched to breaking point of the shadow Treasury team. Nor could the task in hand be done by a group of sympathetic part-timers. We needed professionals and we had some of the best.

Advice for many another Labour policy was offered at bargain basement prices.

Within months of the general election victory, Labour abandoned its promise to regulate Andersen and its rivals, and settled the DeLorean unpleasantness. The Tories hadn't been prepared to let it drop. The Conservative Northern Ireland minister Michael Ancram said in his last months in power that he remained determined to get the public's money back. New Labour arrived, and in November 1997 government lawyers working for the Treasury solicitor cut a deal. Andersen agreed to pay just over £21 million – which barely covered the government's legal costs, and was one tenth of the £200 million demanded by the Tories. Andersen staff were seconded to the Treasury team. Andersen went on to help create such triumphs of New Labour's first term as the ripping up of London Underground, the management of Railtrack, and, but of course, the Millennium Dome.[5] Andersen also produced all manner of seemingly authoratitive reports which stated, *inter alia*, that Britain was the best place in the world to do business (which was possibly true for the shyster) and that the Private Finance Initiative was great value for money (which was palpable nonsense, as academics at University College, London, proved within days). Both studies were quoted by ministers as author-

itative, independent evidence from ajudicators whose impar-
tiality and good judgement could be trusted. Matthew Taylor,
the Liberal Democrat Treasury spokesman, noted that
'Although a series of reports [on the PFI] have been published,
the government always quote the Arthur Andersen report
because it is the only one to support their position.'

Andersen went from being shunned to being Whitehall's
favourite consultants. The fees rolled in and the tosh rolled out.
Was Andersen's rehabilitation dishonest? Certainly not, said the
government. The DeLorean affair had been settled by lawyers of
unimpeachable probity. No pictures of ministers taking brown
envelopes had been produced. No witnesses had testified to a
pact being struck. Favours had been given and received, but
that was correlation not causation. Where was the conclusive
proof? Where was the smoking gun?

Enron's entry from the cold was as speedy. Margaret Beckett
was put in charge of energy policy after the 1997 election and
kept Labour's promise to save what was left of the coal industry
by imposing a moratorium on gas-fired power stations. Enron
seemed snookered. Its clout was with the old regime. Lord
Wakeham had joined its board after obligingly opening the
British market to Enron and firms like Enron. But he was a Tory
and the government was Labour. His Lordship couldn't be
expected to have a voice in public policy in the new era. Wakeham's public duties were confined to more than a dozen direc-
torships on company boards and the chairmanship of the Press
Complaints Commission, which gave the man from Enron's
audit committee the task of regulating the morals and manners
of me and my colleagues. His regulatory touch was light.

In the United States, Enron had learned that it was an easy
matter to befriend both parties. Enron's lobbyists got to work
on New Labour. They were drawn from a smarmy sub-culture
of Third-Way influence peddlers which appeared within
months of Blair winning the 1997 election. Karl Milner was typical of the species. He resigned as a special adviser to Gordon
Brown and joined GJW, a lobbying firm which had shown its

friendship to the new regime by giving Labour £15,000. Milner was pitching for the Enron account. He explained to Greg Palast, an *Observer* reporter who posed as a businessman, how Enron's problems might be managed. First Enron had to find new friends who could whisper in the right ears. GJW 'had many friends in government. They like to run things past us some days in advance to get our view.' Milner proved he wasn't a braggart by producing an unpublished parliamentary report on the future of energy policy. There were ways round the ban on new gas-fired power stations, he continued:

> The way you go about it is that you play on the existing prejudices within the Cabinet for coal, you play on the existing prejudices within the Cabinet for competition and you play the forces off against each other. It's intimate knowledge of what is going on that produces results in the end. That's how GJW makes money.[6]

Enron sponsored the 1998 Labour Conference in Blackpool, and gave £38,000 to the party in total. True, the party's fund-raisers didn't know at the time that Enron was a criminal organisation. All they could have known was that Enron threw jobs and money at American politicians and regulators, espoused a free-market fundamentalism which would have made Margaret Thatcher blink and presided over the mass beatings of peasants in the Third World. Enron also gave £25,000 to the Tories. As in America, all bases were covered. Even though the Tories weren't going to win, they couldn't make a fuss about Enron's friendship with New Labour when their relationship was as chummy.

Just after the Blackpool conference, Peter Mandelson allowed Enron to buy Wessex Water. Enron saw water as the successor to the power, a boring regulated industry it could profitably chop up. The world's water market was worth $300 billion, Enron estimated. The householders of the West Country were to form a base from where Enron's water arm could flex its muscles all over the planet. It seemed a profitable notion, and Rebecca Mark, who had presided over the Indian deal, was in charge of 'making it happen'. Wessex Water was split off from Enron and sold for $695 million. Mark's share options were worth $50 million. Within two years, Enron's water business was bust. Mark paid way over the odds for an Argentinian water company. Her business was financed by off-balance-sheet special-purpose entitites, whose debts would help bring down Enron. But at the time it seemed that Mandelson was giving Enron what it wanted.

The Clinton administration meanwhile was lobbying hard to end the protection of the British coal industry. A description of how sustained the pressure could be when Clinton's people got behind their corporations came from John Kachamila, the Natural Resources Minister for Mozambique, who received a bid from Enron to run a natural gas project in his country:

> There were outright threats [from the US Embassy] to withhold development funds if we didn't sign, and sign soon. Their diplomats pressured me to sign a deal that was not good for Mozambique. We got calls from US senators threatening us with this and that if we didn't sign. They put together a smear campaign . . . everyone said I wouldn't sign the deal because I wanted a percentage, when all I wanted was a better deal for the state.'7

For whatever reason, New Labour caved in. In 1999 it gave Enron permission to build a gas-fired power station in Kent. In July 2000 it made Ralph Hodge, the boss of Enron Europe, a Commander of the British Empire, for his 'services to the gas and power industries'.

Enron was at the heart of New Labour. Far from shunning Lord Wakeham, Blair put him in charge of the Royal Commission on the reform of the House of Lords. All other democracies had a second chamber which was elected directly or indirectly. They realised that democracy rather depended on elections. Wakeham disagreed. He and his great-and-good colleagues recommended a House of Lords where only a small fraction of the members would condescend to put themselves before the electorate. The majority would be quangocrats chosen by the party machines. A director of one of the most odious companies ever to come to the market was denying the British people democractic goverment. In the end, the Enron man's plan for Parliament was too democratic for Blair. He decided that the Lords should consist of quangocrats and the rump of the aristocracy. There wasn't to be a single elected member. Not one.

Among the many academics and journalists Enron had on its pay roll was Irwin Stelzer, an elderly American free-marketeer, who would have been an obscure figure had he not struck a friendship with Rupert Murdoch. A column in the *Sunday Times* followed. Stelzer was always in Downing Street to advise Blair on how the British should be governed. On one splendid occasion in early 2001, Gordon Brown invited Enron's adviser to a seminar in his official residence. The subject was how to restore a 'moral sense' to a depraved society. Among the ideas run up the flagpole by the blue-sky thinkers was the need for a religious revival. A *Guardian* journalist who was present said, without naming names, that one speaker explained to the Chancellor of the Exchequer that 'moral revival may involve locking up single mothers in institutions to ensure their offspring are taught virtue'.[8] The rich would cash in, while the poor slopped out.

Were Labour's political and financial dealings with Enron dishonest? Ralph Hodge CBE suggested that they were. 'I don't think that we would have been successful at getting [to] the top table without donations . . . It is clear in the current climate, sponsorship and donations are the most efficient ways of gaining access.'[9] The government indignantly spluttered that the relationship was proper. The takeover of Wessex Water was a normal takeover of a privately owned business which Mr Mandelson had no reason to stop. The moratorium on building gas stations had always been a temporary measure, and by 1999 its usefulness was at an end. In any case, where was the smoking gun? Where were the finger-prints on the warm barrel which proved beyond reasonable doubt that the government was guilty? All conspiracy theorists had done was assemble facts into an order which suited them. They weren't being clever and they weren't being funny. The Prime Minister's official spokesperson dismissed the affair as the 'great Enron yawnathon'.

Presumably Bernie Ecclestone (the tycoon who ran Formula One), Rupert Murdoch (the media tycoon) and Lakshmi Mittal (the steel tycoon) were as dull. Ecclestone provided a taste of what was come when he slipped New Labour £1 million just before the 1997 election under conditions of the strictest confidentiality. New Labour had been committed to banning the tobacco companies from sponsoring sport. Ecclestone collared Blair and warned him that Formula One would be driven overseas if the prohibition was enacted. There weren't many who understood the economics of motor racing who agreed with him, but Blair did. He ordered his health ministers to make Formula One a special case, while imposing the ban on Old Labour sports such as darts, greyhound racing and snooker, which would suffer more from the loss of tobacco money. This was a shocking betrayal. Most of the progressive middle classes regarded smoking as an unpardonable sin. It was a greater social error to light up a fag in their living rooms than sexually assault the family pet. After weeks of lying, the government admitted that it had been paid by Ecclestone. The whole affair reeked. But, as the government pointed out, there was no smoking gun to settle the matter. 'Closure' was obtained by Blair going on the BBC's Sunday political show and saying:

> I hope that people know me well enough and realise the type of person I am . . . I would never do anything to harm the country or anything improper. I never have. I think that most people who have dealt with me think that I am a pretty straight sort of guy.

'How did I do?' Blair asked Alastair Campbell when the cameras stopped rolling.

'It did the job,' Campbell replied.[10]

Murdoch gave New Labour a gift worth more than money, the backing of his *Sun* newspaper. Blair lobbied for Murdoch in Europe and, in 2003, presented a Communications Bill to Par-

liament which debased the legislature by asking his whipped
MPs to do the tax-dodging monopolist another favour and
pave the way for his media empire to take over Channel 5.

I've saved the best to last. Mittal was a peach. The steel magnate gave New Labour £125,000 before the 2001 election. Blair
then wrote to the Romanian government and attempted to persuade it to sell a steel works to Mittal. Every explanation for
Blair's behaviour fell apart, until just one remained.

Downing Street told lobby correspondents that Mittal's
LNM steel firm was a 'British company'. It was nothing of the
sort. LNM employed only a handful of people in London. As
with so many others who donated to political parties, profits
went to the tax havens – in the Dutch Antilles in this instance.
Mittal had a home in London and could vote in British elections. The *Guardian* discovered that he had the rights but not
the responsibilities of the rest of the population because of a
loophole in the law which allowed wealthy foreigners to avoid
personal tax. In opposition, Labour denounced the scam as
'indefensible', but in office, the party couldn't find the time to
stop the abuse. Enron paid virtually no tax in the 1990s. The
Hindujas hid their documents in Swiss bank vaults. Rupert
Murdoch's newspapers harangued the scrounging poor while
sending their profits off-shore. It was hard to resist the impression that a large proportion of the people who funded politics
were using a small proportion of their tax-free gains to keep in
place a world order which tolerated the tax havens that served
them so well.

Blair's letter to the Romanian prime minister was presented
by Downing Street as a polite note which simply congratulated
him for concluding an agreement with Mittal. The Welsh
Nationalists and the *Sunday Telegraph* showed that Blair intervened at the moment when the Romanians were thinking of
selling their steelworks to Mittal's French rivals. The Romanians took Blair's letter as an endorsement of Mittal's bona fides.
The Prime Minister, the *Observer* found, couldn't have injured
the interests of Labour-voting steelworkers in Britain more

grievously if he had tried. Blair was helping a billionaire whose American subsidiary was calling on George W. Bush to impose tariffs on steel from Britain and elsewhere (which Bush duly did).

The Mittal scandal came shortly after the Enron and Andersen scandals, and for a few weeks in February 2002 men and women of moderate temperament stuggled to come to terms with the painful thought that Blair was bent. It was too much for them to handle. On the BBC Six o'Clock News, journalists broke the first rule of journalism and said that the Enron and Andersen affairs were 'complicated'. Hacks should never say a story is complicated because they know that viewers will switch over or off if they do. (In any event, how was it complicated? Money was given and services were rendered. Did I lose any of you when I set out the train of events? You kept up at the back? Excellent.) Blairites in the *Independent* warned that those who investigated corruption were reviving the nihilism of the Weimar Republic. Respectable pundits trumpeted that Britain wasn't as corrupt as Italy, while showing no stomach for the fight to keep it that way. Where was the smoking gun? they demanded. Where was the prosecution case proven beyond reasonable doubt?

There was no smoking gun in the Mittal affair, nor in any of the other scandals, for the plain reason that guns are found by detectives at crime scenes. Journalists and opposition politicians can't produce them unless they are flukishly lucky. They don't have powers to subpoena evidence or interview witnesses under oath or send officers into Downing Street with a search warrant. The police do, but the police have never in my lifetime investigated allegations of honours being sold or favours being given in return for campaign donations. In France magistrates investigating the Elf-Aquitane scandal have revealed the corruptions of the Franco-German political classes. In Italy magistrates put Silvio Berlusconi on trial for corruption. British judges don't investigate. They deal with cases brought to them by the Crown. In the United States, Congress can call witnesses and question them under oath. There is a separation of powers between the legislature and the executive. The president and the Cabinet aren't drawn from Congressional ranks. Members of Congress are prepared on occasion to take on presidents, even when the president is from their own party. The British executive is drawn from the legislature. About 100 office-holders are MPs from the governing party. They must give up their jobs if they wish to investigate real or alleged abuse. Behind them are MPs who covet their jobs. They too have no inclination to ask embarrassing questions. The monarchical power of the Prime Minister is such that he decides what business the legislature should discuss. Only the Commons select committees show a faint pulse of life. But they can't force witnesses to give evidence or civil servants to release documents. The 'Where's the smoking gun?' question is well chosen. It's the best shot in the establishment's locker. For Britain is a land where the guns never smoke. All the British can do is look at the correlations and judge men by the company they keep.

The millennium bubble proved than none of the checks of modern capitalism worked. Contrary to assurances given by several generations of Nobel Prize-winning economists, investors turned out to be as rational as a sack of ferrets. The banks lied to their customers. The share options which were meant to give executives an incentive to act in the interests of shareholders encouraged them to loot and defraud. The accountants who were meant to police business let the thieving continue for fear of losing fees.

Capitalism's collapses normally have the beneficial side-effect of making overdue reform an imperative. After the Wall Street Crash of 1929, Franklin Delano Roosevelt was elected President. In his inauguration address in 1933 he declared:

> The money changers have fled from their high seats in the temple of our civilisation. We may now restore that temple to the ancient truths. The measure of the restoration lies in the extent to which we apply social values more noble than mere monetary profit.

Roosevelt introduced restrictions on capitalism which protected America until the Clinton administration abolished them in
the 1990s.

The end of the millennium boom forced even Bush's America to imitate FDR in a small measure. Hardly anyone went to
prison because while the taking of $100 is theft, the taking of
$100 million is a 'market failure'. Nonetheless, Bush was com-
pelled to require the chief executives of companies trading on
Wall Street to swear to the veracity of their accounts and to
impose restrictions on the services accountants could sell. After
British troops had risked their lives in Afghanistan, Blair tried
to call in the favours Bush owed by attempting to persuade him
to exclude British companies from the minimum standards.
Law officers in New York and other states and cities seized the
emails which showed how the investment banks were passing
off worthless goods. The Financial Services Authority said it
believed the same con was going down in London – the same
banks were operating in the City and Wall Street, so the suspicion was plausible. However, it didn't send in detectives. Instead
it asked the banks to own up to wrongdoing. None did.

The accountancy giants could count themselves lucky that
Patricia Hewitt, formerly of Arthur Andersen, was Secretary of
State for Trade and Industry when the world of the 1990s fell
apart. PricewaterhouseCoopers, KPMG, Arthur Andersen,
Ernst & Young and Deloitte & Touche had sold themselves as
global operators. Until the crash, the global reach of global
firms was a phenomenon so obvious it was scarcely worth men-
tioning. But after Enron, WorldCom and the dotcoms there was
an unnoticed economic revolution. The same politicians and
business leaders who assured the public that globalisation was
inevitable now denied that globalisation existed. National differences were rescued, and British businessmen were discovered to be uniquely virtuous. An honesty gene in the Surrey
stock-market belt or a mystery element in the Thames water
ensured that the City was place of probity and honour whose
accountants couldn't be more different from the vulgar and

grasping Yanks. It transpired that there was all the difference in the world between accountants from the same firm in London and Washington. There was no need to protect pensioners and investors, because the City wasn't interested in grabbing as much money as possible by whatever means it could. Melanie Johnson, Hewitt's deputy, said the 'greed-based culture' of the States 'is not nearly as prevalent in the UK'. Peter Wyman, the leader of Britain's accountants, agreed. His colleagues were guided by solid principles, he said, whereas the American cow-boys were always trying to see 'how close to the line' they could get. The police demurred. The National Criminal Intelligence Service complained in 2001 that only 1 per cent of the reports of possible money laundering its officers received were from accountants. Their protests were in vain. The culture which produced DeLorean, Enron and Andersen was allowed to con-tinue on its way unmolested.

In 2003 as in 1993, the political class's response to public unease was more gestures on crime and more bashing of asylum-seekers. In 2003 as in 1993, public services were to be improved by privatisation and commercialisation. You couldn't hear yourself think for the noise of the barking dogs, but the wretched caravan never moved on.

Everything changed, except New Labour.

Unable to adapt, sooner or later it will die. Blair might have gone during the Iraq crisis, and may have gone by the time you read these lines. I know I'm partial, but there doesn't seem to be one good reason for New Labour to remain in office when its ambition is so puny. Lack of exercise wastes away a political body. It atrophies because it has nothing to do.

The 1990s system of manipulation, however, is a sturdier beast which may have years of life left in it. In the financial mar-kets, universities, media and politics it depends on the assertion that the élite holders of power are acting in the name of 'the People'. The failure to provide a coherent response to this absurdity has been the greatest failure of the opponents of the status quo. A start might be made by accepting that there is no monolithic 'people'. There are barbaric and democratic sensi-bilities on the left as well as the right. There are different classes and interests, which the rhetoric about 'the People' disguises. The stock-market crash and the robbery of the middle classes which followed has produced a country in which the majority of those classes and interests no longer benefit from the dereg-ulated markets and regurgitated policies of the bubble world. This is a potential coalition for change. But the greatest success of the bubble world was to disable the only vehicle for change, the Labour Party. Without the prospect of reform, anger is directionless, and the new élite can carry on as if nothing has happened.

Acknowledgements

Harry Fletcher kindly allowed me access to his files on the recent history of crime policy. Vanessa Thorpe, Chris Blackhurst, Antony Barnett, Richard Heller and Robert McCrum were my guides around the Dome. Thomas Frank was an invaluable source of information on American capitalism in the 1990s. Professor Prem Sikka, Caroline Attfield, David Oliver and Peter Allen helped me understand the City. I owe a debt of gratitude to Francis Wheen and Euan Ferguson, who read the manuscript and were irrepressible sources of inspiration. Natasha Fairweather at A. P. Watt and Jon Riley at Faber and Faber stayed calm and thoughtful as deadlines whooshed by. Above all, Anne-Marie Ellis helped me with my labours until the moment she went into labour. This book is dedicated to my mother and father, who tried their best to bring me up properly. Neither they nor anyone else are responsible for its errors of taste and judgement. They remain, as always, the sole responsibility of the author.

Nick Cohen
London, 2003

References

ONE Snobs and Mobs

1 Nick Cohen, 'The Fear, the Shame, the Guilt', *Independent on Sunday*, 21 February 1993

2 Gitta Sereny, *Independent on Sunday*, 6 February 1994 and 13 February 1994

3 Euan Ferguson, 'How the Death of Bulger Hardened us to Pity', *Observer*, 31 October 1999

4 Even Blair's sympathetic biographer John Rentoul, the author of *Tony Blair*, Little, Brown, 1995, noticed that something stank about Blair's reaction. 'His speech was of no direct relevance to the Bulger case ... It was like a Conservative politician's speech, responding to a moral panic induced by an atypical case by condemning moral decline.'

5 Quoted in Donald Macintyre, *Mandelson: The Biography*, HarperCollins, 1999, p.241

6 Philip Gould, *The Unfinished Revolution: How the Modernisers Saved the Labour Party*, Little, Brown, 1998, pp.162–71

7 Rentoul, *Tony Blair*, p.281

8 Christopher Hitchens, *No One Left to Lie To*, Verso, 1999, p.33

9 Hitchens, p.35

10 Gould, p.188

11 *Financial Times*, 21 November 1994. Quoted in Nyta Mann and Paul Anderson, *Safety First: The Making of New Labour*, Granta,1997, p.255

12 *Guardian*, 8 October 1994

13 Melanie Phillips, 'One Boy's Cycle of Despair', *Guardian*, 14 December 1990

14 'Rough Justice for Juveniles', *Independent*, 28 August 1996

15 Alan Travis, 'Child Jail "Overuses Force"', *Guardian*, 15 January 1999

16 'Blair Wants On-the-Spot Fines for Louts', *Guardian*, 1 July 2000

17 Count of bills: National Association of Probation Officers. New offences: series of written answers given to Simon Hughes MP,

beginning with response to question of 8 April 2003. Crime initiatives: Oliver Letwin, interview on the *Today* programme, 12 March 2003

18 Hitchens, p.25

19 *The 2001 British Crime Survey*, Home Office London

TWO Elected Every Day

1 George Walden, *The New Élites*, Penguin, 2000, pp.42 and 65

2 Greg Philo, ed., *Market Killing*, Longman, 2000

3 Philip Gould, *The Unfinished Revolution*, Little, Brown, p.293

4 Richard Stengel and Eric Pooley, 'Masters of the Message: Inside the high-tech machine that set Clinton and Dole polls apart', *Time*, 6 November 1996

5 Gould, p.326

6 Sir Patrick Devlin, 'Trial by Jury', Hamlyn Lecture, 1956

7 The figure is based on estimates from the National Association of Probation Officers, the First Division Association of senior civil servants and the Association of Magisterial Officers. See Nick Cohen, 'Who Needs 12 When One Will Do?', *New Statesman*, 3 December 2001

8 Quoted in *Century of the Self* by Adam Curtis, broadcast on BBC2 in 2002. See also Nick Cohen, 'Primal Therapy', *Observer*, 31 March 2002

9 Walden, p.174

10 Geoffrey Wheatcroft , 'Who's In Charge?', *Guardian*, 12 March 2001. Nick Cohen, 'Hacking Their Way to a Fortune', *New Statesman*, 3 April 2000

11 Graham Allen MP, *The Last Prime Minister: Being Honest about the UK Presidency*, Politico's Books (also available at www.grahamallen.labour.co.uk)

12 Figures quoted in the *Economist*, 8 March 2002

13 Quotes and figure from Steven Barnett and Emily Simpson, *A Shrinking Iceberg Travelling South: Changing Trends in British Television*, University of Westminster, 1999

14 Quoted in Geoffrey Wheatcroft, 'The Press and the Swinish Multitude,' *New Statesman*, 11 December 2000

15 Hansard, 6 December 2000

16 Kevin Maguire, 'Muckraker Who Feeds off Bins of the Famous', *Guardian*, 27 July 2000

17 *Guardian*, 27 July 2000

THREE 'They Hid Their Gold and Fawned and Whined'

1 *Daily Mail*, 3 February 1900

2 'Scandal of How it Costs Nearly as Much to Keep an Asylum
   Seeker as a Room at the Ritz', *Daily Mail*, 2 February 2000

3 'Why Begging is Such a Threat', *Daily Mail*, 10 March 2000

4 'The Betrayal of British Couples', *Daily Mail*, 10 July 2000

5 'Nailing Press Myths about Refugees', Refugee Council, December
   2002

6 Jason Bennetto, 'Warning to Editors on Racist Reports', *Independent*, 17 December 1998

7 Nick Cohen, 'A Terrible Viciousness is Born', *New Statesman*, 24
   February 2003

8 *The Final Report of the Committee of Inquiry into Hunting with
   Dogs in England and Wales*, HMSO, 2000, found that 'methods
   involving guns probably account for the greater part of foxes
   killed'. With unsurpassable bureaucratese it continued: 'We are
   satisfied that this experience [of being hunted by dogs] seriously
   compromises the welfare of the fox. We are satisifed that the activity of digging out and shooting a fox involves a serious compromise of its welfare.'

9 Quoted in Alan Travis, 'And Still They Come', *Guardian*, 25 January 2000

10 In 1998 only 0.9 million of the 22.4 million people recognised as
    refugees by the United Nations were in the developed world's
    countries' asylum systems: *United Nations High Commissioner for
    Refugees by Numbers*, Geneva, 1998. For country comparisons see
    By Invitation Only: Australian Human Rights Policy, Human Rights
    Watch, 2002 (available at www.hrw.org)

11 David Held and Anthony McGrew, *Globalization/Anti-Globaliza-
    tion* (Polity Press, 2002), p.120

12 *Asylum Statistics 2001*, Home Office, London

13 'Nailing Press Myths About Refugees', Refugee Council, 2002: it
    quotes Home Office figures from the second quarter of that year

14 For sacking of staff to pay for the useless system see Mike Simons,
    'PAC Slams "Ridiculous" Attempt to Hide Immigration IT Deba-
    cle', *Computer Weekly*, 22 February 2001. For phone calls see Nick
    Cohen, 'This Far and No Further', *Observer*, 9 May 1999, and
    Hansard, 27 July 1999, column 254. For how Siemens got its cash
    see 'What Difference Did Labour Make?', *Computer Weekly*, 5 June
    2001

15 *Whitehall and the Jews 1933–1948: British Immigration and the Holocaust*, Cambridge University Press, 2000, pp.60-61

16 For the neglected story of Saddam's racial purity campaigns see 'Iraq: Forcible expulsion of ethnic minorities', Human Rights Watch, March 2003 (www.hrw.org/reports/2003/iraq0303]

17 Hansard, 2 November 1992, column 38

18 The standard rejection letters were put on the Home Office's website. See Francis Wheen, 'Refuge Refused', *Guardian*, 21 April 1999

19 Figures and anecdotes given by Earl Russell in House of Lords. Hansard, 30 April 1996, column 1619

20 Hansard, 2 November 1992, column 42

21 John Morrison, 'The Cost of Survival', British Refugee Council, 1998

22 Hansard Special Standing Committee on the Immigration and Asylum Bill, 20 April 1999

23 From the transactions of the Standing Special Committee on the Immigration and Asylum Bill, 11 May 1999

24 For the short, miserable history of vouchers see 'Token Gestures: The Effects of the Voucher Scheme on Asylum Seekers and Organisations in the UK', Oxfam Policy Papers, December 2000 (www.oxfam.org.uk/policy/papers/vouchers/main.htm)

25 Alan Travis, 'Sainsbury's Hits Back on Vouchers', *Guardian*, 15 March 2000

26 David Blunkett abolished vouchers in the autumn of 2001 after a campaign led by the unions and back-bench MPs. The government was forced to promise changes to the fines on lorry drivers after a challenge in the courts in 2002.

27 For a full discussion see Lejla Mavris, 'Human Smugglers and Social Networks: Transit Migration through the States of Former Yugoslavia', UN High Commission for Refugees, December 2002

28 'Home Office Announces Budget Settlement', press release, 9 April 2003

FOUR Have a Nice Holocaust Day

1 Zoe Williams, 'Grin and Bear What Exactly?', *Guardian*, 12 November 2002

2 Jeevan Vasagar, 'History Teaching in UK Stokes Xenophobia, says German Envoy', *Guardian*, 9 December 2002

3 Ian Kershaw, 'The Thing About Hitler', *Guardian*, 29 January 2003

4 For the strange history of Holocaust commemoration see Peter

Novick, *The Holocaust and Collective Memory*, Bloomsbury, 1999

5 Novick, p.202

6 Novick, p.193

7 Nick Cohen, 'The Holocaust as Show Business', *New Statesman*, 20 November 2002

8 Norman Finkelstein, *The Holocaust Industry*, Verso, 2000, pp.21–37

9 Finkelstein, p.130

10 Paul Berman, *Terror and Liberalism*, Norton, 2003, pp.56–7. Christopher Hitchens, 'Saddam: He's Hitler, he is Stalin . . . why did we tolerate him for so long?', *Daily Mirror*, 21 March 2003

11 Oliver Burkeman, 'Harvard Bars Oxford Poet', *Guardian*, 14 November 2002. After months of fuss, Paulin said that his views had been misrepresented.

12 Berman, pp.139–41. Berman has a fascinating chapter on what happens to intellectuals when they try to find rational causes for irrational phenomena – Nazism in the 1930s, the Islamic death cults today.

13 Novick, pp.14, 256

14 Novick, p.220

15 Faber and Faber, 2003

16 Julian Stallabrass, *High Art Lite*, Verso, 1999, p.129. By one-liner art, he meant that Britart produced the instant responses of the audience at a stand-up show who hear a gag, chortle, then wait for the next hit. As in, 'Oh look, someone's put a dead shark in a tank filled with formaldehyde. You've got to laugh. Next!'

17 Quoted in David Aaronovitch, *Benn and Saddam*, Guardian, 4 February 2003

18 The details of the purges of the Baath party, orders given for the genocide of Kurds and Arab Christians and the dual use of plastic shredding come from witness statements and evidence collected by Indict, which was established in 1996 to campaign to bring the perpetrators of crimes against humanity to justice. Read www.indict.org.uk, if your stomach's strong enough. The figure of 500,000 deaths from malnutrition and disease comes from Unicef; other estimates lower it to 300,000. For accounts of the failed CIA assassination plot and the slaughters of the Kurds and Shia in 1991 see Andrew and Patrick Cockburn, *Saddam Hussein: An American Obsession*, Verso, 2002

19 Channel 4 News, 15 March 2003

FIVE The Second Battle of Stalingrad

1 Philip Webster, Tom Baldwin and Michael Evans, 'The Day Straw and Blair Nearly Quit', *The Times*, 26 April 2003. Patrick Wintour, 'When Blair Stood on the Brink', *Guardian*, 26 April 2003. The transcripts of the 26 February and 18 March debates can be read in the daily debate section of Hansard (www.parliament.the-stationery-office.co.uk)

2 Approval ratings: *Guardian*, 26 April 2003. Opposition to war: *Financial Times*, 28 April 2003

3 Figures from Fareed Zakaria, 'The Arrogant Empire', *Newsweek*, 24 March 2003

4 *Guardian*, 23 April 2003

5 For a ludicrous and self-serving prediction that the bombing of Afghanistan would lead to mass starvation see Nick Cohen, 'Bread Not Bombs', *Observer*, 14 October 2001

6 The love of Clinton is discussed in Perry Anderson, 'Casuistries of Peace and War', *London Review of Books*, 6 March 2003

7 George Monbiot, 'A Discreet Deal in the Pipeline', *Guardian*, 15 February 2001

8 John Pilger, 'Australia's under side', *Guardian*, 5 October 1999

9 John Bulloch and Harvey Morris, *No Friends but the Mountains: The Tragic History of the Kurds*, Viking, 1992, p.95

10 Bulloch and Morris, p.140

11 Letter in *New Statesman*, 14 April 2003

12 Nick Cohen, 'Strange Bedfellows', *New Statesman*, 7 April 2003

13 Nick Cohen, 'The Left's Unholy Alliance with Religious Bigotry', *Observer*, 23 February 2003

14 David Margolick, 'Blair's Big Gamble', *Vanity Fair*, June 2002

SIX The Big Tent

1 The minutes of the meeting were leaked by a minister anxious to escape blame for the subsequent shambles; see *Mail on Sunday*, 12 November 2000

2 Adam Nicolson, *Regeneration: The Story behind the Dome*, HarperCollins, 1999, p.141. As the Dome's official historian, Nicolson had unrivalled access and is a valuable source for students of the folly. Unfortunately, he published just before the Dome opened. His failure to spot the oncoming train-wreck and his raving predictions that the Dome would be a 'Teflon Ayers Rock . . . a Pantheon on the beach, a sunshade for an entire seaside resort, an

envelope for something, or for nothing in particular,' make *Regeneration* a late but credible contender for the title Most Misconceived Book of the Twentieth Century.

3 Michael Grade, 'It's Unignorable: The Dome Exerts a Firm Hold on Visitors, for all the Complaints about its Pointlessness', *Guardian*, 15 January 2000. Nicolson, p.172

4 *Patriots: National Identity in Britain 1940–2000*, Macmillan, 2002

5 *Observer*, 30 March 1998

7 In *How the Emperor Got His Clothes. Rupert Murdoch: The Untold Story of the World's Greatest Media Wizard*, Crown Business, 2002, Neil Chenoweth explains: 'Kelvin McKenzie, probably the world's greatest tabloid editor (certainly the most obnoxious), used to stalk the newsroom [of the *Sun*] urging his reporters generally to annoy the powers that be, to "put a ferret up their trousers". He would do this until the moment it became clear that in the course of making up stories, inventing quotes, invading people's privacy and stepping on toes, the *Sun* had committed some truly hideous solecism – like running the wrong lottery numbers – when he would rush back to the newsroom shouting, "Reverse ferret!" This is the survival moment, when a tabloid changes course in a blink without any reduction in speed, volume, or moral outrage.'

8 Nicolson, pp.196–7

9 'Murdoch's Newscorp has paid no tax since 1988', *Guardian*, 19 March 1999

10 McNulty's research and the line from 1970s therapy to Blairism was shown in *The Century of the Self*, a four-part series by Adam Curtis broadcast on BBC2 in 2002

11 *Daily Mail*, 11 November 2002

12 Report by the Comptroller and Auditor General, HMSO, 9 November 2000

SEVEN The Cashondeliveri Brothers

1 Copies of the correspondence between the Hindujas and Downing Street were released by the Conservative MP Andrew Tyrie in 2001

2 Chris Blackhurst, *Independent*, 2 March 2001

3 Sir Anthony Hammond KCB, QC, *Review of the Circumstances Surrounding an Application for Naturalisation by Mr SP Hinduja*, HMSO, March 2001, pp.93–4

4 Hammond, p.110

5 'Guns and the Dome', *New Statesman*, 15 November 1999, and
    'Have Faith and Pass the Bofors Gun', *Observer*, 19 December 1999
6 The Penguin paperback edition of Andrew Rawnsley, *Servants of
    the People*, has a full account
7 Hammond, p.12
8 Hammond, p.13
9 Hammond, p.21
10 Hammond, pp. 45–6
11 Hammond, p.61
12 Hammond, p.60
13 Hammond, p.64
14 Hammond, p.71
15 Hammond, p.70

EIGHT 'A Complication of Knavery and Cozenage'

1 Quoted in Thomas Frank, *One Market Under God*, Doubleday,
    New York, 2000. Essential reading if you want to understand the
    mess we're in.
2 Charles Kindleberger, *Manias, Panics and Crashes*, New York, 1989
3 Gary Hamel, *Leading the Revolution*, Harvard Business School
    Press, 2000
4 See Robert Gordon, *Does The New Economy Measure Up to the
    Great Inventions of the Past?*, National Bureau of Economic
    Research, Working Paper No. 7833
5 Will Hutton, 'Please Sir, I Don't Want to be an Economist',
    Observer, 13 June 1999
6 Edward Chancellor, *Devil Take the Hindmost*, Macmillan, 1998, p.95
7 John Maynard Keynes, *The General Theory of Employment, Inter-
    est and Money*, Macmillan: St Martin's Press, 1936, p.156
8 Biggs's story is told in John Cassidy, *dot.con: The Greatest Story
    Every Sold*, Penguin, 2002
9 Cassidy, p.210
10 David Teather, 'The Whores of Wall Street', *Guardian*, 2 October
    2002
11 Chancellor, p.67
12 Malcolm Balen, *A Very English Deceit*, Fourth Estate, 2002, p.155
13 Chancellor, p.56
14 John Kenneth Galbraith, *The Great Crash 1929*, Penguin, p.59. It's
    still in print and a charitable reader could consider giving a copy
    to Gordon Brown.

NINE Bribed and Unbribed

1 San Diego *Union-Tribune*, 2 February 2001
2 Peter C. Faruso and Ross M. Miller, *What Went Wrong at Enron?*, John Wiley & Sons, 2002, p.28
3 Faruso and Miller, p.51
4 Marie Brenner, 'The Enron Wars', *Vanity Fair*, April 2002. Robert Bryce, *Pipe Dreams: Greed, Ego, Jealousy and the Death of Enron*, Public Affairs Ltd, 2002, pp.36–43
5 *Washington Post*, 28 July 2002
6 *Blind Faith: How Deregulation and Enron's Influence over Government Looted Billions from Americans*, available at www.citizen.org. The exemption for contracts designed to defraud and mislead was reported by the Minority Staff Committee on Government Reform of the US House of Representatives on 7 February 2002 in 'How Lax Regulation and Inadequate Oversight Contributed to the Enron Collapse'.
7 Bryce, p.84
8 Jonathan Weil, 'Accounting Gets Scrutiny', *Wall Street Journal*, 4 December 2001
9 Brian Cruver, *Anatomy of Greed: The Unshredded Truth from an Enron Insider*, Hutchinson, 2002
10 *Vanity Fair*, April 2002
11 See the Center for Responsive Politics: www.opensecrets.org
12 Bryce, p.87
13 'How the Texas Tort Tycoons Spent Millions in the 2000 Elections', Texans for Public Justice
14 Duncan Campbell, 'Blackouts Bring Gloom to California', *Guardian*, 19 January 2001. Scott Thurm, Robert Gavin and Mitchel Benson, 'Juice Squeeze', *Wall Street Journal*, 16 Spetember 2002. 'California Power Probe', *Wall Street Journal*, 14 August 2002
15 'The Enron Corporation: Corporate Complicity in Human Rights Violations', Human Rights Watch, 1999
16 *Multinational Monitor*, July 1995
17 The case that the deal was corrupt was made in The State of Maharashtra versus DPC and the MSEB, Civil Suit No. 3392 of 1995 at the Bombay High Court. Extracts from the inquiry's findings can be found in the Human Rights Watch report, pp.134–52
18 *Multinational Monitor*, July 1995. Human Rights Watch, p.118
19 Khozem Merchant, 'Work Stops on Indian Power Plant', *Financial Times*, 17 June 2001

20 Cruver, p.177

TEN Because I'm Worth It

1 These and succeeding quotes are from Charles Leadbeater, *Living on Thin Air*, Viking, 1999
2 Radical scholars have argued that *We're Going on a Bear Hunt*'s narrative of a long quest which ends in headlong flight should be taken as a subversive parable of Labour's eighteen-year journey to a reckoning with Conservatism. See Tim Minogue, letter to the *London Review of Books*, 11 November 1999
3 Cruddas' criticism of the New Economy can be found in *A Charter for Workers' Rights*, The Institute of Employment Rights, 2002, p.24
4 *Charter for Workers' Rights*, pp.24–32
5 *Management Today*, 25 July 2001
6 Heather Connon, 'Glaxo in Bid to Stave Off Shareholder Revolt', *Observer*, 11 May 2003
7 Survey in the *Lawyer* magazine quoted in Nick Cohen, 'Let's Kill Half the Lawyers', *New Statesman*, 6 November 2000
8 Cohen, 'Let's Kill Half the Lawyers'
9 Tax-dodging losses to Treasury from Prem Sikka and Austin Mitchell, *No Accounting for Tax Havens*, Association for Accountancy and Business Affairs, 2002. Deaths from cold and benefits lowest in Europe, ibid. Joke transport system, sources too numerous to mention. Useless police, Home Office 2002 detection rates quoted in 'Figures of Fun or Real Ratings?', *Guardian*, 26 February 2003. Cumulative under-investment in NHS: Derek Wanless, 'Securing Our Future Health: Taking A Long-Term View', HM Treasury, 2002
10 Survey results quoted in 'British Pay Their Accountants Best', *Guardian*, 7 December 2001
11 From the introduction to Michael Young, *The Rise of the Meritocracy*, Transaction Publishers, 1994 edn.
12 Quotes from Francis Wheen, 'Satirical Fiction is Becoming Blair's Reality', *Guardian*, 14 February 2001
13 Nick Cohen, 'In the Firetrap Bubble', *Observer*, 1 December 2002
14 Example quoted in Polly Toynbee, 'Halt This Fatcat Feast', *Guardian*, 7 September 2001
15 Michael Young, 'Down with Meritocracy', *Guardian*, 29 June 2001

ELEVEN Thank You for Not Smoking

1 For the DeLorean case see Jason Manning, *The Rise and Fall of John DeLorean*, 2000; Flynn McRoberts, 'A Final Accounting', *Chicago Tribune*, 1 September 2002

2 Arthur Levitt, *The Numbers Game*, Pantheon Books, 2002

3 Robert Bryce, *Pipe Dreams*, Public Affairs, 2002, p.223

4 Levitt, pp.128–43

5 David Osler, *Labour Party Plc*, Mainstream Press, 2002, p.201

6 Milner quoted in Nick Cohen, *Cruel Britannia*, Verso, 1999, pp.194–9

7 Nick Cohen, 'Back to the Bad Old Days', *Observer*, 20 January 2002

8 David Walker, 'Brown Holds Court with the Moralists', *Guardian*, 1 February 2001

9 *Daily Mail*, 29 January 2002

10 Tony Blair interview, *On the Record*, BBC1, 16 November 1997. Campbell quote from Andrew Rawnsley, *Servants of the People*, Hamish Hamilton, 2000, p.104

Index